Writing, Revising
and Editing

Famous Writers School
Westport, Connecticut

A reader for people who
put words on paper

Writing, Revising
and Editing

Foreword by Herbert R. Mayes

Produced by Gordon Carroll
with the cooperation of the Instructional Staff
and the Guiding Faculty of the Famous Writers School,
as well as contributors to the *Famous Writers Magazine*

Doubleday & Company, Inc., Garden City, New York, 1969

Library of Congress Catalog Card Number 74–76987
Copyright © 1969 by Gordon Carroll
All rights reserved
Printed in the United States of America
First edition

Dedicated to
the students of the Famous Writers School
who have taught us so much about
the teaching of writing

Foreword

There isn't anything in this book that I, as an editor, would take out; nor anything more that I would put in. Its purpose is clear: to help people who already write to write better; to help people who are beginning to have that delicious feeling that makes them want to write, to write.

From the beginning, what I have admired about the Famous Writers School is its modest, unflamboyant approach to its objectives. Every student is provided with a plan, a course, a direction, and professional help that enable him to become more adept in the use of language. The School cannot instill talent. It does ensure the *development* of talent.

Today, as always, much more is written than is printed; but there is a peculiar satisfaction involved in writing that only writers can know, even when what they write is for their eyes alone, whether it be a diary, a short story, a novel, or a series of letters. Nevertheless, most of us prefer to see our names in print. It is a laudable ambition, and the School fosters it.

This may be more a commercial for the School than a foreword to an excellent book, but that does not bother me. I am interested in the School, and its success, but primarily in its students, because my life has been spent with authors, not institutions of learning. Anybody concerned with writing will find something good in this book. Everybody concerned with writing will find something good in the School. But I do not want to see any persons, young or old, enroll unless they mean to take their assignments seriously. If they do, they will find ample gratification. If they do not, there are other schools, less costly and obviously less demanding.

Herbert R. Mayes
New York City

Introduction

The professionals who have written this book have, in one way or another, worked their way from the bottom to the top in a highly competitive business where achievements are vastly more valuable than theories. Not every contributor to the volume offers the same guideposts to the student of writing. Not every contributor agrees on the exact "best way" to teach writing—nor indeed to the oft-heard argument that there *is* any "best way." If they have learned nothing else from their lives spent at the typewriter, they know writing is not amenable to hard and fast rules and that each person has to indulge his own aptitude if he hopes to rise from the novice class to the level of the reliable and capable performer.

Another point: the contributors to this volume agree with the philosophy of the School of which I am Director. Simply expressed, the philosophy says that "it takes success to teach success." Or, to put it another way, that a logical way for a person to learn is to hark to what top performers have to say about the particular field under discussion. That is truly the purpose of this book—to let the reader "listen" while some of the best practitioners of writing talk about their craft in a way the student will find both practicable and applicable.

Almost all the material in these pages appeared first in the *Famous Writers Magazine,* a publication distributed to some 60,000 active students of the Famous Writers School and also to hundreds of editors, publishers, literary agents, and others who have to do with the world of writing. The magazine made its bow in 1963, when the FWS student body totaled only 15,000. Since then, it has become the most widely read writer's magazine in the world—a fact which gives understandable pleasure to its editor and to its staff, which works so hard in an editorial field never too well supplied with either ideas or contributors.

The selections in this volume come from three kinds of authors. First, members of the Guiding Faculty of the School. These men and women of renown were the original creators of the School. In addition to the material they contributed to the course textbooks, they continue to contribute to the *FW Magazine* in the subject areas where they specialize—namely, fiction, non-fiction, business communications, and advertising copywriting. Their contributions are not only welcomed by the School's students but are also widely quoted by outside publications.

The second source of material for this book is the instructional staff of the School, whose members handle the flow of student assignments to and from Westport. These lesson manuscripts, varying in subject matter, length, scope, and purpose, come from students in the fifty states of the Union and from countries all over the world. Through analyzing and evaluating this mass of material, instructors learn about problems that commonly plague students, and in this volume they have discussed many such problems in enlightening terms.

These instructors, it must be added, are also professionals in every sense of the term. Like the Guiding Faculty, they have spent their lives earning a living from writing or from their editorial pencils. With years of experience behind each of them, they work full time as resident teachers at the School— the only correspondence school in the world which so maintains a large permanent teaching group on the premises.

The third group of contributors to this book are writers who are not officially connected with the School but who are familiar with the School's operations and have contributed material of their own to the *Famous Writers Magazine.* They include such people as a woman columnist for a prominent newspaper; the editor of one of America's best-known women's magazines; and the editor of a publication designed chiefly for juvenile readers. These contributors bring to the volume still another set of viewpoints, based upon their own commercial success in writing. Also, they touch upon areas and subjects not emphasized in the School's textbooks and thus give supplemental help to the student of fiction or non-fiction.

A separate book could be written about the School, its Faculty, its staff, and its teaching methods. Some day, perhaps this will be done. But for the time being the present volume will serve, I conceive, a worthwhile purpose. To the beginning writer, it offers much counsel and guidance on how to go about mastering the fundamentals of the craft. To the more accomplished writer, it offers some keys and secrets to producing more polished and thus more salable prose. To the professional writer (some of whom will indubitably scan the book, out of curiosity if nothing else), it offers reasonable proof that the mechanics (not the art) of writing can be taught—if the teachers are capable and patient and the students are receptive and willing.

Gordon Carroll, Director
Famous Writers School
Westport, Connecticut

Contents

Writing, Revising and Editing

FW

Section I Some basics of writing

Bergen Evans

By nature, all of us are skillful talkers,
but when it comes to putting thoughts into
words, we need more than a glib tongue

Writing begins with the basics

Dr. Samuel Johnson once said of a friend of his that the man was "as brisk as a bee" in conversation but that the touch of a pen managed, somehow, to make his hand numb.

Every writer knows exactly what Johnson meant. Ideas crowd into our minds, clothed in apt and witty phrases and loaded with wonderful illustrations. We try them out, in talk, on our friends and are a great success. But the minute we sit facing that blank sheet in the typewriter, it all evaporates. The ideas elude us and what we can remember of them seems dull and trivial. The witty phrases come out as colorless clichés and the illustrations illustrate nothing but our own fatuity.

"Look into your heart and write," Sir Philip Sidney advised the stymied author. But there's a laugh, and a bitter laugh. How do you do it? We can look into our hearts and *talk*. But the writing just won't come.

Why not? The answer is simple: from enormous practice we are skillful talkers. From an almost total lack of practice, we are unskillful writers. The practice that most of us need is in the rudiments.

Actually, talking is more difficult and complex than writing. We must not only find words for our meaning, but we must find them instantaneously and shift them quickly to meet the ever-shifting moods and currents of conversation. Further, communication in speech depends to a great extent upon stress and rhythm and intonation, upon facial expressions and gestures. It must be agile, immediate, and responsive.

That we do this incredibly difficult thing well is because we do it more and have done it longer than anything else we do, excepting seeing and breathing. We have been talking a blue streak since we were three years old – every waking minute we could persuade someone to listen – and sometimes in our sleep, just to keep in practice.

But we are infants at writing. Add up every word we've ever written in our lives and – for most people – it probably won't come to 100,000 words. Yet we can speak 100,000 in a good, gabby day.

So we are, as you might say, only a day old as writers. That means that we have to learn the equivalent in writing of the basic sounds in speech – the equivalent to the phonetics we practiced when we were hanging on to the edge of the playpen. We have to learn, for instance, how to indicate in writing those pauses which, in speech, direct stress and emphasis. In speaking we do it without thinking. If we fail we know it at once from the other person's answer or, even before that, from the look on his face. But in writing we do it by means of punctuation or, more subtly, by prose rhythms that enforce the desired pauses by the beat of their pattern.

That's all punctuation is – an agreed set of symbols to indicate meaningful pauses and certain relationships. They are purely utilitarian. But learn them we must, and learn them so well that we never have to stop and think whether we want this one or that. The right one must come naturally or the whole flow of our thought can be dammed up.

The two sentences – "I know you know" and "I know, you know" – say totally different things. The comma isn't in there just as a mark of elegance. Or consider a headline I read several years ago: Tree Ninety-Nine-Year-Old Bears. Did the writer of the news story mean what the headline said – and, if he did, how did he know the exact age of the bears? Or did he mean, as I suspected and as the story bore out: Tree, Ninety-Nine-Year Old, Bears?

The student who wrote in an examination paper, "No Disraeli was far from being a saint" admitted to me later that he meant the exact opposite: "No, Disraeli was far from being a saint."

It isn't solely a matter of omission, either; unnecessary punctuation can distort meaning. When a young lady in a theme referred to the attractiveness of "a tall, bronze, skinned young man," I could only conclude she was either careless or a cannibal.

Richard Brinsley Sheridan, one of the wittiest men who ever spoke English, was once ordered in Parliament to apologize for having called a fellow-member a liar. He answered, "Mr. Speaker I said the honorable member was a liar it is true and I am sorry for it." Then Sheridan added that the honorable member could place the punctuation marks where he chose.

Grammar serves the same purpose as punctuation: it makes our meaning clear. Grammar that serves this purpose is good grammar and that which doesn't is bad. Students are warned against what are called "dangling" participial phrases, for instance, not because they are wrong but because they are confusing.

A girl in one of my classes once wrote an essay describing an overnight journey in a Pullman. It was her first trip away from home and she found herself unable to sleep. She was homesick. The noise of the train was disturbing. She was uneasy at the lack of privacy and particularly disturbed by the snoring of a man directly across the aisle. Then, after a sleepless night, she had to endure his hearty greetings as he, fully refreshed, climbed out of his berth. At least propriety compels me to assume that is what happened. But it isn't what she said happened. She wrote, "Climbing out of my berth in the morning, the man who had kept me awake asked me cheerfully how I had slept."

In a student theme, such writing brings a laugh. In commercial writing, it brings a rejection slip.

Grammar, punctuation, a knowledge of the basic mechanics of expression, are the writer's tools of which, to be effective, he must have easy mastery. He must be able to use them with assurance. He will never get anywhere until he has freed himself from the burden of figuring out each problem and how he may best deal with it. Like any other good workman, he reaches for the proper tool, knowing that it will do the job.

He will know, for instance, what constitutes a complete sentence, and he will know when it would be wrong to use anything less than a complete sentence. He will know what punctuation will make his meaning unambiguous. He will have learned that for organizing a piece of expository material, some kind of outline can speed the writing and save him time and stress.

These things will in time – much less time than the beginner realizes – become automatic and liberate the writer's energies to experiment with style, to develop individuality, and to refine expression. He will no longer be encumbered with the awkwardness of his ignorance.

Efficiency, however, is not the same as effectiveness, and it is effectiveness the writer wants. He wants to be able to convey *precisely* what he has in mind with force and clarity, with persuasiveness if he is advocating something, and with emotional impact if he is writing any form of fiction. To achieve these things he needs to know, in addition to the mechanics of writing, the devices of rhetoric. He must be able to organize a piece with coherence, to put his ideas in meaningful order, to work up to a clinching climax.

He should learn to value conciseness and to shun pomposity. He must develop an appreciation of the ways in which word order can affect emphasis. He should be able to recognize a cliché, in words or thought, and avoid it. He should cultivate a sensitivity to shades of meaning in words by referring to a good dictionary, by observing admired writings, and by applying selected words thoughtfully in his own writing.

Rightly or wrongly, a reader who is stopped by a mistake or slowed down by a confusing passage or is compelled to explore several possibilities by an ambiguity will question the mental capacities of the writer, will wonder whether he is one from whom to accept judgments or even facts. An airline pilot who seems uncertain of the location of the cockpit isn't likely to inspire confidence in the passengers.

The sense of control that comes with a knowledge of basic principles serves the same purpose in writing that it does in any other activity – playing the piano, selling real estate, cooking a meal, running a meeting, trying a case in court. It gives self-assurance, assurance that one is not doing the wrong thing or making a fool of himself or going off at a tangent. This is a point often overlooked—perhaps because it is so obvious. But the effect of insecurity is definite and pervasive. It can be frustrating, inhibiting, paralyzing.

Only when a writer knows that he is capable of expressing himself correctly and clearly can he write freely. The truth of this is felt at once when we think of trying to write in some foreign language that we haven't fully mastered. What man would want to negotiate an important transaction in any other language than his native tongue?

Another perquisite of the confidence that comes with, and can only come with, a mastery of basic principles, is the pride we can take in work well turned out. This is intangible but it's very important. Without it we would hardly dare to go on to another piece of work.

Bad or careless writing is an affront to a reader, for it implies either that the writer is not putting forth his best effort (a discourtesy in itself) or that he believes the reader will not know the difference. This won't do. You can't affront the reader. Usually, you have no hold on him whatever except by attraction. That doesn't mean that you have to flatter him. Indeed, crude flattery will arouse immediate hostility in any reader worth having. But you have to interest him and to hold his interest. This is the function of style.

Sometimes the content of what the writer is saying is so important that it gets through to the reader regardless of how it is presented. But most of the time a writer has to depend on style – a style appropriate to his material – to hold the reader's interest. And here, more than he has any idea of, a grounding in basic principles will keep him from alienating the reader.

None of this means that rules can never be broken, but a writer can break the rules with confidence only when he knows exactly what he is doing. James Joyce's mastery of the resources of the language was the key to his brilliant experimentation. He could never have taken the extraordinary – and highly valuable – liberties with the language that he did take had he not been absolutely sure of himself. No reader, no matter what he may think of the method or the result, can fail to sense Joyce's control of his medium.

For one who writes, then, it is important to know the rules of his craft, in order to improve efficiency and effectiveness, and to promote self-confidence in himself and confidence in his reader. The more successful he is in achieving these objectives, the more attractive and persuasive he will be to his audience. Whether his range is limited to personal letters or extends to reports of national importance or experimental fiction, he needs a knowledge of basic principles to function as a writer.

Such a knowledge will enlarge his competence and contribute to the development of his artistry. It won't make him an artist if he hasn't any talent, but it will provide an indispensable foundation for creative ability to build on, the means to project his individuality and to mold his style into a unique instrument of expression.

The artist is an inspired craftsman, but he's still a craftsman, and a good craftsman must have a mastery of his tools.

Don't be afraid to cut

Every writer hits now and then upon a thought that seems to him so happy, a repartee that amuses him so much, that to cut it is worse than having a tooth out. It is then that it is well to have engraved on his heart the maxim: If you can, cut. – Somerset Maugham

A tip from E. B. White

Advice to young writers who want to get ahead without any annoying delays: don't write about Man, write about *a* man. – E. B. White

Gordon Carroll

*For the beginning writer, nothing
pays bigger dividends than the impulse
to "play around" with words*

How to write better sentences

To start this little exercise, let's set up a simple sentence and then see
what can be done with it. As a sentence, nothing could be simpler – and
clearer – than this: "The man walked down the street." As a declarative
statement, anyone will accept it; but as a literary effort, it rates close to
zero. How can we go about improving it? First, it may be broken into three
logical parts:

The man/walked down/the street.

Each part is a clear thought, but in order to embellish style, we can pose
a few questions:

What *kind* of man – tall, short, old, young, erect, stooped? *How* did he
walk – fast, slow, straight, crooked? What *kind* of street – city, town, village, American, European?

By answering these questions we come up with an amplified version of
the sentence:

The *young* man/*ambled* down/the *village* street.

Now the reader has a clear picture of what we want to convey; he knows what kind of man, and how he's walking, and where he is. But from a writer's point of view, the sentence can still stand much improvement. So let's continue our questions and see if we can't produce still another sentence. What time of day was it? What kind of weather? What distinguishing characteristics did the man have?

Suppose we say that the time of day is late afternoon, that the weather is cold, that our man is blind, and that our street is in a big city. The sentence could then read this way:

> Late on a cold afternoon, the blind man shuffled down the city street.

We're making progress in our search for a richer, fuller sentence, but we can do better. Since cold weather means winter, and since a blind man usually has certain characteristics, what about using our imagination and producing this sentence?

> On a wintry afternoon, the blind man shuffled down Broadway, one hand holding a tapping cane, the other a battered tin cup.

In going through the above steps — and always thinking about what we want to say *before* we say it — we've revised a simple sentence into something palpably better. And thus, we've learned something quite valuable about the writing process.

Our next step is to carry this business of sentence revision into another exercise — one based on a paragraph of description, consisting of seven sentences placed in proper continuity. Each sentence conveys a thought, each helps to develop the paragraph, each helps to round out — and complete — the description. But each is too similar to the next in construction, too stereotyped, too monotonous in tone and value, too likely to stifle the reader's interest before he reaches the end of the paragraph.

First of all, we want you to read the paragraph just as we present it below — seven dull sentences strung in a row. Then we want you to join us as we go back over the sentence and, one by one, see what can be done to give them life, variety, vigor, and color. However, we must first repeat something that has been said many times by many writers: *There is no one best or perfect way to write anything.* There are countless ways, depending on the nature and talent of the individual writer.

In this exercise of revising descriptive prose, we merely show you *one* way in which the final sentences were arrived at. You might prefer some other way — and so might thousands of other writers. Nevertheless, the exercise is well worthwhile, since only by testing and experimenting can you hope to reach the high level of competency which must always be your writing goal. Now, here is the paragraph of seven sentences:

> The sun rose in the sky. The street shimmered in the heat. The dust surrounded the walking men. The horses and mules in the street were dirt-caked. The surface of everything reflected the sun's rays. The air above the town wavered. The new pine bank building glared white in the sunlight.

In a sense, this paragraph does an orthodox job of description. We know from reading it that the writer is talking about a sunny, hot, and dusty town – probably a Western town, since there are horses and mules mentioned. We also know the town has a new bank building. In other words, we have a description of the town – a word picture of a setting – but the words themselves are put together in a dull and lifeless way. So, what can we do?

We will take up the sentences, one by one, and see if we can improve them. Let's start with Sentence One: "The sun rose in the sky."

By concentrating on imagery – and adding words here and there – we come up with:

> The sun rose higher in the sky and grew in strength.

We have supplied "higher," which, though obvious in the case of a rising sun, adds definition, and we have appended "grew in strength" – another obvious observation but still a useful touch of style. Now for another revision:

> The sun climbed higher and seemed to glow in the sky.

Here, "climbed" has been substituted for "rose" (an improvement in verb usage); "in the sky" has been put at the end of the sentence for strength; and "seemed to glow" has been supplied for richness. Next, a third revision:

> The sun climbed higher, grew fiercer, and glowed in the sky.

We've kept the first four words, then added "grew fiercer" (a helpful phrase), and removed "seemed to," since this wasn't necessary in the longer version of the sentence. Let's try once more for improvement:

> The sun climbed higher, grew fiercer, and seemed to glow in the burnished sky.

This version retains some of the previous changes, takes back "seemed to," and adds "burnished." All in all, this final revision gives us a stronger sentence – one that builds up its descriptive message more appealingly, more powerfully, than did the simple Sentence One of the original paragraph.

Now, what about Sentence Two: "The street shimmered in the heat"?

Although the thought expressed here is permissible, it hardly seems important enough for a whole sentence in itself, since any street, anywhere, will likely "shimmer" in the heat. Let's drop the sentence as such and use the thought as an introductory phrase to Sentence Three: "The dust surrounded the walking men." For example:

Along the shimmering street, dust surrounded the men as they walked.

This improves the original, but we can continue with revisions in search of a sharper word picture. Since "along the shimmering street" seems in the right place, what can we do about the "dust" part of the sentence? Here's one possibility:

The dust followed the men as they walked and almost choked them.

Nothing wrong with this expansion, but don't let's stop yet. A third effort:

The dust trailed along with the men as they walked, choking them.

"Trailed" is better than "followed," and by putting a comma break after "walked," we've removed the "and" construction and created a smoother style. However, we can make one more try at describing the scene:

The men drew in the swirling dust with every breath they took.

Looking back on the four revisions made so far, can we combine some of the best features of each and come up with a final version? We can—and here it is:

Along the shimmering street, the dust trailed the men as they walked, and they drew it in with every panting breath.

Remember—there is no one best way of writing this sentence—or any other sentence in the English language. Here, we're merely striving to refine and strengthen descriptive writing by using our imagination and our knowledge of words. And, if we've accomplished nothing else so far, we've gotten rid of the original paragraph pattern in which every sentence begins with "The."

It's time now to turn to Sentence Four: "The horses and mules in the street were dirt-caked."

First, can we make the scene clearer, can we add some details about this sunbaked town?

The horses and mules, standing beside their hitching rails, were caked in dust.

Better, yes, but still more detail can be added:

> Horses and mules, hitched in front of the shabby stores, had rings and lines on their faces where the moisture from their eyes had caked the dust.

The reader now knows how and why the dust became caked, but let's make one last try at improving the sentence through minor but valid changes:

> Horses and mules, hitched in front of the shabby stores, had deep lines on their faces where moisture from their eyes and mouths had caught the dust and turned it into mud.

What about Sentence Five? In the original paragraph, it reads: "The surface of everything reflected the sun's rays."

This is a sound sentence: it conveys a thought; it helps to complete the writer's picture of the town; it comes at a logical place in the continuity of the paragraph. But it is stereotyped, lacks color or tone, and can be improved.

> The surface of everything mirrored the sun's bright rays.

Not much change, but "mirrored" is better than "reflected" and "bright" accents "the sun's rays." Yet we must continue revising, always in search of something better.

> The heat was everywhere, and a hundred surfaces mirrored back the sun's merciless rays.

These changes speak for themselves; we've played around with language; we're seeking to individualize our style; but we still have a "The" opening. First, however, we'll forget "The" while we revise a little more.

> The heat was all around, and a thousand surfaces reflected the intensity of the sun's rays.

By spending additional time and effort, we continue to give the sentence more style, more individuality – and get still further away from the flatness of the original. And now, one final attempt (in which, among other things, we get rid of "The" and the repetition of "sun"):

> Heat lay everywhere – above, below, and around – and a thousand glistening surfaces reflected the intensity of the sky's glare.

Next, Sentence Six from the original paragraph: "The air above the town wavered."

This is another needless observation on the writer's part, since we've already established the kind of heat that would create "shimmering" or "wavering." However, let's keep "wavering" in mind to be used in Sentence Seven: "The new pine bank building glared white in the sunlight."

Picking up the "wavering" touch, here's a first revision:

> Although the town moved in wavering lines, the new bank building stood out clear and white in the sun.

Not bad, in fact, quite good – but this isn't the time to stop. Remember – practice, and more practice, is what makes a better writer. In our next revision, we can forget the "wavering" for a moment and concentrate on the bank's appearance. For example:

> The white pine front of the new bank stood gleaming, like old bones in the sun.

We have strengthened our imagery, and used "new" and "old" in logical contrast. Now, it's time to put all our thoughts into one final revision:

> While the rest of the town moved in wavering lines, the pine front of the new bank stood out sharply, gleaming like old bones in the sun.

With this final effort, the revision of the original seven sentences is complete. The paragraph now reads:

> The sun climbed higher, grew fiercer, and seemed to glow in the burnished sky. Along the shimmering street, the dust trailed the men as they walked, and they drew it in with every panting breath. Horses and mules, hitched in front of the shabby stores, had deep lines on their faces where moisture from their eyes and mouths had caught the dust and turned it into mud. Heat lay everywhere – above, below, and around – and a thousand glistening surfaces reflected the intensity of the sky's glare. While the rest of the town moved in wavering lines, the pine front of the new bank stood out sharply, gleaming like old bones in the sun.

By comparing the revised paragraph with the original, you'll find that the monotony of tone and style of the original is gone; the rhythm and variety of the sentences are improved; the reader has a clearer picture of the scene; and the writer can feel encouraged because his efforts have paid off. He has learned a fundamental fact about writing: if you merely jot down the first thing that comes into your head – and stick with it – you'll probably be a beginner forever. In short, the more you revise, the better you write.

The above exercise in sentence revision should challenge you to do more of your own. To help you get started, another exercise is presented below – but an exercise with a big difference. First, we give you a set of seven sentences, each of which states a fact or facts, each of which offers material for a paragraph of colorful description. But between the seven simple sentences and the final paragraph are all the steps we went through above.

Why don't you take the seven sentences and find out for yourself how each might be revised (up to five times) to produce the final result? Of course, since the final result is in front of you, you might say: "What's the use? It's all been done for me—why should I waste my time?" The answer is simple: You learn to do by doing! Even though we give you the final result in advance, who is to say it is the *best* result? By working over the seven sentences, by following the dictates of your own mind and imagination, by using words and phrases that seem fitting to you, you may well come up with a better paragraph, one that satisfies you more than the version offered here.

Here are the seven sentences, strung together in paragraph form:

> The rancher was the last to dismount. The rancher's companions waited for him at the saloon door. The rancher dusted off his vest. The rancher seemed bigger than all the rest of the men. The rancher was fifty, tanned, and had a moustache. The rancher's hat and boots were expensive. The rancher drew the eyes of passersby.

So much for the facts. Now, here is a paragraph that resulted from persistent revision of the seven sentences:

> The straw-haired rancher from Nogales was the last to get down from his horse, while the rest of the men waited respectfully on the sidewalk, hanging back from the doors of the saloon to let him approach. As he stood knocking the dust from his corduroy vest, he seemed bigger than all of them put together, not only because of his bulk, which was considerable, but also because of his confidence, his obvious affluence, his air of command. He was tall as well as broad, not more than fifty, with a tanned face and a yellow moustache beginning to turn gray. His hat was the best of Stetsons and his boots had clearly come from a fine leatherworker. A few idlers, moving along the dusty street, eyed him curiously as he turned to stare with pale blue eyes at an old reward notice posted beside the saloon entrance.

As we remarked at the beginning, don't get us wrong: the revised sentences are not presented as the best or the finest or the most "literary" or the most of anything else. Our purpose is to activate your mind and your imagination, so that the next time you write a sentence, you'll give it extra thought *before* you go on to the next. By following the techniques outlined here, we believe you can effect a noticeable improvement in your writing— and have the fun of playing a "word game" at the same time.

George Lowther

*Many a successful author has found that
going to the typewriter – and staying
there – produces best results*

Don't wait for inspiration!

Few occupations by which man earns his daily bread and butter (and perhaps a bit of jam) are as easy and pleasant as that of the writer. Being his own boss, accountable to no one but himself, he enjoys a life free of the pressures that others must face daily.

The writer works when the mood urges or fancy bids – unless, of course, he prefers to be doing something else at the time. There can be no happier way of life, no more delightful means of earning a livelihood, no more satisfying mode of existence than that of the writer. Or . . . so think those who have never written! . . .

However, those of us who actually write for a living know better. We are all too aware of the discipline needed to conceive an idea and, once conceived, to nourish it with imagination and, once nourished, to place it properly on paper. No writer is unfamiliar with the agony of courting his muse, with those moments when in despair he pushes the typewriter away and knows himself to be utterly alone in his misery.

But, fortunately, he is not alone. He is, if he only knew it, so surrounded by sympathetic companions, by veteran wayfarers on the road to literary success, that he need only reach out to find a supporting arm from somebody who has trod the path before him. Listen, for instance, to Joseph Conrad writing to his friend and editor Edward Garnett:

> I sit here religiously every morning – I sit down for eight hours every day – and the sitting down is all. In the course of that working day of eight hours I write three sentences which I erase before leaving the table in despair. . . . At night I sleep. In the morning I get up with the horror of that powerlessness I must face through a day of vain efforts.

Lonely, confused, and so wearied he felt he couldn't go on, Conrad *did* go on – to write some of the great classics in the English language. And his words would have found echo in the hearts of such writers as Arnold Bennett, H. G. Wells, Virginia Woolf, and many others over the years. Let's continue with this theme and listen to Pearl Buck's plaint:

> Writing is hard work, demanding the utmost of mind and body. Writing a novel is the hardest work of all. A young farmer whom I once employed on my farm came to complain of something or other and he began by saying, "Of course, I know you earn your living the easy way . . ." I listened in stunned silence. I? The easy way?
>   I can think of nothing easier than sitting on a tractor through hours of dreaming spring and summer, the mind half-sleeping, the body at rest if not at ease. Summer and winter my typewriter does not rest. Brain must work if I am to do my job. It takes a perfected discipline, this job of being a writer.

One of the great masters of deceptive simplicity with words growls:

> I start with blank paper and put all that I know at the time on blank paper. Most of the time it is tough going.

His name? Ernest Hemingway.

The groan of writers who feel they have "dried up" will find an echo with Stuart Cloete, author of the best seller *Rags of Glory:*

> I have cycles of writing. I work like hell for three months, and then for a month or more I'm certain that I'll never have another word to say. So I suffer. And then I resign myself. And then the month is up, and I start to make a little headway again. A couple of weeks more of trying before suddenly I'm back in the groove.

Whatever your methods, when you have a great sigh of desperation as your fingers lie limp on the typewriter, think of these words by Marjorie Kinnan Rawlings:

I have no free swing in what I write, no little miracles. I let my novels mature for several years, know almost exactly what I want to do in them and slowly do it. I make the first draft as perfect as I can and do comparatively little rewriting, because what I toilsomely put on paper is the best that I can do. For me there is no improving it. The phrase, the line, the paragraph – they never are quite right, as it seems to me, but I keep plugging, getting them as near right as is possible for me. Every thought, every description, every bit of dialogue, is as compressed, as tight, as I can fashion it. It is all self-conscious and perhaps that is wrong, but it is the only method I can use.

When it comes to writing that appears informal and casual, the late Frank O'Connor had no peer. To read an O'Connor story is as if he himself sat in your living room and told it to you. Yet he rewrote "endlessly, endlessly, endlessly! And I keep on rewriting, and after it's published as a story and then after it's published in book form, I usually rewrite it again. I've rewritten versions of most of my early stories and one of these days, God help, I'll publish them as well."

You have trouble getting started on a piece of writing? You say you sit before your typewriter for hours with your brain as blank as the paper before you? Many a successful author has the same problem. Let William Styron, Prix de Rome winner for his novel *Lie Down in Darkness* speak for all:

I get a fine warm feeling when I'm doing well. . . . But that pleasure is pretty much negated by the pain of getting started each day. Let's face it, writing is hell. When I'm writing steadily, I average two-and-a-half or three pages a day – longhand on yellow sheets. I spend about five hours at it, of which very little is spent actually writing.

I try to get a feeling of what's going on in the story before I put it down on paper, but actually most of this breaking-in period is one long, fantastic daydream in which I think about anything but the work at hand. I can't turn out slews of stuff each day. I wish I could. I seem to have some neurotic need to perfect each paragraph – each sentence, even – as I go along.

Georges Simenon joins you on what you thought was a solitary journey. Simenon's approach to one of his famous Inspector Maigret suspense novels requires that he complete it in a span of eleven days under unremitting strain!

After I have started a novel, I write a chapter each day, without ever missing a day. Because it is a strain, I have to keep pace with the novel. If, for example, I am ill for forty-eight hours, I have to throw away the previous chapters. And I never return to that novel.

When I am doing a novel I don't see anybody, I don't speak to anybody, I don't take a phone call—I live just like a monk. All the day I am one of my characters. I feel what he feels. It is in this character's skin I have to be. And it's almost unbearable after five or six days.

That is one of the reasons my novels are so short—after eleven days it's impossible. I am too tired. That is why before I start a novel I look to see that I don't have any appointments for eleven days. Then I call the doctor. He takes my blood pressure, he checks everything. I have to be sure I am good for eleven days.

Or, if you prefer other company, here is Kenneth Roberts' account of what he went through in the writing of his best seller *Arundel:*

9:00 A.M. Retire to the workroom, wrap an overcoat around the feet to keep out the chill that rises from the tiled floors of all Italian buildings [he had rented, dirt cheap, a villa in southern Italy], sit down at the desk and devote one hour to revising and rewriting the work done on the preceding two days.

10:00 A.M. Dip into eleven reference books to make sure of dates, weather, costumes and sundry other matters having to do with the day's writing, and try to go on with the story until . . .

1:00 P.M. Unwrap the overcoat from the feet and emerge for lunch, read the *Paris Herald* and the morning mail. Play three games of cribbage, piquet or backgammon with Mrs. Roberts.

2:30 P.M. Retire to the workroom, adjust the overcoat around the feet and work for five hours.

7:30 P.M. Emerge for dinner, complain about the small amount of work accomplished during the day, and play three games of piquet, cribbage or backgammon with Mrs. Roberts.

9:30 P.M. To bed with an armful of reference books, to brood morosely over the next day's work.

So, you see, as a writer you have many a companion in courting the muse.

To the "bleeder"—the poor soul who writes and tears up, writes and tears up, who cannot create an outline to save his neck and must feel his way through page after page, often with dire results—Aldous Huxley offered consolation:

. . . work away at a chapter at a time, finding my way as I go. Sometimes I will write a great deal, then find it just doesn't work, and have to throw the whole thing away. I like to have a chapter finished before I begin the next one. But I'm never entirely certain what's going to happen in the next chapter till I've worked it out. Things come to me in driblets and when the driblets come I have to work hard to make them into something coherent. It is hard work . . . very absorbing and sometimes exhausting.

Franklin P. Adams once told the following story about Robert Benchley, the eccentric humorist. Benchley had contracted to write an article for a magazine and, as the deadline approached, found himself devoid of ideas. In desperation he rented a room at New York's Algonquin Hotel, locked himself in, sat at the typewriter and, in an effort to force the muse to his bidding, wrote the single word *The*.

As he sat frowning, the telephone rang. The caller was George S. Kaufman, the playwright, who informed Benchley that a poker game was about to start in Kaufman's suite down the hall. Would Benchley care to take a hand? Benchley would, and did.

Hours – many hours – later he returned to his solitary room, sat down at the typewriter, stared bleakly for a long time at that one word *The* and then, with a sigh of resignation, typed *End*.

Writing is like tennis

Your problem is to communicate with the reader – to get your message past the barrier of cold type into his mind and emotions. You have three sets of tools to work with: words, verbal and rhetorical forms, modes of approach.

To visualize this division with a rough approximation, let's look at tennis as a game. The ball is roughly the equivalent of the writer's words: without it, there can be no game at all. The strokes (serve, drive, volley, etc.) represent the verbal and rhetorical forms: they are the various ways in which the ball can be hit. The style of play (backline, midcourt, net – conservative, tactical, aggressive) corresponds to the writer's mode of approach: the player *chooses* his style by reference both to his skill and to his judgment of his opponent's response.

Reverse this categorical sequence, and you find that his style determines his strokes and his strokes determine the delivery of the ball, just as in writing the mode determines the forms and the forms determine the delivery of the words – Mark Wiseman

Gordon Carroll

The use of word bridges is one way by which
the writer can impart smoothness and movement
to his prose

Transitions: a key to style

When you talk about style in writing, you are talking about a variety of qualities: for example, tone is a part of style, and so are pace and rhythm, as well as color, imagery, sensitivity, and those old favorites – unity, coherence, and emphasis. All of these points are important, but just how do you go about isolating and defining them so that the writing student can put them to work in his own manuscripts? In other words, although they offer much opportunity for theoretical talk, how do you use them *practically?*

Unhappily for the student who's interested in style (and what student isn't?), theory usually wins out over practice, since style is basically a matter of individual talent – the ability of a person to put words on paper in a way indisputably his own. To teach style in this sense of the term is as impossible as it is to teach talent. Neither can be packaged and sold to the person who wants to bring his writing skills to a high level of competency.

There is, however, amidst all the theory and preachment about style, a method through which the writer can vastly improve his output. It is almost mechanical in that it involves specific words and the ways in which they may be used in sentences and paragraphs to create a smoothness, a flow, a harmony of language that keeps a piece of writing moving ahead for the reader, from beginning through middle to ending.

The procedure is called *transition* – the use of "bridging" material to blend your ideas together so that they come out as a coherent and pleasing whole.

Unless you use the right kinds of words, phrases, and sentences to move your piece ahead, step by step and thought by thought, your copy will lack not only smoothness but unity, too; sentences and paragraphs won't flow smoothly, one out of the other; the reader gets lost because unsuitable words and phrases interrupt his eye and his mind; and the overall result is not "style" in the literary connotation of the word but a rough, uneven, and often confusing collection of verbal fragments.

While transition is fundamentally a matter of word mechanics, there are no rigid rules or alphabetical formulas to guide the writer. All you can do is start with the simpler devices used by writers to bridge thoughts and then go into the more complicated areas where the individual develops his own style by trial and error.

The simpler devices are those used, mostly in non-fiction, to move the reader forward from one completed thought or set of thoughts to the next. Like paragraph indentions, they break the flow of copy without breaking the author's unity. And most of them – like the indention – come at the beginning of a paragraph. For example:

What's more	Therefore
Anyway	In short
In other words	Besides
Of course	Finally

There are many more of these familiar connectives or word bridges, and they've served generations of authors, from the fabulist to the classicist to the essayist to today's article writer. In fact, a number have been put to work in this article you're now reading – paragraph two starts with *Unhappily;* paragraph three, *There is, however;* paragraph five, *Unless;* and paragraph six, *While.* None of these is the ultimate in transition: rather, they are cited as evidence of the technique under discussion.

In addition to (there's *another* word bridge to tie this paragraph to its predecessor) the more hackneyed connectives, there are endless other forms that transition may take – endless because here we become involved with literary style, which, as pointed out above, is so individual a matter that it defies teaching. But at least many of these forms can be isolated and analyzed (the number depending entirely on how many examples of writing you want to select) and, from a scrutiny of them, the writer can often learn a great deal more than he has reason to expect. Let's make a random selection from contemporary writing and see what it reveals.

First, some excerpts from magazine articles in which the authors have tied the end of one paragraph to the beginning of another, so that the reader moves ahead with ease. However, in order to evaluate the excerpts helpfully, we shall have to give "wrong" and "right" versions so that you can compare them and see how the "right" transition achieved the authors' objectives. This example is from the lead of an article in *Reader's Digest:*

> George Thomas was on his knees, weeding, when the dizziness crept over him. A gray veil fell across his eyes and the world seemed to spin. His left arm buzzed with a "pins and needles" feeling, which then gave way to numbness. Slowly he realized that neither his left arm nor his left hand could move.

This is a dramatic opening: it sets the stage and hooks the reader. Now, how does the writer carry his reader into his next paragraph without "bumping"? Here are some *wrong* ways to start paragraph two:

"George Thomas was alarmed." This thought is too obvious to be mentioned.

"He thought it might be caused by overexertion." A plausible idea, but does the reader really care at this point? Hardly.

"This had never happened to him before." By implication, the reader has already assumed that George Thomas was in *sudden* and unusual trouble.

What, then, is a logical beginning for paragraph two? The authors of this piece – Ronald M. and Patricia Deutsch – had a wide choice, but they came up with a good one.

> After ten frightening minutes, some sensation began to return to his paralyzed arm.

Note how the phrase *After ten frightening minutes* does a job. It ties in naturally with the closing words of the preceding paragraph – "could move." And it recognizes that the word "after" or "afterward" is a good bridge, for it conveys to the reader, in more ways than one, the forward movement of the piece. Although the Deutsches could undoubtedly have carried on with equal effect by using other phrases, the one they used is worthy of attention.

Quite often, it is not only a particular phrase that ties one thought to another but, more important, *where* it appears in the bridging sentence. Let's look at the first two paragraphs of a non-fiction book whose setting is Melbourne:

Across the street, beyond the brooding shade of the big fig tree, the sunlight lapped the gates of the Hidden Gardens as Ted Carse left the bar of
the Botanical and began to walk up Domain Road.

At the corner he stopped for a tram to swing, then went on under the
dappled leaves, up the sloping street . . .

The transitory phrase here is *At the corner* – and it works well. Do a little
word juggling yourself, and see how results might have been otherwise. For
instance:

He stopped at the corner. . . .

OR: *He stopped* for a tram to swing by the corner. . . .

OR: *A tram swung* past the corner. . . .

OR: *He stopped so* that a tram could swing past him. . . .

Any or all of these would be permissible, but by starting the second paragraph with *At the corner,* the author carried the reader along with a minimum
of jarring. The tone and the rhythm of the three words were just right for
the author's purpose.

In a *Saturday Evening Post* article about children, Richard Lemon showed
a fine grasp of the connective. Here are two paragraphs from the body of
his article:

Most adults like to think of the years from five through twelve as the
essence of childhood, a simple time cut off from adult cares. In their
reveries, boys still earn money by mowing lawns or pitching newspapers
onto front porches. Girls play with lovely dolls in costumes from all over
the world. And toys, if not actually made by elves, are lovingly hammered together by a little old man in square spectacles in Switzerland.

It is time for adults to lay aside such fantasies and face the realities,
which are astonishing . . .

Note the opening of the second paragraph, *It is time for adults.* How much
stronger, smoother, interest-holding than if the second paragraph had
started:

Adults should lay aside such fantasies. . . .

OR: *Such fantasies should* be laid aside by adults. . . .

By using the phrase *It is time,* the author gave greater emphasis to his
thought and, at the same time, vastly strengthened the style of his sentence.
Whenever you feel hesitant in moving from paragraph to paragraph, try
variations on the first transition that comes to your mind. Chances are, you'll
please your reader – and improve your style, too. Before you know it, you'll
have taken a long step toward creating a style that you can truly feel is your
own.

So far, we've been looking at transitory devices used by the non-fiction writer. In non-fiction, these devices are easier to detect, easier to evaluate, easier to improve than in the world of fiction. But the fiction writer, too, has to know transition, for if he can't move the reader ahead with the same ease and plausibility that the article writer achieves, then his full creative talents will never come to the surface.

Since the fiction writer is consciously more of a stylist (and more consciously strives for style in everything he writes), his use of transition is loose, informal, and subject to few restrictions. For one thing, his reliance on dialogue removes the need for careful word-bridging in much of his work. Further, he knows the fiction reader will accept inferences and asides more readily than the non-fiction reader, who wants his articles solid and factual yet fast-moving in style — the kind of style so often supported by the clever use of transitory phrases.

Nevertheless, the fiction writer often employs recognizable word bridges, even though they may come in countless shapes and guises. Below are several examples, selected at random from the novels or stories of contemporary writers. The first is from *In the Red,* a British thriller by Joan Fleming:

> In the carefully worked out timetable, he had made allowance for a quarter of an hour in the public house near the station at Ealing; time for a glass of stout and a sandwich before taking a train to the air terminal. But first he had to go to his flat and pick up the suitcase which he had left ready.
>
> If he had had any sense, he meditated, he would have brought the suitcase with him on his way to work . . .

If he had had any sense is a good transition: it keeps the prose flowing and it adds to the reader's awareness of the character's mental processes at this point in the novel. How much smoother is this style than if the author had written:

> *He reflected that* if he had had any sense, he would have . . .

Now for another example, this from James Gould Cozzens, an acknowledged master of style in both the short story and the novel. The passage is from "Farewell to Cuba," one of the stories in the Cozzens anthology *Children and Others:*

> His fingers found it to be an envelope and he was immediately angered, thinking that after all they had disobeyed his instructions downstairs. He was about to take it out with him when, standing still, he had another idea.
>
> *Without moving, barely breathing,* he ripped the flap. He pressed a hand into his pocket and brought out a cigarette lighter. The wheel

rasped his thumb twice and a flame jumped up, yellow on the enclosed
sheet.

He looked at it quietly. He had never, it seemed to him, heard a
silence so tremendous. . . .

The transition between paragraphs one and two is precisely right. By itself, *Without moving* would do quite well, but Cozzens has added a second
phrase — *barely breathing* — which strengthens the bridge and adds to the
imagery. Then, at the beginning of paragraph three, he uses a more abrupt
transition — a sentence of five words which, despite its simplicity, takes the
reader along.

Unquestionably there are many other ways in which Cozzens could have
tied these paragraphs together and exemplified his qualities as a fine stylist,
but the ones he did use offer a useful lesson to students of writing.

For a third example from fiction, let's look at an excerpt from a novel by
Daphne du Maurier, *My Cousin Rachel*. Many of Miss du Maurier's novels
are set in times past and have the flavor of the language of the period. Here
she is writing of eighteenth-century England:

Apart from my school days at Harrow and afterwards at Oxford, I have
never lived in any place but this house, where I had come at the age of
eighteen months after my young parents died. Ambrose, in his queer gen-
erous way, was seized with pity for his small orphaned cousin, and so
brought me up himself, as he might have done a puppy or a kitten or any
frail and lonely thing needing protection.

Ours was a strange sort of household from the first. He sent my nurse
packing when . . .

Despite the deliberately archaic style of this writing, the bridge to the
second paragraph is interesting. At first, you might think that a "bump"
must occur between the words *protection* and *ours*. But read along with the
author and you find that the contrast, if it can be so called, between the end
of the first paragraph and the beginning of the second, is well handled by the
phrase *Ours was a strange sort*. It keeps the narrative moving ahead and also
emphasizes the background point that the author felt was important to your
understanding of the character.

Similar examples of good transition can be found at will in the work of any
professional author in either non-fiction or fiction. The professional has
learned the technique so well that he erects his word bridges automatically:
he moves ahead as he writes, rarely pausing to think how he is to get from
one point to another, one paragraph to another. But the professional did not
learn this technique overnight: it came to him only after long periods of trial
and error — periods during which he, like almost every beginning writer,

despaired of ever finding his own style or achieving smoothness in his prose. The moral here for the student is clear:

If you want to master the art of transition, read and read and reread the work of professional authors, paying special attention to how they move from one paragraph to another – indeed, from one sentence to another within a paragraph. Take out your pencil and underline the transitory phrases, just as they have been italicized in this chapter. Study them slowly and lovingly; copy them off on your own typewriter; try to grasp the "feel" of the words as they move past. By constant exposure to good prose, by constant experimentation with your own, you will learn, more quickly than you now anticipate, how the good writer carries his reader along with a minimum of verbal interruptions and digressions.

An editor and his staff

Observers have often remarked that an editor is no better than his staff. Perhaps – but there is a corollary here: a good editor trains his staff in his own image. Unless each subordinate knows the working of the boss's mind, senses his likes and dislikes, appreciates what he is trying to do for the welfare of the organization as a whole, then confusion is compounded and editorial direction is lost.

It is not easy, however, to acquire and train a staff – and for a number of reasons. For one, each staffer is understandably an entity in his own right, subject to the characteristics of the individual. Until certain idiosyncrasies are removed, the staffer functions not as a team member but only as a spectator. For another reason, many of today's junior editors are peripatetic by instinct: they shift around from office to office, playing their own version of musical chairs. When they come to a new job, they are likely to bring with them the policies of the last office they tenanted.

For still another, younger editors tend to hold a pretty high opinion of themselves: they are members of a "fraternity" – the brotherhood of those who work with words – and they assume powers that are not concomitants of the job. Authority and conceit go often hand in hand; a tendency to dictate editorial policy is usually present, along with the urge to lord it over the writer so that the latter won't get any silly ideas about the importance of *his* craft. – Gordon Carroll

Morton Freedgood

*When an author submits a piece stolen from his
betters, he starts a chain of events that can
lead anywhere – even to prison*

Curious cases of plagiarism

Of the large and flavorsome assortment of nightmares that plague the
dreams of editors and publishers, the choicest is plagiarism. Unlike Vol-
taire, who rather offhandedly dismissed plagiarism as "the least dangerous to
society" of all forms of theft, the editor and the publisher regard it as one of
the cruelest crimes man can commit against man.

No precise definition of plagiarism to cover all contingencies has ever
been arrived at – nor does it seem likely that it ever will. Even great legal
minds have disagreed, and most plagiarism lawsuits are determined as much
by common sense as by writ. However, shorn of all nuance or nicety,
plagiarism may be defined simply as the copying by one man of another
man's work, in whole or in significant part.

Each time a plagiarist submits a story or book he has stolen from his betters, he threatens to inflict a triple wound on the editor he has chosen to
honor with his secondhand goods. The purchase of a plagiarized work by
an editor means that he has been victimized by a literary holdup man; has

become involved in a knotty copyright problem with the publisher and author of the original work on which the theft was based; and has been made a fool of. This last is the unkindest cut of all, because it plugs him squarely in the soft underbelly of his self-esteem.

You may ask: Shouldn't an editor or publisher know *when* a plagiarized story crosses his desk? Most of the time he does; but not always. Despite his wistful image of himself as omniscient, he simply can't have read – or re-membered – everything that was ever printed. And everything that was ever printed constitutes the hunting preserve of the plagiarist. If the literary crook is incautious enough to copy a story of, say, Hemingway, or a sonnet of Shakespeare, the editor will probably know it. But the editor's defense is spread too thin to protect him against the plagiarist who steals from an obscure author.

The most gruesome of all editorial mistakes lies in printing a story or book – usually accompanied by hearty self-congratulations at having dis-covered a genius – which then turns out to be a less-known work of Tolstoi or Flaubert. Fortunately, this doesn't occur too often, mainly because most plagiarists are too lazy to update the language or customs of a story written in a different century. So they usually steal the work of a modern author. Even then, many of them won't take the trouble to change the title of the story, the names of the characters, or the locale. That would be *work*.

For the plagiarist who doesn't find the task of thinking up a new title too onerous, the results can sometimes be highly rewarding – if only temporarily so. Take, for example, the novel called *Positions Unknown,* which arrived unheralded in the editorial offices of the venerable Boston publishers Little, Brown. Signed by an unknown, Robert E. Preyer, Jr., the novel was a highly professional performance, bearing all the earmarks of a best seller. Little, Brown was delighted to offer Mr. Preyer an advance of $600, and to schedule the book for early publication.

Positions Unknown was, as the saying goes in the trade, a hot property. Exactly *how* hot, Little, Brown discovered a few weeks before publication when Virginia Kirkus, who runs a well-known book-rating service, read a set of advance proofs and recognized *Positions Unknown* as a word-for-transcription of a best seller by Ernest Gann called *Island in the Sky*.

Little, Brown had no recourse but to remove the book from its list, destroy pages and the plates, and take its loss. What – since the path of plagiarism leads but to the prison cell – happened to the enterprising Mr. Preyer? Not very much, since he was already an inmate of Ohio State Penitentiary.

Plagiarists are rarely as "successful" as Mr. Preyer. Luck – or hard luck, depending on whether you're sitting in the editor's chair or the plagiarist's – plays an important part in the drama. Certainly luck was looking the other way when a Montana miner many years ago made his bid for immortality by sending a story called "The Luck of Roaring Camp" to *Munsey's Magazine*. It was, of course, a word-for-word copy of the famous story by Bret Harte, including the title.

Editor Robert Davis's reply has become a classic. "As much as I admire the story you submitted," he wrote, "I am unable to publish it for a very peculiar reason. Many years ago I promised my old friend Bret Harte never to print 'The Luck of Roaring Camp' by anyone else but himself."

Equally unlucky – and unforgivably careless – was the thief who submitted a poem to Charles Hanson Towne, editor of *Delineator*. Mr. Towne returned the manuscript to the contributor with the following letter: "I beg to acknowledge receipt of your verses and to inform you that I have found them admirable. I cannot praise them highly enough. Indeed, I liked them so well that I wrote them myself two years ago."

In most cases, would-be plagiarists are nipped in the bud by editorial vigilance. But even when their theft actually blossoms in print, inevitably the deception is unmasked. When all else fails, the public, that inquisitive, knowledgeable genius, eventually puts the finger on the larcenist. Thus it was a reader of *Esquire* and not – understandably – one of the magazine's editors who revealed that a story called "The Perlu," which appeared in a 1935 issue of the Magazine for Men, was actually a more than reasonable facsimile of "The Damned Thing," one of the most famous of Ambrose Bierce's stories. A year later, *Esquire* – which has had more than its share of unsolicited trouble with plagiarists – proudly published a story titled "The Tale of Three Cities." It remained for an eagle-eyed reader to point out that the story was an almost exact transcription of "The Eternal Triangle," printed in *College Humor* some five years earlier.

Sometimes plagiarism is strictly a family affair. Scott Fitzgerald's wife, Zelda, after reading her husband's novel *The Beautiful and the Damned*, remarked wryly: "On one page I recognized a portion of an old diary of mine which had mysteriously disappeared after my marriage, and also scraps of letters which sounded vaguely familiar. Mr. Fitzgerald – if that's how he spells his name – seems to believe that plagiarism begins at home."

So far as is known, Fitzgerald never took the trouble to deny his wife's whimsical charge. But neither, in all likelihood, did he admit it.

More candid in this regard was Dmitri Tiomkin, who, in accepting his Oscar for having composed the award-winning score for a movie, said, "I want to thank my collaborators – Ludwig van Beethoven, Johannes Brahms, Peter Ilyitch Tchaikovsky. . . ."

Although plagiarism might be called the last resort of the untalented, it has frequently enough been the first resort (and sometimes the second and the third) of the great. Lord Byron – who was himself not above lifting some little tidbit he admired – wasn't kidding when he declared, "The most original writers are the greatest thieves." Among those who have been accused of plagiarism, with more than a modicum of justice, are such august names as Marlowe, Spenser, Goldsmith, Milton, Pope, Coleridge, Keats, Dickens, Wilde, Kipling, Stendhal, Rabelais, Molière, Dumas, Hugo, Melville, Burns, Shakespeare, Izaak Walton, etc., etc.

Edgar Allan Poe, one of the most righteously outspoken foes of plagiarism, was recently shown to have patterned his best-known poem, "The Raven," after the raven "Grip," which appears in Charles Dickens' novel *Barnaby Rudge*. As for Dickens, he drew heavily on Boswell's *Life of Johnson* and the tales of Washington Irving for *Pickwick Papers*. Ben Jonson mined rich nuggets from such classical writers as Juvenal, Suetonius, Horace, Plutarch, Pliny, and others, and his famous song, "Drink to Me Only with Thine Eyes," is a suspiciously tight "paraphrase" of Philostratus. Laurence Sterne, author of *Tristram Shandy,* helped himself boldly and shamelessly to large portions of Burton, Swift, Erasmus, Rabelais, and Cervantes.

Samuel Taylor Coleridge lifted whole pages of his critical masterpiece *Biographia Literaria* from Schelling; and Poe, in *his* critical writings, took heavily from Coleridge. Bryon transferred a great deal of the action and some of the actual words of Goethe's *Faust* to his own *Manfred*. Keats made free with Spenser. Oscar Wilde stole from Whistler's writings on art, and Whistler memorialized the theft by saying, "Oscar has the courage of the opinions . . . of others!"

Stendhal, one of the great French prose masters, was also one of the stickiest-fingered. He swiped the idea for his first novel, *Lucien Lewen,* from a manuscript belonging to one of his mistresses; his *History of Italian Painting* from the Abbé Lanzi; and his *Memoirs of a Tourist* from Prosper Mérimée. Robert Burns, one of the most original of poets, nevertheless copied the third stanza of "A Red, Red Rose" from the Motherwell collection of chapbooks.

Benjamin Franklin, that avatar of probity and the golden rule, combed the writings of Dryden, Pope, Swift, Bacon, and La Rochefoucauld to eke out the homiletics of his famous *Poor Richard's Almanac*. Thomas Jefferson, in writing the Declaration of Independence, snitched two of its most ringing phrases from others – "life, liberty and the pursuit of happiness" originated with Locke, and "all men are born free and equal" with Ulpian. Confronted with the evidence of his borrowings, Jefferson calmly admitted them, pointing out that, in taking on the assignment of writing the Declaration, he had not promised to "invent new ideas altogether" and "offer no sentiment which had never been exposed before."

The greatest highwayman of all was the noblest writer of all – William Shakespeare. It would take more than a page to list the debts this titan of the literary ages owes to other writers. Coolly, without an ounce of compunction, Shakespeare plundered the literature of all times and all countries. Yet time has handed down a curious – and curiously correct – verdict. Where most of the writers he copied from outrageously are forgotten or half-forgotten, Shakespeare lives on in the majority opinion as the greatest writer of all time.

The moral is not – in case you're getting ideas – that if Shakespeare could plagiarize with impunity, so can *you*. The moral is this: If you're going to plagiarize with impunity, you'd better be darn sure before you start that you're as singular a genius as Shakespeare. Even if you *have* convinced yourself of this, it's still a good idea to think twice before you embark on a course of literary piracy.

In Shakespeare's day, the chances were that the plagiarist's worst punishment consisted of his becoming the object of moral indignation or derision. Today, there are stringent legal deterrents, and the perpetrator of arrant plagiary usually winds up swinging a hammer on a prison rock pile.

Why, then, in view of the odds against success, do people continue to roll this particular pair of fixed dice? In at least one instance, the motive is exactly like that of any other form of thievery – the lure of easy money. The man who exhumes a story by de Maupassant or Marquand, signs his own undistinguished name to it, and sends it off to a magazine hopes thereby to collect some cold cash. To another copycat, the cash, though not to be despised, is of secondary importance to the glory of seeing his name in print and becoming established as a full-fledged author in the eyes of his friends and neighbors.

Still others, blinded by admiration for a favorite author, lose track of where imitation ends and copying begins. Then, of course, there are the pathological crooks – literary versions of the kleptomaniac, who steals compulsively rather than for gain.

Unless the theft in question is clumsily obvious – and most cases are – plagiarism is not always an easy thing to prove in a court of law. A few decades ago, Jack London brought suit against a film company, charging that a movie called *Love of Gold* was a flagrant steal of his short story "Just Meat." Despite the striking – and seemingly damning – similarities between the two, London lost the case. The judge, although he took due cognizance of the resemblances, pointed out that the contested plot had been used earlier in Kipling's "The King of Ankus," and still earlier in Chaucer's "The Pardoner's Tale," and earlier yet in a long succession of oriental tales!

In the same view, Horace Walpole's "I would have been a handsome man but they changed me in the cradle" was shown to have come from Cervantes' *Don Quixote*. But Cervantes had picked it up from the Greeks, and the Greeks had gotten it from the Egyptians, who may or may not have filched it from the Israelites or the Philistines.

Although plagiarism is usually an ill wind that blows no good to anybody, in at least one case a flagrant instance turned out to be a disguised blessing. For years, Charles E. Van Loan had been writing baseball stories for the pulp magazines, but hadn't been able to make the *Saturday Evening Post*. Then somebody stole one of his yarns and, after making a slight alteration or two, sent it off to the *Post,* which bought it and printed it.

A friend of Van Loan thereupon wrote to George Horace Lorimer, editor of the *Post:* "If you like Van Loan stories, why not buy them direct from the original author?"

Lorimer found the logic of this appeal irresistible, and so began Van Loan's long and prosperous career as a writer of stories for the *Saturday Evening Post!*

> (*Author's Note:* Wilson Mizner, a celebrated wit of the twenties, once said, cynically but with deadly accuracy: "If you steal from one author, it's plagiarism. If you steal from many, it's research." The piece you have just read was researched from a number of sources, most notably Alexander Lindey's definitive book, *Plagiarism and Originality.*)

Reading helps your writing

Reading for profit (or for pleasure) is a habit most successful, ambitious men discover to their advantage early in life. People who get ahead in most businesses and professions consciously take time out for reading. The most successful ones instinctively knew early in their lives that to get the better of their competition, they would have to use high-powered mental ammunition. They got it largely by reading. Having developed the reading habit early in life, they used it to become successful.

Janet Van Duyn

*There are many reasons . . . and all of them
add up to the current increase in literary
output across the country*

Why women want to write

The world is full of women who want to write. We see them at work in a
variety of places – in offices, on trains, taking notes at lectures, hunched over
desks in libraries, tapping out copy on card tables in living rooms. In fact,
there are few modern settings into which we can't put a woman and a typewriter. The question, however, is not so much where are the women writers –
but *who* are they?

We can start by looking at a few "types." A Minnesota housewife, let's
say, wants a permanent record of her grandparents' migration to this country.
Another, a high school dropout who used to be "pretty good in English,"
realizes that she's capable of doing more than caring for a home, husband,
and four children. A college professor wants to make a significant contribution
to her field or to communicate her knowledge to a wider audience.

From the poet who must grope for phrases to convey her depth of personal
feeling to the busy woman-of-affairs who has much to say and no time to say
it, there's a common denominator, a motivating force which prompts a

woman to roll a clean sheet of paper in the typewriter and begin. Apparently, she's reached a plateau in her experience from which she wishes to view the world and tell others what she sees. Why?

In the past few decades, the social analysts have knocked themselves out trying to find out where "woman's place" is — to "factor her in" on the vast, complicated scheme of things. If she stays home and likes it, she's imprisoned in some kind of "mystique." If she goes out and likes it, she's restless, irresponsible, even disturbed. If by some miracle she manages to do both, she's a phenomenon and therefore suspect.

Whatever her motives for writing may be, she's certainly written *about* — by members of her own and of the opposite sex. Under the subject heading of *Women,* our library catalogues offer about four inches of cards that imply the going is rough: problems of marriage, adolescence, single blessedness. Problems of dress, morality, job-hunting. Admonitions to go home, cut loose, save, spend. The challenge to women doctors, lawyers, mechanics, ministers. The biology of women. The psychology of women. And finally, like a melancholy amen — the trouble with women.

The magazines and newspapers enrich the confusion. Most articles about women represent her as "going through" an almost endless series of phases, all of them sinister. With all this treachery lurking about, no wonder the besieged, problem-ridden female takes to her typewriter. Surely she's got something to say.

Even before she caused such a flutter among journalists, woman was represented as a creature of whims and fancies, always changing her mind. But there is also the centuries-old image of the wise woman who lives on the hill. How do you reconcile these two sides? Perhaps it is woman's inconsistency which actuates her deep-rooted urge to write.

"I'm not sure why I want to write," a housewife recently told the Famous Writers School. "It seems as though some part of me, not logical, urges me to try."

No one can dispute the fact that a writer, man or woman, can rarely analyze his motives until he has marshaled them from the subconscious and set them down. Ideas lie far beneath the level of day-to-day living. But with a woman, the subconscious is often a stronger guiding factor; she must follow that "hunch" even before she's able to express it in words. Hence her seeming lack of logic in making decisions.

Professional women authors frequently describe this feeling of wanting to write and not knowing why. "Will another novel swim up?" Virginia Woolf asks in her *Diary.* "If so, how?" And Simone de Beauvoir, sitting alone in front of a blank sheet of paper, could say: "I felt the need to write in my fingertips and in the taste of the words in my throat, but I didn't know where to start. . . ."

During the busy years when a young woman is concerned with home, husband, and children, she may have little time for searching her subconscious. Often she feels she must keep her impressions submerged until the tumult is over. Frequently a middle-aged housewife says: "My love of writing goes back to sixth grade when I wrote a play the class acted. Our teacher urged me to continue writing because I had talent. . . ."

Next comes high school, perhaps college, with real promise from this woman's pen. Then comes marriage – and literary blackout.

It's a familiar story, but it's fatuous to blame the institution of marriage. As most women will admit, their first allegiance is to the home, and when there are children around, there's simply too much to do. During those years this type of woman is easy prey to distractions, emergencies, groups and it takes a strong drive to produce manuscripts.

Other women do manage to contrive a few minutes or hours a day for the typewriter. "It isn't that I dislike making peanut-butter-and-jelly sandwiches," a young mother of five said wearily. "I'm just sick of it. That's why I want to write – to get out into a world where people are more than four feet high."

Seated alone at her typewriter, a woman can reach out to the adult world. Writing satisfies her longing more than the passive act of reading, because when she's finished, she's got something to show for her efforts uniquely hers. Nor does she have to go far to find her material. Women writers from Jean Kerr to the incomparable Mrs. Gaskell have proved that the small events of home and village can be delightful entertainment.

"It pleases me to describe everyday happenings in a way that makes life at our house sound like a Broadway comedy hit." Here's a woman laughing at her own situation and giving life a new dimension.

This kind of standing aside suggests solitude – and this is what creative persons need and crave. In *A Gift from the Sea,* Anne Lindbergh enjoys new insights after getting off on an island by herself. Alone, but not lonely, a woman has for a time escaped her categories – Wife, Teacher, Mother, Secretary. But why writing, we may ask? If a woman needs a creative outlet, why doesn't she choose painting or music?

Very often she does. But the mere act of writing is a simple one: all it requires is a chair, a table, and a typewriter. Not even any special manual dexterity.

As an art form, writing is intangible. It requires an ability to think, to match words and phrases to fleeting impressions, to observe, to invent. Most people have an urge to master a part of its complex technique, just to be

able to say what's on their minds. For women, who often must live in a con-
stricted world of a household or a 9-to-5 office job, a reaching out through
the medium of words is a natural outlet.

However, the articulate woman is a relatively new phenomenon. Until the
late 1700s, woman was almost mute. In a world of men, the women were
subservient, with no voice of their own. Unless uttered by men, women's
words were unimportant. "They were content," writes Agnes de Mille. "They
were speechless."

In the latter part of the eighteenth century, women began to make themselves heard. One of the first women's names to appear on a published book
was that of Lady Mary Wortley Montagu, a widely traveled aristocrat who
learned the Turkish language, went about enthusiastically in Turkish dress,
and wrote colorful letters about what she saw in the Levant. They appeared in
1763.

In London, a Mrs. Vesey gathered a group of intellectual men and women
about her for evening "conversations." Gradually, novels by women appeared.
Mary Ann Evans, a woman with spirited notions of reform, guarded her
reputation under the name of George Eliot. On a bleak Yorkshire heath,
three pathologically shy sisters named Brontë wrote romances under the
names of Currer, Ellis, and Acton Bell. And on the other side of the Atlantic
an equally shy New England spinster, Emily Dickinson, penned delicate
lyric poems, which in an age of tasteless amplitude were remarkable for
their pith and meaning. Little did she realize that she was to usher in a whole
generation of American poets – notably Sara Teasdale, Edna St. Vincent
Millay, and Elinor Wylie.

By the time the nineteenth century was in full swing, the cloak of gentility
had been shed. Women were writing furiously about factory workers, slaves,
social outcasts; no social problem was safe from their pens. In America,
Harriet Beecher Stowe and Louisa May Alcott became household words.
(In an article in *Harper's Magazine,* Ellen Moers appropriately dubbed
these nineteenth-century novelists "angry young women.")

Yet they weren't all angry; some were simply good storytellers with sharp
powers of observation. Jane Austen, queen of them all, brightened her
uneventful life by writing novels about life around her. Sitting quietly at her
desk, she tossed literary darts at the fads and fashions of her time.

Eventually the lady of letters became so entrenched that she became a
caricature. With relish, Charles Dickens created in *Bleak House* one of his
most believable women characters – a cause-ridden, indolent housewife
named Mrs. Jellyby, who, "sitting in quite a nest of waste paper, drank coffee
all evening and dictated at intervals to her eldest daughter."

At the end of the nineteenth century and at the beginning of the twentieth came the great surge of brilliant women novelists, short-story writers, poets, essayists: Wharton, Stein, Mansfield, Sitwell, Woolf, Cather. Women, as spokesmen for their own sex, were coming into their own.

Mary Johnston, whose romantic novel of colonial days, *To Have and to Hold*, had been an unprecedented best seller in 1899, turned her talents to Civil War novels written from the Confederate point of view. Elizabeth Madox Roberts wrote perceptively of life in Virginia. Perhaps the most significant of all was Ellen Glasgow, a native of Richmond, who could write both realistically and satirically of the social ferment below the Mason-Dixon line.

As America grew and spread, women were motivated to describe home and heath in living terms. Sarah Orne Jewett's stories of Maine began appearing in the early 1900s; in them one can smell the salt and spray, sense the sweep of landscape, hear the echoes of an empty house. Julia Peterkin's classic, *Scarlet Sister Mary,* evoked the pride and sensitivity of the Gullah Negro of South Carolina. Names of certain writers became permanently associated with places they wrote about: Gertrude Atherton with California, Marjorie Kinnan Rawlings with Florida, Willa Cather with Nebraska, Katherine Anne Porter with the curious, shifting population of Mexico and the Southwest.

Both America and England have produced some amazingly prolific women writers, who have spent years learning their craft, developing their style, and often trying out many forms of expression. Edna Ferber is an outstanding example of novelist, short-story writer, and playwright. Daphne du Maurier has a long list of successful titles to her credit. As a young writer, Faith Baldwin first turned her hand to poetry, then went on to write more than seventy-five novels and countless short stories.

Ladies often turn out to be excellent sleuths. *The Lodger,* one of the first crime-suspense stories, based on the activities of Jack the Ripper, came from the pen of Mrs. Belloc Lowndes. Mary Roberts Rinehart—and later, Agatha Christie and Dorothy L. Sayers—have had phenomenal success all over the world. Mignon G. Eberhart and Leslie Ford, with their flair for atmosphere coupled with their ability to invent, continue to imbue their charmed readers with a "cosy sense of peril."

Despite all this female success, certain critics have lately remarked that "complacency" has crept into women's writing. They mourn the damping out of fire and ask why, with all her intuition, the woman writer hasn't produced more noteworthy material. Is it true that the female renaissance is about to end?

Hardly. Today, more women are writing about more subjects than ever before in history. To be sure, a lot of it is trivial and passing, but writing is no longer a specialized art – a megaphone for a Big Woman with a Big Cause. Often it is a necessity, and in a technical sense, a skill which few can afford to be without. Whether in fiction or non-fiction, the writer's first duty to the reader is to be interesting.

And why shouldn't we point pridefully to women writers who have been cited for their efforts? To Margaret Mitchell, whose *Gone with the Wind* justly deserved a Pulitzer Prize. To Pearl Buck, winner of both a Pulitzer Prize and the Nobel Prize for literature for her novels of Chinese life. To Lillian Hellman, playwright and scenario writer, who won the award of the New York Drama Critics Circle for *Watch on the Rhine*. To Eudora Welty, whose short stories of Mississippi have brought her a Guggenheim Fellowship and three O. Henry awards.

With all these clacking typewriters, there's bound to be not only variety but also experiment and competition. With woman's world changing and enlarging at such an unprecedented rate, we can look forward to more sky-rockets in the future. And although some of our female literary output is complacent, some noisy, some "beat," women are achieving stature as scientists, sociologists, historians – and are also turning out to be brilliant writers.

A hundred years ago there would have been no place for a Rachel Carson, a Margaret Mead, a Ruth Benedict. Who would believe that a woman like Edith Hamilton, having concluded a distinguished career in teaching, would carve out a second career through her books on the world of ancient Greece? Or that there would be writers of the caliber of Barbara Tuchman and Catherine Drinker Bowen, who would turn their scholarship and insight into history and biography?

With her peculiar brand of intuition and integrity, a woman writer often notices small, insignificant details a man may pass over. Thus she can light up the past, giving it new perspective and life and meaning.

One thing we cannot do is to accuse today's women of slighting their opportunities or wasting their dreams. A woman's freedom is dearly bought. She drives a hard bargain with Time. She's too much of a realist to waste what she's struggled for centuries to acquire.

Give her a typewriter and a room of her own, and this Mistress of Illogic will make a brave thrust into what Virginia Woolf calls the "loose, drifting material of life." Winding it on her special distaff, she will patiently smooth, sort, and spin until she has fashioned it into a pattern of many colors.

Getting rid of characters

You should think carefully about the four elements in a story – character, setting, situation and theme. But the time always comes when you've just got to get words on paper, and when you transfer your ideas into words, your characters, settings, situations and themes are bound to change somewhat. Many things come out of the typewriter that you hadn't imagined. But as they develop clearly, they give the whole project better focus.

I know for my own part that I seem more and more likely as my characters come out of the typewriter to understand what that kind of person would do. I also find, occasionally, that I have created a character who has no relation whatsoever to the plot. He's a fifth wheel. I thought of him, I put him into the story. But he never came alive; he proved to have nothing whatever to do with the story. So I had to remove him. – Mignon Eberhart

The theme is vital to juveniles

If your story is important enough for young people, you ought to have something which you want to say about it. Not a sermon, not a lesson, but an underlying idea which will hold it together. Why did you want to write about this material? What does it hold that you value, that you want to contribute? Ask yourself what you want to say about it, and when you can formulate your idea into a statement, you have a theme. This underlying idea, invisible as it is, may be the most important part of your story.

If this generation, like those before it, repeats the blunders of the past, we writers might possibly be to some degree at fault. Though we compete with movies, with comics, with television and radio, we still have a power which none of them possesses. The young reader takes his book into the quiet of his mind, and there he stays with it until it has become a part of his thinking and his feeling. You have entered into him and become a source of his growth. – Mabel Louise Robinson

The definition of a book

When you sell a man a book, you don't sell him just a few ounces of paper and ink and glue – you sell him a whole new life. Love and friendship and humor and ships at sea by night – there's all heaven and earth in a real book. – Christopher Morley

Section II   Articles
and
features

Morton Freedgood

For the average author, the largest editorial
market lies in the field of factual and
informational writing

The wide world of non-fiction

For reasons having little to do with anything so disagreeable as reality, the fiction writer currently enjoys more "status" in the eyes of the public than the non-fiction writer does. Like most questions involving status, this one is as bright and iridescent as a soap bubble, and just about as substantial. As writers themselves know, the sole valid standard for measuring status in the world of writing is quality. Whether a man writes fiction or non-fiction, only one thing matters—*how well he writes*.

Bedazzled by the occasional "runaway best seller" and the occasional Broadway "smash hit," the public tends to regard the novelist and the playwright as literary Glamor Boys. But this view is a mirage. The best seller and the smash hit constitute a tiny minority of all the novels that are published and all the plays that are produced. And even in the case of these rare birds, glamor is no more than skin deep. Just beneath the surface are the blood, sweat, and tears of hard work and craftsmanship. So far as writing goes— *any* kind of writing—the glamor is mostly in the eye of the beholder.

It would be foolish, in defending the status of non-fiction, to do so at the expense of fiction. Each genre has its place in the scheme of things, each reinforces the other, both together are vital forms of communication in a world which may depend for its survival on the ability to communicate.

Whether because of the myth of glamor or not, fiction is chosen by a good many beginning writers whose talent might be better suited to non-fiction. Actually, a good argument could be advanced – if such arguments were anything but fruitless – for persuading students and beginners that opportunities in the non-fiction field were, if anything, greater than in fiction. Certainly this is true in terms of the marketplace. Glamor or no glamor, many a non-fiction writer, to quote a popular entertainer, cries all the way to the bank.

At a conservative estimate, the non-fiction writer produces roughly 95 percent of all the words that are printed and read. Does this figure seem outlandish? Let's examine it. We can quickly list the writing the fictionist does: novels, plays, short stories, movies, television shows, poetry. Everything else in the expanding universe of writing falls to the province of the writer of non-fiction. This includes books and articles on every possible subject in the human spectrum, ranging from the ingredients of a cough syrup and the instructions for operating an electric can opener. It includes the reading matter on a dollar bill and almost everything that is printed in a newspaper. It includes the contents of legal documents and circulars and fliers and birth certificates and passports and the Articles of War and the charter of the Elks. It includes advertisements, publicity, captions accompanying photographs, traffic information on road maps, and letters from collection agencies. It includes the manual for operating your convertible top, your air conditioner, your hair drier, and your lawn mower. It includes mail-order catalogues and theater programs; greeting cards and subway cards; rubber stamps and postage stamps; speeches, orations, and eulogies; announcements and pronouncements and political platforms; and the copy on a gum wrapper.

It includes the news and the weather and the commercials on radio and television; radio and TV documentaries and station breaks and charity appeals; dictionaries and encyclopedias and how-to books of every conceivable – and occasionally inconceivable – description; the major portion of all the books written for the burgeoning juvenile market, which in recent years has favored non-fiction over fiction in ever-increasing proportion; reminiscences and memoirs and personal histories; chronicles from the Bible to Winston Churchill.

The catalogue could be continued indefinitely. But perhaps it can be most neatly summed up with this revealing little paradox: barring the fictional examples that are quoted, every word contained in the two volumes of the

Fiction Course of the Famous Writers School is obviously non-fiction!

A relevant point about each of the varied forms of non-fiction writing cited above is that somebody got paid for writing it. But, important as this is, it's not the only point. The same operative satisfactions that exist for the writer in the "glamor" field of fiction exist in the not-so-mundane-as-you'd-think field of non-fiction.

Granted, few souls would conclude that they had fulfilled the American Dream by writing the instructions for assembling a beach chair, or composing the directions for applying a home permanent, but such huge satisfactions are few in any area of writing. Instead, the satisfaction is the simple and rewarding one of having written to good purpose – to have communicated and been paid for it. But there are additional gratifications. On its upper levels non-fiction is unqualifiedly creative, and shares with the very best of fiction the permanency of what we call "literature." There are a hundred, or a hundred hundred, examples that might be adduced of non-fiction books which have made a seminal contribution to the sum of man's knowledge of himself and the world he lives in – great works of science, economics, history, religion, philosophy.

The argument can be proved – if it needs proving – without leaving home. Let's consider the case of one of our own Guiding Faculty, Bruce Catton. Significantly, Catton started out with the intention of becoming a novelist. But he was, by his own admission, a poor novelist, and so he turned his crea-tive energies to the writing of non-fiction; specifically, to the Civil War. Working in a field which had already been tilled to near-exhaustion, in which every conceivable facet had been turned and re-turned, every fact picked over a thousand times, Catton has produced a series of books which have been hailed all over the world for having cast new light on their subject.

How did he do it? The answer – if not the doing – is simple. He brought to the task the fully dedicated powers of his imagination and intelligence and perception. In other words, he functioned at the same white heat of creativity as the good writer of fiction. As the novelist takes imaginary characters and events, intensifies them, and brings them to life in a plausible environment, so Catton takes real people and events out of the past, intensi-fies them, and makes them live vividly in the present. The point hardly needs making that bringing the dead to life in print, as Catton does, is a fully equivalent achievement to bringing the nonexistent to life, as the novelist does.

The opportunities to pull off this kind of trick on a grand scale in magazine non-fiction are limited. But, nevertheless, the magazine writer, too, can experience the high adventure of writing creatively and imaginatively. Let's take a look at still another member of our Guiding Faculty, J. D. Ratcliff. Ratcliff, who couldn't write fiction if the penalty for failure to do so was burning at the stake, brings to his non-fiction curiosity, a keen mind, sound editorial judgment, and respect for, but not enslavement to, facts. There's no question but that he works with as much absorption and devotion on a brief article for *Reader's Digest* as a fiction writer does on a short story. Every one of his articles is massively researched, carefully thought through, intelligently and creatively attacked. Each is, finally, a distillation of fact and opinion that contributes its scruple to the weight of man's knowledge.

While it's true, as a crude generality, that most writers have a vocation for either fiction *or* non-fiction (and it's only good sense to play one's strongest hand), it's equally true that many others work both sides of the street. Although this jack-of-all-trades versatility is more prevalent in Europe (where the man of letters often does novels, plays, short stories, literary criticism, political pieces, and even journalism), it has begun to flourish in this country as well. Hemingway, whom most people think of exclusively as a novelist and short-story writer, is the author of three non-fiction books — *Death in the Afternoon, The Green Hills of Africa,* and *A Moveable Feast:* John Steinbeck's most recent best seller, *Travels with Charley,* was strictly non-fiction; Scott Fitzgerald's famous autobiographical series, *Crack-Up,* was as widely read as his novels; Saul Bellow, author of the best-selling novel *Herzog,* frequently writes reviews and criticism; James Michener has published a number of non-fiction books dealing with oriental art: Mary McCarthy, author of *The Group,* has published several volumes of non-fiction ranging from literary and theatrical criticism to social commentary. There's no lack of evidence to prove the point — from Washington Irving and Mark Twain to John Hersey, Herman Wouk, and Norman Mailer.

Again, let's refer to the Guiding Faculty of Famous Writers School to illuminate our thesis. For three decades, Faith Baldwin was strictly a fiction writer, and as such, one of the most widely read of all popular novelists. Then, on invitation, she accepted the writing of a monthly non-fiction column for *Woman's Day.* Called "Open Door," the column quickly established itself as a prime favorite with the magazine's large audience — and with Miss Baldwin herself. She had discovered the wide, wide world of non-fiction and become a convert to its fascinations. Not that she gave up fiction. Instead, she now "mixes 'em up" the way a good baseball pitcher varies the speed of his delivery, writing her non-fiction pieces and continuing to produce stories and novels.

Miss Baldwin recommends this change of pace highly, but only to those who are suited to it. She's more concerned with those people — and there are a significant number of them – who are trying to fit the square peg of a talent for non-fiction into the round hole of fiction.

"Everyone wants to write fiction," she acknowledges, "yet they may be barking up the wrong literary tree. Non-fiction is a tremendous field, and materially, as far as books and magazines are concerned, more rewarding than fiction. . . . For example, humor is a wide-open field, and both book and magazine publishers are panting for it. Incidentally, everybody now recognizes that humor is not exclusively a man's field. We have a number of women humorists who write books, articles and light verse. The names of Jean Kerr, Phyllis McGinley and Cornelia Otis Skinner spring quickly to mind. And look at other fields, once considered strictly masculine, in which women succeeded – medicine, physics, engineering, law, the ministry. Why should they not go forward in non-fiction and with enormous success?"

Miss Baldwin continues: "I have found in my particular field of non-fiction more reward, emotionally and spiritually, than I ever knew before. So I hope that other women will bring to this branch of writing their patience, sympathy and comprehension. They make people and places and things come alive for us, make actual struggles real by understanding both the successes and failures of those about whom they write. There is no reason why they shouldn't; they are equipped for this kind of writing. More power to them!"

Without trying to make invidious comparisons, there's little question that non-fiction, by its very nature, is a more "outgoing" form of writing than fiction. From conception to completed work, the non-fiction article or book contains much of the excitement of a chase, or a good detective story. The writer tracks down facts wherever they may exist – in the library, in the museum, in "the field." In many instances one fact leads to another in a kind of fascinating paper chase at the end of which is the prize – perhaps, if you're lucky, a little gem of information which nobody else has yet uncovered.

But it isn't all paper work. Much of it involves travel – not necessarily to far places, but certainly to interesting, off-the-beaten-track places. And much of it is dealing with people – interviewing experts, people with unusual personal stories or backgrounds, people with odd occupations, public officials. Then there's correspondence, not only to gather facts, but with editors and, from time to time, there will be face-to-face conferences with editors to discuss one aspect or another of a piece. As a vehicle for getting to meet people, to learn new things, to enlarge your own perspectives, there's nothing to compare with the preparatory work – the research – for a non-fiction article or book. It comes as close to being sheer fun as anything connected with the serious business of writing can be.

Writers who inhabit the wide, wide world of non-fiction know all this, of course, and most of them wouldn't change places with the fiction writer for all the money in the world . . . well, perhaps for *all* the money in the world, but not for a penny less. The non-fiction writer doesn't pine for the glamor of the fiction writer because he knows it doesn't exist in any real sense. He knows that all writing, fiction or non-fiction, is difficult, exasperating, terrifying, discouraging, anguishing, and, ultimately, infinitely rewarding.

So — if you want to write fiction, fine, go to it. If you feel you can combine fiction *and* non-fiction, that's fine too. But if your natural inclination is definitely toward non-fiction, don't let yourself feel for a minute that you're a stepchild. There are no stepchildren in the family of writers, only, as in any family, brothers and sisters who are slightly and engagingly different from each other.

Women make successful writers

Any woman, given some talent, the urge to express herself and the will to work, can write successfully — and her sex will not deter her. There are as many successful women fiction writers as men. One factor attributed to women which has often been (as far as the critics are concerned) a detriment in other professions does not hold true in writing. Women lawyers and doctors, for instance, are always accused of being "too emotional." Yet in writing, emotion is certainly no drawback. Instead, it's an enormous help. For you have to *feel* in order to write. — Faith Baldwin

Through a writer's eyes

No writer should be afraid to describe the world he sees, even if it is different from the world of others. He is the only one who sees it. After all, all a writer has to give is himself. — Somerset Maugham

William B. Hartley

A husband-and-wife team proves
that geography is no obstacle to
successful writing

Formula for free-lancing

In 1957, shortly after I settled in Miami to write national magazine articles, I received a one-line letter from William Lindsay Gresham, a friend, a former editorial associate, and the author of *Nightmare Alley*.

"Since you have obviously gone crazy," he wrote, "did they use a straight-jacket or did you go quietly?"

I had gone quietly. But Bill Gresham's observation summarized a general attitude about writing articles from Florida. Everyone agreed it was possible and even pleasant to produce fiction under the palms. There was also agreement that you could write non-fiction in the area – provided you had an indulgent uncle, a private income, or a job on the side. But no one believed a writer could make a living in Florida solely from writing non-fiction for national magazines.

Yet my wife and I have been doing it for ten years under the by-line "William and Ellen Hartley." We have produced at least 350 articles for major magazines, plus one hard-cover book and several paperbacks – all non-fiction.

I am absolutely sincere when I say this doesn't reflect unusual merit on our part. There are non-fiction writers in every part of the country, Florida included, far more talented than we could ever hope to be. Moreover, I don't believe luck has played much part in our survival as unaffiliated Florida writers; luck could not be consistently good over a ten-year period. Nor do I think that a background in editing has been particularly helpful. Magazine policies have changed since Ellen and I occupied editorial chairs.

If any "secret" exists, it might be found in our continuing evaluation of the out-of-New-York writer's problems and our insistence on viewing article writing *as a business*. "Business" is a dirty word to some writers; we, however, are flattered when an editor tells us, "You people are so businesslike."

When I resigned as executive editor of *Redbook,* I spent almost a year writing a remarkably bad novel that still haunts me as an equally bad movie on the Late Late Show. (Earlier, I had been editor or managing editor of some half a dozen other magazines, and had written since 1936.)

By chance, I visited Miami, where Ellen had arrived to work in an advertising agency. She had been on the staff of *Sales Management* magazine and had also done professional writing. I started writing almost at once and Ellen joined me on a full-time basis shortly after we were married. Our first problem was to overcome a suspicion on the part of many editors, close friends included, that Miami-based writers were inevitably involved in Miami publicity – and also spent most of their time fishing. We also tried to get across the thought, now generally accepted, that there is much more to Florida than pretty girls and oranges.

As an initial step in convincing editors that we really worked, we purchased businesslike stationery. Even today, our queries go out on paper bearing the heading: "Suggestion for Your Publication." This form identifies us immediately with any query we submit to an editor. And although this sounds pompous, our best means of letting editors know that we *really* work (despite sun and fun) has been to work. For example, during Hurricane Donna, when our home seemed to be blowing into the next county, we finished a manuscript by candlelight.

In order to produce an assigned paperback book, I worked daily from 4 A.M. until 3 P.M. Ellen then took over, working until 2 A.M. A catering service provided food. We also produced three articles during this period. (Our experience with the catering service later was described in *The Better Way* section of *Good Housekeeping.*)

Early in our activity as Florida-based writers, we made two important decisions. One was never to be typed as "Florida regional writers." The other was to avoid specialization.

Without turning our backs on regional stories, which would have been silly, we decided we could do broad national articles as readily from Miami as we could from Tarrytown, New York. The research techniques were essentially the same. Miami has an excellent public library; the University of Miami has a fine law and medical library as well as a good general library. Anything not locally available can be obtained through inter-library loans.

In addition to these facilities, we began a source index that has since grown to huge proportions. If an editor asks us to write an article on widget making in Idaho, it is quite possible that we can tell him the name of the chief widget manufacturer within two minutes. (In a delightful switch, the local public library has sometimes called us for information.)

Building a source index is boring work, but it has paid off. We have no hesitation researching and writing an article for the *Reader's Digest* on the misuse of tranquilizers; an article for *Good Housekeeping* on conciliation courts around the nation; a piece for *Science Digest* on what the space program has taught us about human stress factors; or an article for *Pageant* on dyslexia, a reading disorder.

Editors have come to realize we can handle these jobs as well from Miami as we could from New York. I estimate that 75 percent of our work is *not* identified primarily with Miami or Florida. Our subject matter has included travel, history, education, general science, medicine, social problems, current affairs, biography, profiles, self-improvement, safety, adventure, religion, such specialties as the space program, and doubtless some subjects I have forgotten. Politics, for example. And pieces involving youth problems and activities.

Aside from financial advantage, the wide range of activity has offered rewarding stimulation. We find it fascinating to hunt wild boars in northern Florida one week, interview a prominent scientist several days later, profile a visiting VIP, and then shift to a piece on school-bus safety throughout the United States.

There is a disadvantage, as well. In order to know something about a multitude of subjects, we have to scan and assess literally hundreds of articles a month. We receive more than fifty weekly or monthly magazines. And enough brochures, pamphlets, and specialized journals to fill a small public library. Ellen is best at digesting science and medical material: I favor education, social problems, and current affairs.

Material is clipped and filed for reference. We also read and clip four daily newspapers. Filing day, a horrifying experience, comes when we can no longer face the accumulation of clippings. A table, forty feet long and four feet wide, is put together with pieces of plywood. Thereafter, while Ellen hums a monotone of protest, we sort all our material for the filing cabinets.

But the files are tremendously helpful. No library collection could substitute for them, because no library is in the writing business. We have sometimes sought a particular bit of information in every public facility Miami has to offer, only to find it later in our own files. As a result, there is now a sign on the crowded filing room – our garage – that reads: Look Here First.

Here, briefly, is how we operate in producing articles from Florida. Some of our work is unsolicited: an editor phones or writes and asks us to handle a particular job. We also solicit work through queries, based on assessment of the current needs of the particular magazine and its policy. There is nothing unusual about this; every writer follows the same procedure.

Since we are far from our markets, however, and usually unable to discuss ideas across the editorial desk, we face the problem of saying either too much or too little in a query. The solution is to research the subject, describe our idea briefly, and note that we will provide an expanded outline upon request. Some editors appreciate detailed queries; others like them short. If we don't know, we ask. And when an idea is particularly timely we sometimes query by phone.

Needless to say, before a query goes out we check the *Readers' Guide* for past use. We also check our own index – the contents pages of many magazines not listed in the *Guide*. These are clipped from some twenty-five magazines and filed for reference. There is no foolproof way to avoid suggesting something an editor may already have in inventory – we try.

When an assignment comes in, our first step is to increase our basic knowledge of the subject. Let's use three illustrations – a piece on Jackie Gleason's ideas about ESP, an article about the war between Florida game wardens and alligator poachers, and a story on dangerous or inadequate school construction.

The Gleason piece was an unsolicited assignment from the editor of *Pageant*. He learned that Gleason was seriously interested in extrasensory perception and psychic phenomena. Would we interview Jackie and also profile him in the process?

You could fit our knowledge of ESP into a thimble and still have room left over for Gleason. So first, we read everything we could find on the subject and also checked past articles on The Great One. After establishing that he would see us, we prepared a few interview questions (not many, since we have found it best to get a person talking and then permit the interview to flow along naturally). The final step was to tape record the interview. Witty, articulate, highly informed, and competently supplied with champagne by a little man who kept popping in and out, Gleason provided us with magnificent material and, incidentally, some understanding of a complex personality.

The article on alligator poachers was cooked up by my wife and the executive editor of *Popular Mechanics*. A letter from him said something like this: "I'm glad to hear you are going into the Everglades to hunt alligator poachers with the game warden. But please be careful. I understand the poachers shoot back."

I took the letter to Ellen and said: "Read this crazy thing. I never told him I'd chase around the swamps after alligator poachers."

"I did," said Ellen calmly. "I must have forgotten to tell you."

The point of this anecdote, however, is that story turned out to be a reasonably typical Florida regional. First, we read everything available on alligators and alligator poaching and taped a preliminary interview with Game Warden Tom Shirley. Then, on a cold night, I found myself whipping over the swamps with Tom in a two-man airboat — a sled-like contrivance driven by a plane propeller. Flying along at top speed *in total darkness,* we covered sixty miles of Everglades terrain. We saw an abundance of snakes and alligators, but no poachers. However, Tom's stories and my experience on actual patrol were sufficient for article construction.

The piece on school construction is typical of a national job. Back in 1961, we spotted a newspaper item that told of a Mississippi high school in which a floor had collapsed. Twenty-two children had been injured. One of us had the bright idea of checking the New York *Times* index on accidents of this sort. They were numerous and shocking.

As we accumulated information, a national pattern began to form. Schools, old and new, were jammed with safety hazards. We queried *Good Housekeeping* and they told us to meet an assignment under the title: "How Safe Are Your Schools?" Then the work began.

Literally hundreds of letters went out to state, regional, and city school authorities with questions on obsolescence, safety hazards, building codes, and local programs designed to improve existing conditions. More letters were sent to the National Safety Council, the National Fire Protection Association, insurance organizations, and other groups. We also talked to architects and building-code authorities, and spent days in the University of Miami law library, checking negligence laws as they applied in the various states.

We ended up with four cartons jammed with research, and a conviction that our basic idea was sound: a shockingly large number of schools were unsafe. *Good Housekeeping* cover-lined our article. I hope it did some good.

The three illustrations provide a fairly good picture of how we write non-fiction from Florida. Our ideas come from many sources – newspaper articles, specialized journals, our own huge files, conversations with lawyers, doctors, teachers, and other professionals, our observations during travel, etc. We try to visit New York at least twice a year, and really should appear more often. We know, however, that we are only a few hours away by plane in the event a personal appearance is required.

There are certain disadvantages in writing non-fiction at a distance from your markets. We miss personal contact with our friends on many magazines. We also miss contact with other writers. I also suspect we miss a certain amount of work by not being able to discuss it across the editorial desk.

But writing from Florida has advantages. Since Ellen's daily stint is over, she is now happily repotting orchids in the patio. I have been typing in the sun all day. The afternoon paper says a blizzard has struck the Northeast.

Presently I will visit a quiet beach to try out what my wife calls "your water wings." (Actually, swim fins and scuba equipment.) You see, there is a new treasure find off Marathon in the Florida Keys, and Ellen just wrote a query. . . .

Working while you sleep

Many writers stop writing at a point where some combat, some struggle, has come not to *the* climax but to a crucial point. Robert Louis Stevenson had a solution to this: He said little elves worked while you slept. I have found it particularly true in writing mysteries. You've stopped work and there you are – you know what you want to have happen but you don't know *how* to have it happen. If you repeat that problem in your mind at night, you say X feels thus and so about a situation, Y feels this way about it – now what is X going to do to implement his feelings and what is Y going to do to implement his feelings – then, as Stevenson said, when you go to the typewriter in the morning, the question has resolved itself. It doesn't sound very practical, but it's the most practical thing in the world. – Mignon Eberhart

Three rewards of writing

The only sensible ends of literature are, first, the pleasurable toil of writing; second, the gratification of one's family and friends; and lastly, the solid cash. – Nathaniel Hawthorne

J. D. Ratcliff

Writing an article is always easier
if you know how to talk to people and
get enticing facts about them

Rules for interviewing

In article writing, interviewing can be the heart of the matter. *Everything* –
note the italics – depends on your asking the right questions. If you depend
on reading alone for your facts, you're simply rewriting what others have
already discovered. Interviewing moves you into new territory, provides the
fresh and original material essential to any good article.

As an interviewer you are like a detective, on the track of elusive fact –
only your job is considerably more difficult than the one which faced, say
Sherlock Holmes. After all, Sir Arthur Conan Doyle had weeks or months to
think up the clever and revealing questions Sherlock asked. You may have
only seconds.

If the interviewer is like the detective, he is also like the gold prospector.
If a gold prospector knew where the nuggets were, he'd simply pick them
up, load them in a truck, and haul them to the mint. He doesn't, of course,
know where they are – and must pan a lot of gravel or dig a lot of tunnel
to find them. The interviewer is in the same position. If he knew in advance

which questions would yield the nuggets, interviewing would be a simple business. But he doesn't know. It may take a hundred questions to bring up a half dozen usable bits of information.

In sum, interviewing is a rather tricky and difficult business. But there are certain ground rules any aspiring writer should know.

The main rule, I would say, is *not* to ask your subject to give you a complete education on the topic at hand. Insofar as possible, go prepared. Read up on your subject. Consult newspaper files. Ask others to fill you in on background. Then type up the questions you want answered. With this framework to build on, the interview will go quickly.

If there are embarrassing questions to ask, always save them until last. Often such questions anger your subject. If you get him in a bad mood at the start, he may end the interview before it gets fairly started. But as with all rules, there are exceptions. As an example, I was interviewing a rather unpleasant man several years ago. He started things going by informing me he had successfully sued one magazine which had run a story unfavorable to him. In a rather menacing way he asked if I objected to his making a tape recording of our talk – for future reference. I assured him I had no objections whatever, so he turned on the machine.

In this case I reversed the usual order of questions. My first one was "Is it true you were once found guilty of embezzling funds of your own organization?" He reached over and turned the tape recorder off. Then we got along to less difficult questions.

Another thing to remember is that interviewing isn't social conversation – any more than is an examination by a trial lawyer. You are there for one purpose and one purpose alone – to get facts. Never make the mistake many amateurs make of intruding themselves into the interview. It makes little difference what you think or feel at the moment. It's your job to find what the other fellow thinks, feels, knows.

Never fancy yourself an expert – no matter how much you may have read while preparing for an interview. After all, it isn't *your* brains that are being picked. And trying to be an "expert" can have calamitous consequences.

Along this line, something happened to me which will illustrate. Fortunately I wasn't working on an article at the time. I was merely talking over my head – way over. It was years ago and I was going from New York to New Bedford, Massachusetts, on a coastal steamer. The dining room was crowded and the headwaiter asked if I minded someone sharing my table. America had gone off the gold standard that day and my table companion and I started discussing it. It was clear he didn't understand the significance of the event, so I proceeded to set his thinking straight. At the conclusion of my lecture he asked what I did. I was a reporter, I replied. And what did he do? He was a banker, he said. His name was Harrison.

"Are you George Harrison, governor of the Federal Reserve Board?" I asked. He was.

"You dirty so-and-so," I said. He burst out laughing. But at least I learned that the good reporter does well to let others do most of the talking.

There are a thousand little tricks to interviewing. Sometimes it's advisable to get the interview subject on *your* home grounds. People who have previously clammed up will often unbend over cocktails, or at the luncheon table. Not long ago I was working on a story in Paris and wanted to interview the head of an international police organization. With the greatest reluctance he agreed to see me – the French hold reporters in something less than the highest regard.

The interview got off to an impossible start. My subject informed me he could spare only fifteen minutes. By any reckoning, at least three days would be required – talking to him and to his subordinates.

With things standing as they did, it was clearly best not to start at all. I suggested that another time would be better since fifteen minutes was a woefully insufficient allotment of time. Would it be possible, I suggested, for him to dine with me, and I mentioned the name of the most punishingly expensive restaurant in Paris. Knowing police salaries, I felt quite sure he'd never been in this glamorous place. He jumped at the bait. After our dinner I got full and wonderful cooperation – and an excellent story.

There are thousands of other tricks. While reasonable acquaintance with your subject is generally desirable, there are times when it pays to play dumb. I doubt if anywhere in the world one will find tighter-mouthed people than Swiss bankers. Interviewing them is much like interviewing statues in a museum. How to get anything from them for a story on the supersecret Swiss banks about which I was writing?

Clearly, the best approach was to ask round-the-rosy questions, always avoiding the point-blank query. In short, to play dumb, keep circling, and hope a few useful crumbs of information would develop from apparently highly interesting information – although my subjects were convinced they had told me absolutely nothing.

One pitfall for many interviewers is deciding in advance what kind of story they're going to write and asking questions which fit in this pre-established pattern. This is suicide. Never flatly decide on the type of story you're going to write until *all* the facts are in. As an illustration, some time ago I set out to do a piece on a doctor I considered a quack. He'd had a bad press and everything pointed in this direction. Naturally I didn't inform him of my intentions. But as I got deeper and deeper into the story it became clear I was on the wrong track. The man had done good work which had been misinterpreted. What started out to be a piece of muckraking turned into a story of praise. Fortunately time bore me out.

Often when you're writing a story, say about a manufacturing company doing some particularly interesting work, it will be suggested that a half dozen key executives assemble to meet you. Avoid this at all costs. When you get a group together there's always one man who will dominate the conversation – and usually he's the dullest and least informative of those present. *Insist* you talk to people individually. When alone, the man who clams up in a group will often be highly informative and helpful.

Another general observation in writing company stories: the help you get is often in inverse proportion to the rank of the man being interviewed. The little guy who works on the factory floor can prove far more helpful than the board chairman.

Where do you begin an interview? Here again the situation is altered by circumstances. If your questions are in order, you can skip around as you please. But if the story is big, a complex and careful development is generally essential. Often the simplest opening question is best. Some years ago I was assigned to write a bone-crusher – on the U. S. Navy. My opening question to an admiral: "How many boats have you got?"

You can guess the response. Somewhat frostily I was informed the Navy didn't call them "boats" and, in the second place, he didn't know. The Navy had no inventory. That was the starting point. And, as it turned out, it was a good one.

Another thing to be remembered: your subjects don't have endless time to spend with you. Be as brief as possible. Ask to be passed along to others. Ask an engineer engineering questions, a financial man financial questions, etc. And another good rule in writing a company story is to save the president or board chairman until last. By then you should have a good idea of how things stand and know exactly what you want from him – probably a few resounding quotes. Chances are he will come up with some unusable generalities. In this case it is permissible to have some quotes ready for him – the quotes you want.

"What you have said really amounts to this, doesn't it?" If he agrees you can put *your* quotes in *his* mouth. This may not sound cricket, but it is.

In sum, the quality of an article can be largely dependent on the quality of your interviewing. If you have a batch of enticing facts to work with, the writing will come easy.

Max Shulman

*One of our most successful humorists sounds a
warning to writers that there's no one kind of
comedy which appeals to everybody*

Humor is no laughing matter

The first—and most difficult—thing a humorist has to learn is that you can't make *everybody* laugh. Good tragedy moves practically everybody. Good melodrama thrills practically everybody. But good comedy, no matter how good, leaves roughly half of its audience unamused.

There is no getting away from the melancholy fact that one man's laugh is another man's yawn. See for yourself the next time you're watching a comedy on television or on the stage or at a movie house. Observe the faces of the audience during a joke. About half the faces will be tilted back in open, uninhibited laughter; of the other half, some will wear tiny, grudging smiles, some will be blank, and some will be frankly annoyed.

Is there no kind of comedy which will amuse everybody? The answer is no—unless we are talking about an audience of very young children. Such a group, every piddler and toddler of them, will go into hysterics over the primitive antics of performers like the Three Stooges or Abbott and Costello. But once a viewer or reader passes the age of pinafores, he becomes not just selective about humor but actually violently opinionated. And, I regret to report, it happens depressingly early in life. Anybody who has ever tried to entertain twelve- or thirteen-year-old kids has been mainly rewarded with sneers for his trouble.

Why people should differ so sharply on what's funny, I can't tell you – and I've been in the humor business for twenty abrasive years. I've seen plays I wrote render an audience practically helpless with laughter at one performance, and then the very next night, with the actors playing every bit as well, I've seen the same play fail to evoke more than a few surly snickers. I've had comic novels reviewed by critics of similar backgrounds and equal intelligence – some of whom hailed me as a new Aristophanes, and some of whom wished to declare me a disaster area.

My *Dobie Gillis* television series brought me a goodly amount of letters each week, some of which put me on Cloud Nine and some of which made me think seriously of selling my typewriter and leaving the country. On everything I've ever written, I've had every kind of response – from the rapturous to the poisonous. The only thing I've never had – nor do I ever expect – is unanimity.

As a beginning writer I was greatly troubled by this divergence of opinion. How could Critic A be so glowing about a book and Critic B be so savage? I made an earnest effort to find out. I went to Critic B, asked him what I'd done wrong and how I could correct it. Critic B told me, and I listened carefully, and the next time I wrote a book, I did all the things he wanted me to, and as a result Critic B loved the next book – but Critic A hated it.

That's when I learned you can't win. There is no board, no committee, no panel of experts you can consult to find out whether what you're writing is funny. There is only one person in the world you can trust – yourself. If *you* think it's funny, put it down. If you're right, you'll find an audience. If you're wrong, you'll starve to death.

Granted that a person has a generalized talent for writing, can he train himself to be a humorist? The answer, in my opinion, is a resounding No. Humor is not so much a technique as an *outlook*. It is not a matter of how to put down words, how to draw characters, how to describe events; all of these things presuppose an *option* on the author's part – he can *choose* his language, his method, his organization. A humorist has no such choice. There is only *one* way he can present his material – the oblique, distorted, unexpected way we call comedy.

A humorist, in short, is a humorist *before* he is a writer. He has, early in life, developed a cockeyed way of looking at the world, and there's no other way he can look at it. Some humorists never learn to write, and so they

live out their days as non-writing humorists – perhaps as professional come-
dians, perhaps as office buffoons, perhaps as classroom cutups – or perhaps
as silent recluses, smiling secretly at a joke they'll share with no one.

The making of a humorist occurs, as I've said, early in life. I honestly
don't believe it possible for anyone whose character has already been formed
along sober, realistic lines to turn himself into a humorist – no matter
how hard he studies, no matter how diligently he practices. How, after all,
can study and practice give you a distorting lens for an eye? This, it seems to
me, you have early – or never.

We come now to the question: what are the forces that make a humorist?
Dr. Freud and his followers, both qualified and non-qualified, have examined
this question at tiresome length. What it boils down to is this: humor is a
defense of the underprivileged. It is not, of course the only defense. There
are many others – such as joining street gangs or advertising agencies. But for
some underprivileged, humor is the answer. If you are born poor, or unloved,
or a member of an oppressed minority, or constitutionally inadequate – and
you find you can't face the world as it is – you develop a distorting lens called
humor that makes the world tolerable to look upon.

A quick investigation of humorists shows a remarkable consistency of
background. Most were poor, most were physically unattractive, most came
from unhappy homes. It's small wonder they chose humor to put a less
inimical face on the world. It helped them get along. In many cases, it made
them enormously successful. It didn't, however, make them happy.

Humorists are – as the cliché has it – a morose lot. The trauma that made
them humorists is never cured. Their personal conditions might be improved,
but not the world around them. They go through life looking through a distorting lens, but they are fully aware they are doing it – just as a man who
must wear armor doesn't mistake the armor for his own skin.

Indeed, many humorists, as they grow older, find humor such an intolerable
evasion of reality that they give it up. Ring Lardner is an excellent example.
From the beginning there was a strong lacing of bitterness in his humor,
a rage at hypocrisy and injustice that kept popping through the froth. A study
of Lardner shows the sugar-coating getting thinner each year, the pill becoming more bitter. Finally his wrath triumphed. He threw away his putty
nose and slap shoes and came out swinging savagely with powerful stories
like "Champion" and "Haircut."

I can't prove it, but I believe Robert Benchley also got disgusted with
humor. Unlike Lardner, he didn't turn to serious writing; he simply gave up
writing altogether.

Thurber, in his last years, was a totally different writer from the ear

Thurber. As his social commentary got more pointed, his humor dwindled to the vanishing point. So, in fact, did Mark Twain's.

S. J. Perelman is the only humorist I know who has stayed true to the same approach for a lifetime. Of course, his technique has gotten more exquisite, his use of language more breathtaking, his skill more dazzling— but "Dawn Ginsbergh's Revenge," written in 1929, and his last piece in the *New Yorker* are the same world viewed through the same lens.

Humorists are fairly rare birds to begin with, and their professional lives are, as I've noted, comparatively short. Hence the steady demand for new humorists, and hence the steady temptation for beginning writers to enter the field.

Let us say you are such a writer. Let us say you are blessed (or cursed) with the necessary distorting lens. How do you go about getting into the business? You go about it the same way you go about getting into any other area of writing: you write. And what do you write about? You write about what anybody else writes about.

Do I mean that the subject of a serious story can also be the subject of a humorous story? That is precisely what I mean. Norman Mailer and Tom Heggen both wrote about the war in the Pacific. Mailer wrote the *Naked and the Dead* and Heggen wrote *Mister Roberts*. Liam O'Flaherty and Brendan Behan both wrote about the Irish Rebellion. O'Flaherty wrote *The Informer* and Behan wrote *The Hostage*. Truman Capote and Mark Twain both wrote about Southern children growing up. Capote wrote *Other Voices, Other Rooms* and Twain wrote *Tom Sawyer*. Nathaniel Hawthorne and George Axelrod both wrote about adultery. Hawthorne wrote *The Scarlet Letter* and Axelrod *The Seven Year Itch*.

What I'm saying is that it's the distorting lens, not the topic, that determines whether a work is funny or not. Even death can be hilarious, as witness *Arsenic and Old Lace*. Any quick look at the current "sick" joke fad will show you how far you can go and still be, according to some, funny.

Let me be perfectly clear here. I don't mean that bad taste, gore, violence, ugliness, and indignity are intrinsically funny. All I mean is that no aspect of the human condition is automatically off limits to the humorist. If his eye sees something as funny, then his pen will make it funny. If, however, his eye betrays him, his pen can't save him. That's another hard lesson for the humorist to learn; unless you honestly think something is funny, don't write it. Don't ever say to yourself, "O.K., it's not a terribly funny idea, but I'll trick it up in the writing." No, friends, that's a snare. You'll find yourself sweating bullets over a piece, and when it's all done you'll have nothing for your pains.

The humorist's eye isn't only his first and most essential tool, it is also a kind of gauge, a kind of litmus paper, an instant test to determine whether something is funny or not. This eye, this distorting lens, this advantage born of adversity, gives the humorist a big edge over all other kinds of writers. He knows before he begins whether he's right or not. Of course, if he gets lazy or sloppy while he's doing the actual writing, he can louse up what started as a perfectly valid idea. Humorists, like any other writers, can't escape discipline.

To sum up – if you truly have the humorist's eye, if you'll learn to trust it, if you're prepared to have roughly half your audience hate what you write, if you're further prepared to grow steadily more disenchanted with your skill as it develops, then by all means you should take up humor.

Good luck to you – and never say you weren't fairly warned!

Write as clearly as you talk

A chemist once came to me with his writing problems. He was trying to perfect a new cigarette lighter which a businessman hoped to manufacture and sell. There were technical problems involved that the chemist found difficult to make clear to the businessman.

"You see," the chemist said to me, "we must make the flame visible. But this flame burns so perfectly you can hardly see it. We've tried to color the flame but that doesn't work too well. What I want to do is to change the torch so it doesn't burn as well as it does now. Then like a match flame, it will show up. You know yourself how you can smoke up a piece of glass with a match flame. That's because there are particles of carbon in the flame that don't get burned. When they're hot they're bright yellow and make the flame easy to see."

The chemist was having no trouble making himself clear. Then I looked at the letter he had written the businessman. It covered the same point. But clear English had been replaced by jargon:

"Neither volatile nor solid additives have proved themselves as flame colorants. It is recommended that the flame be made softer, for in unsaturated hydrocarbons this is a means of increasing the visibility of the incandescent gas."

The letter was *addressed* to the businessman but it was not *written for* him. It was written for other chemists. – Robert Gunning in *The Technique of Clear Writing*.

Theodore Wachs, Jr.

*Knowing how to use a camera effectively
will help the author to crack many editorial
markets*

Writing with pictures

At first I thought (and why not?) that my inspired prose had sold the story
on lake-trout fishing at Lincoln Pond. But when the next issue of *Fishing
World* came out I knew the truth as soon as I opened the pages: without
photographs I wouldn't have had a salable piece at all.

In camera close-ups, the few middling-sized trout we caught that August
afternoon took on noble proportions. And the view of Lincoln Pond, mirror-
ing the mountains and shoreline spruce trees, went far beyond my powers
to describe in words the quiet splendor of the Maine woods. Everything was
there in a glance at the pictures – the setting, the tackle, the clothes we wore,
the boat and motor, even the twisted smile on the face of Peter Silver, our
guide, as he lifted a three-pound trout from the water. Readers of outdoors
magazines love to pore over details like these. Photographs supply them as
nothing else can.

I didn't, however, take those particular pictures. My friend Maury Delman
packed a camera and tripod up four miles of blazed trail and stood waist-

deep in Lincoln Pond while Pete and I performed within range of his telescopic lens.

Maury is a professional writer-photographer who fishes in such faraway places as Iceland and Argentina and sells his stories to the outdoors magazines. He learned the importance of pictures early in his writing career, when editors answered his story suggestions with: "The idea sounds good, but what have you got for photographs?" Today, Maury would leave his tackle box behind before he'd take off on an assignment without his camera.

The editors of travel and adventure magazines feel much the same way about illustrations for non-fiction pieces. "Photographs by the author" has been a familiar credit line on *National Geographic* articles ever since Gilbert Grosvenor started roaming the world with notebook and camera some forty years ago. In a recent issue of *True* magazine, eight of nine features are illustrated with photographs, two of them by the authors. A recent *Argosy* had five photo-illustrated features, two combining photography and art, and two that used art only. It's worth noting that the last two were based on fantasy and humor, subjects that don't lend themselves readily to camera treatment.

In the craft magazine field, the picture-story is standard: either photographs or sketches are part of the author's responsibility. Maybe you can tell a reader in words alone how to build an outdoor patio, but you'd have a hard time convincing the editor of *Popular Science* that this is the best way to go about it. "Top-quality photos are a *must,*" he says in the magazine's requirements sheet for writers. The italics are his.

Does this mean that after mastering the techniques of writing, you must start worrying about mere pictures? The answer is yes – if you want to sell consistently to the specialized markets. If you want, blame it on *Life, Look,* television, and the man who invented the half-tone engraving process . . . but it's a picture-minded world, nevertheless.

Photographs won't turn a bad story into a good one but they'll often guarantee a sale that might otherwise be lost, even when the story is well written. They can also bolster a writer's income and lead to more varied and profitable assignments, once the word gets around among editors that he can deliver a complete editorial package.

Worrying about pictures has other, less tangible benefits for the writer. It helps him to observe more keenly, to look for revealing detail – colors and textures, lights and shadows, expressive forms and movements. This increased awareness of the world about him leads to sharper, more accurate reporting.

I know several writers who use the camera as a visual notebook; going over rolls of film after they come back from an assignment gives them a reliable playback of what they saw and did when they were too busy to stop and take notes.

There are four ways to get good photographs for your articles. One is to team up with a professional like my friend Maury, who is willing to share the risks and rewards of your venture. The second is to marry someone who will, patiently and expertly, take over the photographic chores while you hunt, fish, or build that outdoor patio. The third is to write only for high-budget publications that provide a staff photographer. The fourth is to learn something about photography yourself. I'll address the rest of my comments to the 90 percent or more of all working writers who come within this last category most of the time.

Shooting your own story illustrations isn't as difficult as you might think. Editors aren't looking for prize-winning salon pictures; they expect clear, sharp photographs that put the reader on the scene and help fulfill the promise in the story title. If you have a fair amount of pictorial sense and are willing to study the fundamentals, you can probably meet the editors' requirements and have fun doing it.

Norman Phillips, a West Coast outdoor writer, looks at the matter this way: "Some writers feel that it's necessary to hire a photographer to handle the camera work. I can't see it, because with modern high-speed films and a simplified camera, anyone who can't learn to take an acceptable picture isn't smart enough to be a writer, anyway. And you still have to tell the hired photographer what shots to take and where to take them from; only you know what will tell your story and express your point of view. Having figured it all out, why not push the button yourself?"

Now let's remove another mental block that sometimes gets in the writer's way. You don't need a closetful of expensive equipment to take good illustration photos, any more than you need an IBM typewriter or a gold-filled pen to write good stories. The basic photo kit for writers recommended by the Famous Photographers School staff (see the box on page 70) will start you off. Later, you can acquire all those wonder-working gadgets advertised in the photography magazines.

Consider the experience of a Famous Writers School instructor who took a vacation trip to the Far East last year. With some misgivings she bought one of the new automated cameras and started shooting. She didn't see the results of her work until she got back to Westport and the processor handed her a set of pictures that would do nicely as illustrations for a travel article. Her comment was highly revealing: "You mean I took those?"

In photo illustration as in writing, equipment is a means, not an end. It's far more important that you train yourself to apply your writer's judgment to photographic problems. If that sounds like a contradiction in terms, here are a few suggestions to make the point clearer.

1. *Plan your shots.* When a writer sits down to compose an article he uses some kind of outline, mental or written; he thinks out the story before he writes.

This planning phase is just as important when you turn photographer. Study both picture possibilities and your story needs before you start shooting, then build a rough work plan (photographers call it a "shot list") assuring a photographic record rather than a series of random snapshots.

For example, if you're covering a deer hunt, you'll need more than a pictorial account of the hunt itself. You'll want some pictures of the base camp, close-ups of the hunters, views of the country you're hunting over, and more close-ups of the hunters bringing the deer, if any, into camp.

If you miss some key items on your shot list, or if the light isn't right, you can probably get your companions to reenact the scene for you next day. A good many photos are taken after the event. This isn't harmful fakery, as long as the pictures are a fair approximation of what actually took place.

2. *Put variety into your pictures.* You know how dull a piece of writing becomes when sentences and paragraphs all begin and end the same way. Sameness can be deadly in photographs, too. So vary your shooting distances, camera angles, and lighting effects as much as you can.

Mix long shots (twenty-five feet or more away) with medium shots (ten to twelve feet) and close-ups (as close as you can get). For a change, try shooting up at your subject from a low angle, with the sky as a plain, contrasting background. Then find a rise of ground and shoot down on the campsite, the hunters taking off into the woods, the boat pulling into the pier.

And remember that, whatever the camera instruction book said, you don't have to take pictures with the sun at your back. Often, you'll get richer detail and more interesting composition with the light coming from side or front. Explore, experiment, improvise.

3. *Edit your pictures.* You edit a piece of copy when you pencil out the excess verbiage and pare your sentences down to essentials. You can edit pictures, too. In case you've never watched a picture editor at work, here's how to go about it.

When your prints come back from the processor, spread them out on a table and study them critically, just as you'd study a rough draft of a manuscript. Decide which pictures best tell the story you want to get across and discard the others, including all prints that are technical failures be-

The Famous Photographers School, a companion organization of FWS, suggests the following items as a useful kit for the writer who wants to "write with pictures":

1. Camera. Either a 2¼ inch×2¼ inch reflex or a 35 mm, with controls for focusing, shutter speed, and lens aperture. Lens should be f/3.5 or faster and shutter should have a range of speeds up to $\frac{1}{500}$ second. (Fifty to seventy dollars and up)
2. Lens shade. (Two dollars)
3. A reliable exposure meter, unless camera has a built-in meter. (Ten dollars and up)
4. Skylight of UV filter for color, and medium yellow filter for black and white. (Three dollars)
5. Tripod. Small, with telescoping legs. (Fifteen dollars and up)
6. A compact B-C flash unit. (Seventy-five cents)
7. Gadget bag. (Six dollars and up)

cause of bad lighting, faulty focus, or poor exposure. Remember, the editor will probably want one strong lead shot – a picture that symbolizes or sums up the story – plus a variety of medium and close shots. Choose both verticals and horizontals.

Sometimes you can save a print by cropping it so that only a portion of the picture comes out in the enlargement. With a red or yellow grease pencil, mark off the area you want to keep and instruct the processor to make an enlargement "cropped as marked." You'll be surprised what this can do to bring up in vivid detail the important elements in your photograph.

All prints you mail out with your story should be 8×10 or larger, just as all manuscripts should be double-spaced with ample margins. Many writer-photographers find it's worth the expense to have the processing and enlarging done by a custom laboratory that will take extra pains to bring out the best in their pictures. You can probably locate a custom lab somewhere in your area.

I've saved the most important suggestion about do-it-yourself photo illustration for last, because I think it deserves special emphasis. It's simply this: *start in your own backyard*. Let me explain.

One of my few achievements is a certain adeptness at casting with a fly rod. I enjoy teaching others this pleasant pastime, but I always insist we practice on dry land. I'm convinced that without the distraction of fish and fishermen, anyone who isn't muscle-bound can learn to fly-cast in a few afternoons.

Camera handling takes a little longer, but the principle is the same. Go into your backyard and shoot some pictures of your dog treeing the neighbor's cat; your daughter skipping rope; your son riding his bicycle; the birds lighting on the window-box feeder. Have the film developed and shoot some more, only this time choose new angles and a different time of day.

After you've used up several dozen rolls of film, you'll find you can handle the camera controls with ease and assurance and that you've learned a good deal about selecting and composing a story-telling picture. Then you can go out on an assignment with your writer's mind free to plot the sentences and paragraphs that give meaning and continuity to your illustration.

Hemingway fired a gun

It is interesting how literary style changes, even from one decade to another. Some eras are much more patient than others. Our era is an impatient one.

There's no time to waste. Ernest Hemingway fired the gun, and we've been running ever since. – Marie de Nervaud in *The Writer's Digest*

Clarity and your reading audience

If any part of a story is not clear to any one person, you can be sure that it won't be clear to a great many people. This is one of the first things a writer must learn. You may say: "Why, that editor! Good heavens, doesn't he know what I mean? It's so clear." But if he looks at your manuscript and puts a little mark and says this passage isn't clear, then you can rest assured that thousands of other people would have the same feeling about it. – Mignon Eberhart

Drawing characters from models

The practice of drawing characters from actual models is not only universal but necessary. I do not see why any writer should be ashamed to acknowledge it. – Somerset Maugham

Rufus Jarman

*A veteran master of the article
tells how you can find ideas for
sale – if you'll only look*

Stories under your nose

The first and perhaps the most serious difficulty encountered by both aspiring and active non-fiction writers is choosing a subject. Too often inclination is to write about three-legged calves and three-headed ladies. Of course, I mean this only figuratively. But beginning writers, especially, see possibilities in wondrous, exotic subjects – the bizarre and unbelievable – the startling, the unknown, and remote.

Actually, a writer's best subject is almost always the one with which he is most familiar. Often he ignores as too dull and obvious material that lies right under his nose – good stories in his own backyard.

My first sale to a magazine, which happened to be the *Saturday Evening Post,* concerned a subject that had been lying around for years under the eyes of every writer in town. During the 1930s, *Post* enjoyed the highest editorial prestige and the reputation for paying the highest rates. Every newspaperman worthy of the name aspired to sell his "great story" to this magazine.

As a reporter for the Atlanta *Journal,* I too cherished such ambitions. I forget now the exact nature of my favorite story idea: it wasn't traveling to Tibet to interview the Dalai Lama but something like that. And then, one night while reading the *Post,* a brand-new idea popped into my head.

On the edge of Atlanta is Oglethorpe, a university of limited size, wealth, and academic importance. Even so, Oglethorpe had figured prominently for years in the national news. The reason: its president and founder, Dr. Thornwell Jacobs, was a publicity genius. At each graduation time, we newspapermen looked forward to a fine display of academic shenanigans. Dr. Jacobs always had on hand an impressive collection of prominent figures – they had ranged from Woodrow Wilson to Franklin Roosevelt to William Randolph Hearst – to receive honorary degrees and participate in the publicity gimmick he had dreamed up for that particular commencement. The most spectacular of these was a Crypt of Civilization, an "indestructible" underground chamber that the school and its honorary grads had loaded with great literature reduced to microfilm – with models of trains, planes, cars, and ships – with recordings of classical music and the voices of world leaders, and the like. The crypt was sealed amid much solemn fanfare, to be opened in two or three thousand years so that mankind's survivors could see how things had been during the mid-twentieth century.

Looking back on it now, it all seems pretty obvious national magazine material, but I guess we newspapermen were too close to the scene. The magazine piece I was reading the night my idea came concerned education and it made me think of Dr. Jacobs. Furthermore, I had married recently and needed additional funds. Anyway, suddenly I saw Dr. Jacobs and Oglethorpe in the *Saturday Evening Post.* The big weekly wouldn't object to giving Oglethorpe and its honorary graduates a good-natured kidding. So next day I copied the editor's name from the *Post*'s masterhead and wrote a letter, telling what I knew about Oglethorpe. In a few days a reply arrived, saying it was a fine idea. Several weeks later the *Post* bought my article for 500 dollars. This made me, for a while at least, the richest reporter in Atlanta.

If we Atlanta newsmen seemed slow to recognize a story, consider this experience of a professional free lance. During his assignment in Washington, D.C., he patronized the National Press Club. Among the club's members were several dozen slightly boozy correspondents, each of whom loved to talk about the "great story" he was "going to write" for "a big magazine." None had ever sold such a piece; in fact, their subjects were invariably remote, obscure, and unlikely.

One day our free lance man, bored by the boozy talk, excused himself and went to the washroom, which looks out over the famous Willard Hotel. A long line of buses was disgorging hundreds of high school seniors, arriving on their traditional "class trip" to the capital.

On his way back to the bar, the free lance stopped long enough to phone the editor of a big magazine and suggest a piece on "The Senior Class Goes to Washington." The editor said: Go ahead. The article sold for 2,500 dollars.

One day, while riding the train to Philadelphia with some twenty ideas I'd carefully prepared for the *Post*'s editors, a man sitting next to me in the club car began telling about a trip he'd recently made to Florida along the Intracoastal (or Inland) Waterway. He gave glowing accounts of the elaborate marinas along the way, the splendid scenery, the attractive atmosphere.

I asked if he objected to my using some of his material in suggesting a waterway article to the *Post*. Actually, I had no such intention; I was just being polite. The story was too obvious: undoubtedly the *Post* had either published it or had a good reason for not doing so.

But that day, the editors rejected every one of my carefully worked-up ideas. In desperation I remembered my friend on the train. "By the way," I said, "I have some fine material on the Inland Waterway."

"Haven't we done the waterway?" an editor asked.

Everybody looked blank. They checked the records. No, the magazine had used nothing on the subject.

To research material for "Enchanted Waterway," a photographer and I were provided a fifty-foot yacht and crew. We spent two fine weeks cruising leisurely up from Florida to Atlantic City through the moss-draped bays, islands, and inlets of the southeastern coast, habitat of old-time pirates, ghosts, and romance. And I was paid a fat fee for the finished article.

Although it's preferable to prepare your ideas ahead of time, a writer should be ready to shoot from the hip. A West Coast free lance was an hour late for lunch with a group of New York editors. Californians ordinarily have it tough, adjusting to a three-hour time differential when they come East. But this happened to be the first day of Daylight Saving, and this completely confused the Californian. He mentioned this fact in his apologies for being late.

"You know," he went on, "I think a general story about time would make a good article – the history of clocks and other timekeepers, origin of Standard times . . . how Daylight Saving began and the confusing stories resulting . . ."

The California writer had an unexpected but profitable assignment.

A San Francisco free lance, while doing a newspaper feature on the local U. S. Mint, was impressed by the accuracy of some big scales used for weighing large amounts of precious metals. They showed a weight difference between a plain cigarette paper and one on which he had written his name. This gave the writer an idea for a piece on scales and their importance to world commerce, how they work, weights and measures in general, and how weights are regulated in international trade.

A big magazine liked the idea and bought his story. It became the first popular-type article ever written for an important publication about scales – the most important of all mechanical aids to trade and commerce. Besides selling the story, the writer was invited to be guest speaker at the annual convention of weights and measures experts from leading U.S. cities.

While visiting Syracuse, New York, a Chicago writer noticed something strange about one traffic light in a residential area. The green light was at top, the amber at its usual place in the center, the red at the bottom. The writer knew that the usual order was red on top, amber in the middle, green at the bottom.

The reason for this unusual arrangement, the writer learned, was that this neighborhood was inhabited by Irish families. They felt their pride was insulted when the hated yellow of Ulster was positioned above the beloved green of the Irish Free State. Local residents continued to wreck the signal by rocking it at night until the city fathers finally reversed the colors.

This inspired the visiting writer with an idea for a magazine story on the history, development, and public reactions to traffic signals – perhaps the greatest frustration of our age. He sold the piece to a top-paying publication – another case where it took an outsider to appreciate a story in something locally familiar.

I observed this same phenomenon while researching a piece on country ham. My home state is Tennessee, in the midst of the ham-and-gravy belt. In that part of the world, country ham is more than a food – it is a part of the culture and traditions. And the various theories on its proper preparation have caused more arguments than religion and politics combined.

Yet when I went back to Tennessee to gather material for my story, most of the people with whom I talked, including newspapermen, reacted like this: "What do *I* know about country ham? Well, er . . . I like to *eat* it! Ha! Ha! What is there to *write* about country ham?"

Here was one of the most colorful subjects in the area, yet Tennesseans saw no romance in ham. And I probably would not have, either, had I not lived away from Tennessee and country ham so long that I viewed the subject almost as a foreigner. I sold the article to the *Post*.

When I entered the University of Missouri's School of Journalism, I wouldn't have dreamed of writing about rustic subjects from back home. To my best recollection, the first writing project I undertook at Missouri attempted to show how the philosophy and religion of any people are reflected in their architecture. Of course, I knew nothing about this, but it sounded dignified. The topics about which I could write with authority — the characters (both human and animal), the traditions, customs, and colorful atmosphere of rural Middle Tennessee — were beneath my considerations.

I would have been embarrassed to write about our country music, or the way Old Man Taylor Heron used to pray at the Baptist Church, or country funerals, or religious revivals — or crows, perhaps the most interesting and remarkable of all our native birds. And I knew firsthand about crows. But it required twenty-five years of living away from Tennessee for me to see the crow as a magazine subject.

Early one morning, while walking my dog in Westport, I heard an unusually loud flock of crows in a thicket. The crow as a magazine subject flashed through my mind, as Dr. Jacobs had in Atlanta years before. Now, however, I envisaged the crow as a vibrant and captivating character whose personality embodied the mystery and romance of my native country. I recalled my numerous unsuccessful attempts to stalk and shoot this wily creature. I thought of tales of the crow's superior mentality, of talking crows, of his traditional loyalty to his kind, his hates and other violent emotions — and of how he has survived and increased despite man's efforts to wipe him off the face of earth.

So I made the crow my special spare-time project for the next year. I read all I could find about him, talked at length with various authorities throughout the land, consulted the Audubon society's files and all manner of newspapers, interviewed conservationists, hunters, bird-watchers, ornithologists, and game wardens.

When the *Saturday Evening Post* published the piece that resulted, it turned out to be perhaps the most successful I ever wrote, from the standpoint of reader response. Personally, I have always been especially proud of that piece, probably because I felt I'd written about an old friend.

Red Smith

A man who hates tired words tells how he
and some literate friends got rid of them
with clinking coins

Curing clichés with a club

There was this interview with the author of a soap opera that had outlived every other agony show on the air. Not surprisingly, the author attributed the longevity of his show to the writing, the freshness and originality of the script.

"I think I know every cliché in the book," he said, "and I avoid them like the plague."

"Ten cents," I said aloud, reading the interview. "Maybe twenty cents."

Sometimes during the sermon on Sunday, I see heads turn in the pew in front of me and I realize I've been at it again, muttering, "Ten cents. Ten cents." I should kick the habit, but it is deeply ingrained.

It began years ago when our family was vacationing at an inn in Wisconsin run by an almost-cousin of mine. The cliché club was the idea of Betty, the innkeeper. She proposed that whenever one of us — meaning herself and my bride, Kay, and me — dripped some threadbare bromide into our practically endless gabble, he should be fined one dime.

After that, conversations went like this: "I disagree. For reasons too numerous to mention — "

"Ten cents."

Clink! Sound of silver dropping into a cup on the coffee table.

The rules were simple. If you said somebody was "mean as a snake" and nobody called you on it, you got off free. If somebody hollered and you appealed, the majority ruled. We all tried to be fair. Common expressions in accepted use were permissible, no matter how familiar. It had to be a genuine platitude, a clinker with hair on it.

The cliché club was about a week old when we had word that old friends from St. Louis were arriving the next day. "Now, look," Kay said, "we're not going to play this game with my darling Grace. It would be like taking candy from a baby."

"Ten cents!" Betty and I yelled as one.

You might think this would shoot vacation expenses out of sight, but it wasn't so bad. On the last evening of our stay, Betty, Kay, and I toured the livelier saloons of Wisconsin's Door County peninsula, drinking up the club treasury. Chances are we would have hit those joints anyway, so we wound up about even. With the rules off for that night, we tried to talk in nothing but the hoariest old saws. We sounded like the Madison Avenue Junior Chamber of Commerce. It was enough to frighten the gulls off the beaches.

From Wisconsin we went to Saratoga and took up quarters in the house Joe and Mary Cole Palmer had rented for August. Joe was covering horse racing for my paper, the New York *Herald Tribune*. He was one of the finest writers I ever knew and had the liveliest mind I've ever encountered.

Naturally, we brought the cliché game East. It was agreed that when the pot allowed, we four would blow ourselves to a large evening in New York. Within forty-eight hours, Joe said a night on the town was nonsense; give us a little time and we could afford Bermuda, if not Tahiti.

None of us could be described as the strong, silent type and none was a slave to early bedtime. After dinner we would move the Scotch and bourbon out to the porch, and hour after hour it rained pennies from heaven, ten to a drop.

Most of us don't listen to ourselves when we talk. If we did, we'd be appalled to discover what a tired old language we speak, what hackneyed figures we employ. Perhaps this is excusable in ordinary social intercourse, but at least nine out of ten writers commit the same sin on paper. What may be forgivable in everyday discourse should be a hanging offense when perpetrated on the typewriter. Try rereading that triumph of the trite and true, *Gone with the Wind,* and you may agree.

Playing the Eastern League, we found we needed ground rules. As an escape artist, Harry Houdini wasn't a patch on Joe Palmer, who would start to say, "He fought like a –" and, catching himself in soaring flight, would conclude "– a rabbit."

His footwork shouldn't have surprised me, and didn't. Years earlier on a drive to Florida, our sports editor, Stanley Woodward, had booked an impromptu roulette game and savaged Joe and me something awful. (It was in a bedroom of the Jefferson Hotel in Richmond, Virginia, and we used the ceiling fan in lieu of a wheel.) Joe couldn't understand our defeat because he'd drawn up the odds and he was good at mathematics.

"Dammit," he said, "we should have cleaned him, but he took us like –" Joe was from Kentucky, and at this point he remembered his Southern training "– like Washington took Yorktown," he said.

Anyhow, it was agreed that anybody alert enough to edit himself in mid-phrase need pay no fine in the cliché club. It was provided further that if the speaker chose to use some weary line because he felt it conveyed his thought best, he must raise both hands to the level of his ears and wiggle two fingers of each to make little hooks representing quotation marks. As long as he put the expression in quotes before completing it, he went unpenalized.

About the third night, an awkward quiet settled on the porch on Saratoga's Caroline Street. We'd all grown gun-shy, and more than slightly broke. Then, gradually, the chatter resumed its normal tempo, but with a difference. The turn of phrase was immeasurably more inventive. A remarkable thing had happened to all of us; we'd begun to think before speaking or, at least, while speaking.

It's a pity politicians don't.

We often read that the art of conversation has been lost. I like to believe that for a little while in Sturgeon Bay, Wisconsin, in Saratoga Springs, and – after that race meeting ended – in Malverne, Long Island, where the Palmers and Smiths then lived, we began to rediscover some shreds of the lost art. Unhappily, our little movement didn't spread. Joe Palmer died and the cliché club disbanded. I never knew what happened to the treasury, or cared.

P.S. – If any reader is disposed to take pen in hand and protest that "Houdini wasn't a patch on Joe Palmer" and "gun-shy" in that context are a trifle worn, he needn't bother. He's right as rain, and you can say that again.

Rudolf Flesch

*Some sound hints to follow if you
have the happy idea of producing
a surprise best seller*

Could you write a "sleeper"?

A sleeper, according to *Webster's Third Unabridged Dictionary* (definition 7c), is "a book that sells well year after year without being advertised." This definition covers a wide variety of books: *The Prophet* by Kahlil Gibran; Emily Post's *Etiquette,* and A. A. Milne's *Winnie the Pooh;* Robert's *Rules of Order* and Mrs. Irma Rombauer's *New Joy of Cooking; The Story of Philosophy* by Will Durant; *The Outline of History* by H. G. Wells; *The Theory of the Leisure Class* by Thorstein Veblen; Thoreau's *Walden;* Samuel Butler's *Erewhon; Alice in Wonderland; The Rubáiyát; Peter Rabbit.*

What do all these books have in common? Is there any underlying principle, any secret that makes a book into a perennial seller? Oddly enough, the answer is yes. Go through the titles I've listed and you'll find that each one of them became a hidden best seller *although it was not expected to be one.* A sleeper, by its very nature, is a book that astonishes both author and publisher by its enduring success.

Emily Post's *Etiquette* came into being because Mrs. Post was a well-brought-up society matron who put down on paper what she knew about good manners. A. A. Milne had had success with a mystery novel and had gotten a sizable advance guarantee on another one. So—human nature being what it is—he shirked the job and filled his time by making up little verses for his small son.

Will Durant wrote his essays on various philosophers for the famous five-cent Little Blue Books; the bigger book that was later made out of them was an afterthought. H. G. Wells was world-famous for his novels and scientific romances; his publisher discouraged him heartily when he came up with the idea of writing a one-volume world history. Thoreau went to Walden Pond to seek solitude, not to write a book.

Lewis Carroll was a mathematician who spent an evening spinning a long yarn for two little girls and was prevailed upon to write it down. Edward Fitzgerald was a student of oriental literature who for his own interest and amusement translated Omar Khayyám's epigrams; when a bookseller offered some of his unsalable copies for a penny apiece, the poet Dante Gabriel Rossetti picked one up and made *The Rubáiyát* famous.

I can add two experiences of my own to this illustrious catalogue. I wrote my first book, *The Art of Plain Talk,* because I'd become absorbed in the subject of my doctor's thesis—the scientific study of readability. I made it into a book for the general public, offered it to a publisher, and was promptly turned down. Then I went to a second publisher, who gingerly decided to pay me a small advance and print 2,000 copies. When the book came out, people in the professional writing field discovered it had something in it. It has sold steadily for more than twenty years.

Another sleeper, *Why Johnny Can't Read,* started when a friend and neighbor told me her twelve-year-old son couldn't read. I spent some months teaching him, then decided to turn my experience into a book. When I offered it to my publisher, he was extremely bearish on the project and tried his best to discourage me. Finally he published it anyway. It became a best seller at once and after a year or two it turned into a regular bookstore perennial.

So make your book neither too short nor too long. Next question: How should the material be arranged? Do you serve up the dishes in your cookbook proceeding from breakfast to dinner and from soup to nuts? Or do you start by teaching the young bride how to boil an egg and wind up showing the sophisticated hostess how to serve a perfect baked Alaska? Do you go from the inexpensive to the expensive? Or from the quick to the slow?

Again, my advice is to let things take their natural course. Your own mastery of the subject will suggest the best way of presenting it to others. You yourself will have some reference books that make you feel at home and some others that exasperate you every time you have to use them. (Do you like *Bartlett's Familiar Quotations* with its chronological arrangement of authors? It bothers me every time I use it.)

Often – far more than you'd think – the best arrangement to fall back on is the good old alphabet. After all, if a book is arranged according to the ABC method, the reader can always get at everything he wants with one familiar motion. Don't think the ABC arrangement is stupid, illogical, arbitrary; of course it is, but no plan of your own can possibly beat it for sheer convenience. Remember that Fowler's *Modern English Usage* existed first as the topically arranged *The King's English;* when it had settled down to a life of its own as one of the world's finest sleepers, Fowler had to do the whole job over again by making it into an alphabetical dictionary.

Similarly, Roget's *Thesaurus* – with its highly original scheme of categories – went through edition after edition until in the end the index more or less swallowed up the text. And J. K. Lasser's *Your Income Tax* adds new alphabetical checklists every year.

What's the moral of all these little tales? Simply this: If you want to write a sleeper, pursue a hobby; bury yourself in some unpromising activity, do a job just for the love of it; get absorbed in something that offers no financial reward whatever; swim against the current of fashionable, best-selling writing; and perhaps you'll succeed.

Begin by knowing all there is to know about hooked rugs; or cooking with wine; or collecting a paperback library; or basket weaving; or making doll clothes; or winning at Scrabble. Then, when your accumulated experience cries out for making itself known, start on your own book.

And now let's assume you've reached the point of writing it. How do you proceed? What kind of book are you going to write? Should it be long or short? How should it be arranged? What should go in and what should be left out? What's the proper technique of packaging a useful, humble, unglamorous sort of book?

Let's begin with the question of the proper size. The answer to this one is simple: It will start small and gradually grow until it has reached natural length. In its first version it will naturally contain everything you've learned in your intense preoccupation with the subject; in later revisions it will slowly thicken because by then you'll have become a book author who's keeping up with his chosen field.

Generally speaking, all established dictionaries, encyclopedias, cookbooks, manuals, guidebooks, and how-to-live books have this tendency to grow over the years. However, there are exceptions. Sometimes an author writes a little book that becomes a sleeper and is then compelled to write another one like it – and a third – and a fourth. A. A. Milne's *Winnie the Pooh* books are such a series, and Beatrix Potter's *Peter Rabbit* books and Arnold Bennett's successive volumes of pocket philosophy.

Essentially, though, these cases are just variations upon the basic theme; in the end the sleeper emerges as the sum total of the series of little books, or perhaps as an omnibus volume, like Arnold Bennett's *How to Live on 24 Hours a Day.* (My own books on writing eventually became a combination package entitled *How to Write, Speak and Think More Effectively.*)

If you offer your book to the world in too small a format, it simply won't have enough body to become a perennial seller. An example is the seventeenth-century devotional classic *The Practice of the Presence of God* by Brother Lawrence. Brother Lawrence never wrote anything himself and what exists today is a brief pamphlet made up of some letters and conversations. True, the pamphlet is a classic, but because of its small size it has remained a hidden classic for some 250 years.

Another example is William James's famous essay *The Energies of Men.* Read any one of the widely known inspirational self-help books of the past fifty years and you'll find that James's essay has been its basic source. And yet the essay itself has never become an inspirational standby – there are only twenty-two pages of it, and James never bothered to expand it. He did, however, write the famous two-volume *Psychology,* which is a fine example of the opposite kind of book – a book that was too long to have a career as a sleeper. It had to be cut down to the one-volume *Psychology: Briefer Course* before it caught on with the general public.

H. L. Mencken was another author who let his books grow too long. His *American Language* started as a normal-size book but eventually became a monster treatise in three enormous volumes. His *New Dictionary of Quotations* started out as a simple collection of his own favorite quotations: then, midstream in preparing the book, Mencken was bitten by the bug of all-inclusiveness and turned the book into a 1,347-page catchall for every proverb, quote, and wise saying he could lay his hands on.

If you do adopt an alphabetical scheme as the basic pattern of your book, you'll earn an unexpected reward: it will make your job immeasurably easier. I'll never forget the moment when I got around to the final preparation of the manuscript of my book *How to Be Brief.* Up to then I had written all my books on writing in the standard fashion – an introductory chapter followed by the first topic to be discussed, then the second, then the third, and so on. Suddenly I realized that with the alphabetical scheme I had freed myself of all the labor of devising introductions, leads, transitions, logical sequences, any kind of structural device. I put a large *A* on the first page of my manuscript and there I was – my book had arranged itself.

Find the right size then; find the right arrangement. Next, find the secret ingredient – the formula, the gimmick, the thing readers will remember as the essence of your book. To sell "year after year without advertising," your book will have to have something about it that will make people recommend it to one another across dinner tables and back fences.

Is your book a guide to world literature? Make it into a list of the Hundred Best Books. Are you writing about traveling in Europe? Work out one-week, two-week, three-week tours. Do you have a new diet to offer? Give them meal plans with fixed calorie counts.

Don't despise people's craving for the neatly labeled package, the formula, the memory aid. That's just the way the human mind works – your own, included. As the author of a sleeper, you're in the business of giving people a handy service; make it as easy as possible for them to assimilate what's in your book.

I learned about this principle the hard way. My first book, *The Art of Plain Talk,* contained a formula to measure readability; among other things, people had to count the number of affixes (prefixes and suffixes) within 100 words. After a year or two I realized I'd asked people for too much work; so I sat down during weeks and weeks of a hot summer and refigured all my original statistics to make people count syllables instead of affixes. The change made the formula somewhat less accurate, but vastly more useful to the public.

Come to think of it, that unforgettably hot summer of statistical work was a prize example of the most essential sleeper characteristic of them all – it's a book you have to live with and work on *after* it has been published.

The useful-book author's work is never done. The years go by, the book sells on and on, readers keep writing in and your files grow and grow. You revise the text, you add material, you weed out what's obsolete. The book gets older, but there are nice things about an old book, too. Some passages begin to seem quaint; some features take on a historical flavor. But readers like it that way, and you get letters from Montana or Israel or Alaska, thanking you enthusiastically for something you wrote five, ten, twenty years ago.

It's a good life. Somehow, like gardening or puttering in a basement workshop, it seems to make for a long, peaceful old age. I have no definitive research finds to offer, but I do know that Sir George Grove, editor of the *Dictionary of Music and Musicians,* lived to be eighty; Burton Stevenson, compiler of *The Home Book of Quotations,* died at ninety; John Bartlett of *Bartlett's Familiar Quotations,* died at eighty-five; Peter Mark Roget died at ninety; Liberty Hyde Bailey, editor of the *Standard Cyclopedia of Horticulture,* died at ninety-six. And Thomas à Kempis, who wrote the most venerable sleeper of them all, *The Imitation of Christ,* ended his saintly life at the age of ninety-one.

Those who don't know, of course, will say that the long life of the dictionary or handbook author must be unbearably dull. But they're wrong. Some years ago a friend found me immersed in the thousands of little index cards that eventually made up my *Book of Unusual Quotations.* I told him I'd been at it for six solid months.

Sympathetically he said, "I bet you'll be happy when you're through with this dull job."

Dull? The idea startled me. I thought the job was fascinating.

Making the simple sound complex

A consultant on communication was being escorted through the offices of a company by its vice president when they came to the room housing the central files of the company. Turning to a file clerk, the consultant asked, "How long do you keep things in these files?"

"Normally, we don't keep forms for more than three years. Then you can either tear them up yourself or give them to the janitor." The visitor turned to the vice president. "When we get back to your office, let's see how this situation is described in the Procedures Manual." And here is what the Manual said:

"At the end of the established retention period, which is normally three years, mutilate the forms or carbons to be destroyed by tearing them into small bits or pieces or by shredding them, and dispose of the resulting waste in accordance with the procedures established for the Maintenance Department."

Whoever wrote that statement was attempting to make a relatively simple task sound impressive and complex. The words of the file clerk are a far more effective explanation because she tried to express an idea and not to impress a listener. — Robert L. Shurter in *Written Communication in Business.*

John J. Green

There's nothing like a human-interest item
to start a non-fiction piece or to give it
pace once it's started

Where and when to use anecdotes

When Patti, my small granddaughter, came home after her third day in kindergarten, her mother asked her what the class had done. "We showed and telled," she said, her blue eyes sparkling with the thrill of this new experience.

As my daughter told me about it afterward, I realized I had the lead for an article I wanted to do about non-fiction. And I couldn't help admiring the teacher who had introduced this five-year-old and her classmates to one of the first and most important precepts of factual storytelling. I wish I had had such an introduction in my youth, but in the one-room country school where I got my first education, I doubt if any of the pupils in all eight grades – or the harassed teacher, for that matter – had ever heard of "kindergarten." I had to learn the precept the hard way.

If you want to work with factual material, either in magazine articles or books, you, too, should learn the show-and-tell principle. It's fine to *tell* the reader the facts – their importance can't be overemphasized – but when you can *show* him what you're talking about with anecdotes illustrating your facts in action, you'll have done the perfect job.

First, let's define what an anecdote is. *Webster's Third New International* says it this way: "A usually short narrative of an interesting, amusing, or curious incident, often biographical and generally characterized by human interest." Harry Edward Neal, free-lance non-fiction writer, who uses anecdotes as well as any man I know, says it more simply: "A brief story involving people in action."

Of course, the anecdote isn't new; it's been around a long time. Lincoln was one of the greatest practitioners of the art and the technique was old in his day. Remember the parables of Biblical times? Aesop, too, did pretty well with his fables. Basically, these early stories, whether you call them parables or fables, are anecdotes.

Today, the show-and-tell technique applies to almost every type of non-fiction writing. If you were writing an article about the visit of Pope Paul VI to India and wished to illustrate the kind of atmosphere he found there, you couldn't do better than to use an anecdote as Aubrey Menen did in "The Pope Visits a 'Lost Tribe,'" which appeared in the New York *Times Magazine:*

> Not since the days of the first Roman Emperors has a Pope been among men who do not respect his faith. He will be among people who look upon him much as the first Popes were looked upon – namely, as the head of a regrettable sect.
>
> I know how deep this feeling is. The great majority of Christians in India live south of Bombay in Kerala, where I spent part of my boyhood. I returned there recently and found that the prejudice remains.
>
> I once had an *ayah* there, a sort of permanent nursemaid who also acts as a servant when the children grow up. It was explained to me that she would not be available on Sunday mornings because she was a Christian and went to church. I was, therefore, puzzled when I saw her, each morning, take a saucer of warm milk and give it to a snake which lived in the garden and which was held in reverence by the Hindu peasants.
>
> I asked her about it. She was confused. She said, in her missionary-learned English, that it was really a "Clistian" snake because it had never bitten anybody. But I was not convinced.
>
> I asked my uncle about it. He was a firmly orthodox Hindu. "Once a Hindu, always a Hindu," he said, "and you must not take her religion seriously. She is a rice Christian."
>
> A rice Christian was a person so poor that he went to the mission to eat the bowl of free rice that was daily handed out and who, in gratitude, or to go on getting more rice, was converted.
>
> "Of course," said my uncle reassuringly, "they convert only very ignorant and stupid people by such means."

Certainly, if the mission had tried to convert my uncle with rice, he would have bankrupted them, since he ate at least four pounds of the stuff a day.

Reader's Digest and its art-of-living articles provide a wealth of anecdotes. Here's one from "We Can't Afford It" by Evan Hill. The piece started like this:

In the small city where I grew up, all the kids in high school knew and liked the banker's teen-age son, Win. And we envied him. He didn't seem to have much more than most of us, but what he did have seemed to satisfy him more.

One Saturday afternoon on his back porch, some of us graduating seniors were talking about buying used Model-A Fords. "When are you going to get one, Win?" I asked.

"I'm not," he said. "We can't afford it."

At first I thought he was joking. But he was serious. I felt embarrassed for him and for his father quietly digging in the flower beds nearby. I hadn't known the bank was doing so poorly. "Oh," I said lamely.

Mr. Purcell turned around and smiled. "I'd better explain," he said, "or we might have a run on the bank. When Win says we can't afford it, he doesn't mean we haven't enough money to buy a Model A. He means we have something else we consider more important to save that money for."

I've forgotten now what it was that had a greater priority than a Model A to a 17-year-old boy in the 1930s, but I've never forgotten Win's candid, no-nonsense words: "We can't afford it." I needed them then, and I have often needed them since.

Bruce Catton is recognized as an authority on the Civil War. Not long ago, a reader asked Mr. Catton how he makes a 100-year-old subject come alive. His answer: "With people."

First, of course, comes research – plenty of it. Then, from this mass of facts, he winnows salient points. Let's look at how he handled the events of April 14, 1865, in *U. S. Grant and the American Military Tradition:*

Destiny has a way of working while people look the other way. A man will make a snap judgment on some matter of no importance whatever – will decide, for instance, whether or not he will go to the theater with friends on a certain evening – and this decision, which seems to concern nothing more than the way a few leisure hours are to be spent, will affect all the rest of his life, and the course of a nation's history as well.

On Good Friday in 1865 – April 14 by the calendar – U. S. Grant had such a decision to make. President and Mrs. Lincoln were to go to Ford's Theater to see a popular actress in a so-so play. The President did not particularly want to go, but there was a holiday mood on the town, the theater management had announced that he would be present, and he felt that he could hardly get out of it. Would General and Mrs. Grant care to go along?

Grant liked the theater well enough, but on this evening, less than a week after Lee's surrender, he and Mrs. Grant were anxious to get to Burlington, New Jersey, where their older children were in school. Also, when the Lincolns visited army headquarters at City Point that spring, Mrs. Lincoln had been nervous, irritable and in truth quite hard to get along with, and Mrs. Grant did not especially want any more of her company just then. So Grant made his excuses, and that evening he and Mrs. Grant took the train; and before he went to bed that night Grant learned that he (or, more accurately, Mrs. Grant) had made one of the most momentous decisions of his life.

For John Wilkes Booth was also of the party at Ford's Theater that evening, and he carried out the monstrous, scatterbrained plan which had taken him there. If Grant had been in the box with the President, he almost certainly would have been murdered. Booth had included him in his program for the evening. . . .

All in all, because he went to New Jersey instead of to the theater, Grant got twenty years more life, became President of the United States, knew the pinnacle of fame, and bewilderment and disillusion as well, left his great name to one of the shabbiest eras in American history, and missed the apotheosis that bore Lincoln aloft as in a chariot of fire once Booth's derringer had done its work.

In still another field, medical and health writing, the anecdote can be the real life of a piece. But here, it isn't just an anecdote, it's a "case history." The trick is to make it "human" at the level of the lay reader.

One of the most prolific of all non-fiction writers was the late Dr. Louis E. Bisch, a pioneer in psychiatry, who knew how to present his findings to the lay reader. In one article, "How Childlike Are You?", he showed how hangovers from childhood can make people act more like children than the adults they are. Here's one anecdote he used to illustrate his theme:

I was out driving with a friend not long ago. The traffic was not especially heavy, but he kept getting out of line, weaving and tooting his horn as though we were headed for a fire. But we were not going any particular place – only out for recreation.

"You make me nervous, Fred," I finally said. "What's the rush? We've got the whole afternoon ahead of us."

"You know," my friend replied, not in the least offended, "my wife complains about the same thing. I sometimes give her fits. You're a psychiatrist. What's wrong with me?"

"If you want the truth," I said, "you drive like an adolescent who wants to draw attention to himself – to show off."

"Is that it?" he said. And then there was a silence for a while. "I believe you've got something there," he finally said. "I was like that when a kid. I was always doing outlandish things to make people notice me. I always wanted to be in the limelight – it's strange I never linked the two together."

Another prime field for the anecdote is travel writing. It's especially useful to set the scene, to introduce the subject in a dramatic way, to supply the hook that assures readership. Here's an example in Nick Nicholson's article "Big Entertainment at 'Six Flags,'" in the *Ford Times:*

> The small boy stared wide-eyed. Scarcely ten feet from where he stood in front of the weathered old courthouse, a lean-jawed Texas sheriff had dropped an outlaw in a lightning-fast shoot-out. The bright-eyed youngster had spotted the outlaw sneaking up on the roof of the blacksmith shop to draw a bead on the sheriff. Then he saw the sheriff whirl, heard the blast of the gun, and saw the outlaw's body flung backward by the impact of the bullet.
>
> Now, with the smell of gunpowder tingling in his nostrils, the small boy raced forward with a joyous whoop. A deputy was leading a sorry-looking critter off to the Jersey Lily where, without doubt, Judge Roy Bean would deal out fast and simple justice.
>
> It's not often that a twentieth-century youngster – even in Texas – can prowl the streets of an old frontier town and come up with such high drama. But it happens several times a day at Six Flags Over Texas, the 13 million dollar historical amusement center midway on the turnpike between Dallas and Fort Worth.

Where can *you* find anecdotes to illustrate *your* articles? They're all around you. Perhaps a story in your local paper has an angle you can adapt. Possibly you overhear a conversation in the local supermarket that's ready-made. When you're hot on the trail of a subject, research the published material in the field. Often you'll come up with a nugget.

Suppose you're working on a piece about domestic animals. You have ample material to illustrate their lovable qualities, but you're short on anecdotes showing the headaches they cause. So you hopefully start reading newspapers. And you find this Associated Press item from the West Coast:

> Robert Hall was on a stepladder painting his kitchen when a shaggy dog wandered in through an open door.
>
> "Scram," said Hall.
>
> The dog wagged his tail.
>
> "Get outta here!" Hall commanded.
>
> The dog stepped toward the ladder.
>
> Hall waved a bucket of paint thinner at the dog. There was an explosion. The dog scrammed. The service porch caught fire. The kitchen caught fire. Hall scrambled down the ladder and called the fire department.

The water-heater pilot had ignited the paint thinner, firemen said in reporting the incident. Hall said the damage will cost him $2,800.

And while this little story from life could be worked into a piece on animals, it would be just as effective if you were doing an article on offbeat insurance claims or on unusual accidents in the home.

Newspaper columnists offer a rich field for research, too. You might be able to use this anecdote from Robert Sylvester's column, "Dream Street," in the New York *Sunday News:*

> The other day a truck, a cab and a private car all managed to ram each other at Fifth Avenue and 48th Street. The three drivers were using some pretty strong language. A newcomer to the onlookers' circle asked: "Anybody hurt?"
>
> "Not yet," said another bystander.

Sports writing is another field in which the anecdote plays a major role. In fact, Red Smith admits he'd be out of business if it weren't for stories about people. While covering the Olympic Games in Rome, he started a column this way:

> This town was raised on wolf milk, as any friend of Romulus and Remus could tell you, and the critter is regarded as more or less sacred here. When a guy is a wolf, Romans don't dignify him by calling him that. They call him a parakeet, presumably for the way he whistles.
>
> A parakeet sidled up to Mrs. Olga Fikoyova and made signs that he considered her a right tasty dish. Olga, defending Olympic discus champion, married the Boston strongboy, Harold Connolly, after winning the Gold Medal for Czechoslovakia in Melbourne. She now is competing for the United States while her mate defends his championship in the hammer throw.
>
> "Husband," said Olga, scaling the language barrier like Lee Calhoun clearing a hurdle, "hammer . . . boing!"
>
> When last seen, the parakeet was headed down the Appian Way, lengthening stride at every jump. The moral seems to be that things haven't changed much around here since J. Caesar was making passes at Cleopatra.

Walter Wagner had a fine example of an anecdote with a real point in "He Finds Fortunes in Your Future" in *True,* the story of Herb Saxton's unusual occupation. Here's how Wagner started the piece:

> The burly, full-blooded Oklahoma Cherokee, 15 minutes after ending his shift as an oil-field roughneck, was already half-drunk as he weaved to a seat in the bus heading for Tulsa. He was mean and he was quick-tempered, and he had been followed persistently for two days by dapper Herb Saxton, who had been hoping to catch him privately in a sober moment.

Saxton, an ex-lawyer turned professional hunter of missing heirs, who has handled 20 million dollars in unclaimed estates – to the financial gain of the recipients and the eminent satisfaction of himself – slipped into the seat next to the juiced oil worker. "You're a missing heir entitled to an estate worth $60,000 dollars," Saxton told him.

The news had the impact of an arrow shot into the sea. The Cherokee looked at Saxton through glazed, uncomprehending eyes. He pulled out a pint and, after another swallow, offered the bottle to Saxton. "Have a drink," he commanded.

Saxton politely refused.

"I said, have a drink," the man repeated more insistently.

When Saxton again turned him down, the roughneck slipped a .45 from his jacket and held it parallel with the pint. "You bastard," he bellowed. "You won't drink with me because I'm an Indian!"

This Wagner story gets off to a fast start through the author's use of people. He shows you the picture as he sets the scene and introduces his main character. And note how simple bits of dialogue give added punch to the story.

I've covered many ways to use anecdotes in articles and some of the places where such material can be found. But there's another source I haven't mentioned, though I used an example at the beginning of this piece.

To be honest, I *created* my opening anecdote. I do have a granddaughter, her name is Patti, she has blue eyes, and did go to kindergarten. These are facts. But Patti didn't say, "We showed and telled," and I'll probably have some explaining to do when she reads this article and objects to being quoted ungrammatically. But the anecdote *did* make the point I wanted and it *did* give me a lead for this piece. And there's no reason why you shouldn't go and do likewise.

Autopsy on Charles Lamb

In the 19th century, the terrible-tempered Thomas Carlyle, in refusing even to meet the poet Algernon Swinburne, remarked that he did not wish to know anyone who was "sitting in a sewer and adding to it." As a man who did not believe in masking his feelings, Carlyle called the dignified Ralph Waldo Emerson a "hoary-headed and toothless baboon," and Herbert Spencer "the most unending ass in Christendom." To posterity, the 19th century essayist also bequeathed an acid word portrait of his contemporary, Charles Lamb:

". . . insuperable proclivity to gin, in poor old Lamb," he wrote. "His talk contemptibly small, indicating wondrous ignorance and shallowness, even when it was serious and good-mannered, which it seldom was . . . ghastly make-believe of wit; in fact, more like 'diluted insanity.'"

Yet Carlyle himself did not escape unscathed. Said the elder Henry James, summing up but not quieting down the fiery Scot: ". . . same old sausage, fizzing and sputtering in his own grease." – Myrick Land in *The Fine Art of Literary Mayhem.*

Searching for a plot

G. B. Stern once said to me, "Characters and incidents are like beads scattered on a table; they only become a necklace when you have a thread on which to string them." That is what I mean when I say that I am searching for a plot. I am looking for a theme, a setting, a twist of narrative that will give coherence to the stories that I weave out of the day-to-day experiences of living. A novelist is always telling himself stories about the people he is meeting, imagining how they would behave in this and the other situation, but those dream stories only become a novel when they have been set within the pattern of a plot. – Alec Waugh in the *New York Times Book Review.*

Using words as weapons

In the early 17th century, the poet and pamphleteer Andrew Marvell broke off abruptly after beginning a "dissection" of one of his fellow writers. He should continue, he said, so the public could see at last just what a scurvy creature he was carving up, but he felt compelled to halt because of "the offensiveness of the scent and fouling of my fingers . . ." In the 18th century, the satirist Jonathan Swift was less reticent in examining the defects of the essayist Sir Richard Steele. The coauthor of *The Spectator* might, Swift conceded, become a reasonably good writer if he would pay a little more attention to grammar, learn something about "the propriety and disposition of words" – and, incidentally, "get some information on the subject he intends to handle." – Myrick Land in *The Fine Art of Literary Mayhem.*

You can't pin English down

There is no simple rule about English that does not have so many exceptions that it would be folly to rely on it. For example, one of the best-known rules in English is that a plural subject must have a plural verb. Nonetheless, anyone who has any ear for English knows that "More than one woman *has* changed her mind" is better English than "More than one woman *have* changed their minds." Even though the subject, "more than one," is, by its own statement, plural, the singular verb *has* is required. – Bergen Evans in *Comfortable Words.*

Section III

Short stories and novels

Max Shulman

A noted humorist cautions writers about the vital need for getting facts straight

The payoff in research

Let's say you want to write something light – a story that's zingy, funny, contemporary. Let's say you get lucky; you come up with a sensational idea. It's hip; it bubbles. It takes place in New York in 1967. A charmingly goofy boy meets a fetchingly balmy girl on the upper deck of a Fifth Avenue bus and they embark on a series of engagingly kookie adventures that lead to a wonderfully batty ending. You do a hell of a job. Your characters, zany as they are, remain perfectly believable; your motivations are strong; your plot is airtight. There's only one little thing wrong – one small leak that's going to sink your entire boat! *There haven't been any double-decker buses on Fifth Avenue since 1953!*

Any reader who knows New York – and they number in the millions – is going to reject your whole story because of that single anachronism. It doesn't matter how good the rest of it is. If there's just one detail the reader can't accept, he won't accept any of it.

What's my point? Simply this: don't ever think that serious research is unnecessary when you're writing frivolous fiction. In fact, in my opinion, the more frothy your story is, the more solid your research ought to be.

In any kind of fiction you ask the reader for what is called "the willing suspension of disbelief," but in comedy you're asking for an extra large helping. Your characters are extra broad and your situations are extra wild; therefore, you're putting extra hard strains on a reader's credulity. Mind you, the reader *wants* to go along with you; after all, everyone likes to be entertained. But at the same time the reader does *not* want to be played for a sucker, does *not* want to have his intelligence insulted.

Curiously, you're more apt to offend him in small matters than in large ones. It's the classic case of swallowing a camel and straining at a gnat. For example, a reader will accept such arrant nonsense as love at first sight, but give him one little item he knows is wrong – like a double-decker bus on Fifth Avenue in 1967 – and you've lost him.

Look at it this way; when you're writing comedy, you are in effect asking a reader to follow you down the garden path. So don't put stones in his way.

You may ask: "If inserting facts in a comedy is so fraught with risk, isn't it better to avoid facts altogether?" The answer is no. Facts are essential to comedy. Recognizable facts and verifiable details give the appearance of reality you need to make comedy stand up.

I'd better stop here and define terms. When I say comedy, I mean *story-line* comedy. I do not mean fantasy or burlesque – *Get Smart,* for example, or *Alice in Wonderland* or *The Red Skelton Show.* When you're writing that kind of thing, you are obviously many removes from life and you have no obligation to be lifelike. But when you're doing story-line comedy – like *The Odd Couple* or *Mister Roberts* or *The Dick Van Dyke Show* – you're asking an audience to believe that what they're seeing or reading could actually be happening. It may be exaggerated, but it must not be *impossible*.

That's why I say research is so important for a comedy writer. Research provides the pegs of hard fact upon which you guy down an airborne story. Things a reader knows, places he is familiar with, dates he remembers, events he recognizes – all of these reassure him. They persuade him that you don't think he's a poor fool who'll believe any old nonsense. They buttress your story with touchstones and points of reference which keep him from feeling bamboozled.

I don't mean you should load your comedy with a catalogue of facts; after all, nobody sits around chuckling over the *World Almanac.* But I say use as many facts as you can gracefully weave in. I say further that when you have a choice between a detail that is precise and factual and detail that is vague and general, always go for the precise and factual.

For example, don't say, "She ordered a bottle of good white wine" when you can say, "She ordered a bottle of Pouilly-Fuissé." Don't say, "He bought stock in an electronics firm while it was still cheap," when you can say, "He got IBM when it was 100 dollars a share." Whenever and wherever your story permits, drop in a dollop of reality. As often as you can, plant a detail that rings a little bell in the reader's mind, that makes him say, "Oh, yes! This is true. I recognize it." The more you reassure him about the *trappings* of your story, the more inclined he is to accept its *essence*.

But, I repeat, don't let your facts backfire. Be absolutely sure they're accurate. Is Pouilly-Fuissé a good white wine? Was IBM cheap at 100 dollars a share? Do double-decker buses still run on Fifth Avenue? You'd better be right, or you're through before you begin.

Comedy writing, I am prepared to say after twenty-five abrasive years, is at best a risky business. There are always a certain number of people who aren't going to think you're funny. That's the nature of humor, and there's nothing you can do about it. When for instance, I get a letter which says: "*Dobie Gillis* is a blot and an abomination, and you're about as funny as a carbuncle!" well, I don't exactly dance with joy, but I don't blame myself too harshly either, for I know there's simply no way for a humorist to please everybody.

When, however, I get a letter which says: "In the last *Dobie Gillis* story you said he was taking freshman Latin in high school and you had him translating Cicero. Boy, are you a lousy writer! You don't get Cicero till third year Latin!" then I blame myself—and bitterly. A little research would have prevented this needless error. A little less laziness, a little more care, and I wouldn't have lost a customer.

Lessons like this taught me the value of research. I surely didn't set out to write a definitive text on the Nike guided missile when I did *Rally Round the Flag, Boys!* Nevertheless, I spent weeks in the Pentagon and at Nike bases picking up as much as I possibly could. I was determined that if the book failed, it would fail for reasons literary and not ballistic. Naturally I got some bad reviews on *Rally*—humor always does—but it pleases me to say that nobody attacked the book because the facts about Nike were wrong.

Similarly, when I wrote *Anyone Got a Match?,* a large part of which concerns food additives, I made visit after visit to the Food and Drug Administration. When I worked with Robert Paul Smith on *The Tender Trap,* the hero of which is a pharmaceutical salesman, I got my family physician to introduce me to the local callers for Squibb, Parke Davis, and a few others, and I repeatedly made rounds with them.

A later project was a musical comedy called *How Now Dow Jones,* which, as you expect, is about Wall Street. Now, nothing could be more frivolous than a musical comedy; all the same, I went down to Wall Street and interviewed well over a hundred brokers, bankers, fund managers, and investors.

And in all of the instances mentioned above, I didn't neglect the library. In addition to personal interviews, I pored through the *Readers' Guides,* read stacks of magazine articles, shelves of books. It happens I live in the East, so trips to Washington and New York are not inconvenient. But if I lived a thousand miles away and my research was limited to the nearest public library, it would still have been done. Library work takes longer, of course, than face-to-face interrogation, but if you persevere you will generally find what you're looking for. And if you don't, there's always the U.S. mail.

A letter, brief and to the point, sent to the proper source and including a stamped, self-addressed return envelope, will almost invariably be answered – *promptly* answered. If I've learned anything in all my interviewing, it's that experts are enchanted by their own expertise. There's nothing in the world they'd rather discuss. When you – in person or by mail – ask a man a question relating to his specialty, he practically quivers like a pup with gratitude.

No matter where you live, research materials are available to you. Use them. Dig you must! Dig deep and hard. Don't be afraid of too much digging. To be sure, most of the stuff you turn up will be useless, but at least you'll have the comfort of knowing that the long labors of plotting and outlining and writing and polishing aren't going to go down the drain because you've made some bonehead error in fact.

And, in addition, research often surprises you with a little bonus – a prize, so to speak, in your Cracker Jack. While you're digging you run across something that gives you an idea for a new twist, a new character, a whole new story development you never would have thought of otherwise. You've all had the experience of opening a dictionary to look up a certain word, and while you're thumbing through the pages, you chance upon two or three other words that turn out to be eminently useful. So it is with research. You never know what you're going to uncover once you start swinging that shovel.

Let me add one more item to the virtues of research – a sort of negative item, but nonetheless valuable. Research can sometimes prevent you from writing a story that shouldn't be written.

To illustrate, let's go back to the example at the beginning of this article. You want to do a comedy, laid in New York in 1967, in which the boy and girl meet on the upper deck of a Fifth Avenue bus. I'm assuming you're not a New York resident or you'd know double-deckers don't run any more. You go to your local library to look up New York buses. Maybe the *Readers' Guide* steers you to an article that provides the answer. Maybe you find it in a guidebook to New York City. Or maybe you draw a blank at the library, so you write a letter to the public relations department of the New York Transit Authority.

But however you get the facts, you learn that the last double-decker ran in New York on April 27, 1953. This information leaves you with three alternatives:

a) Is the double-decker bus absolutely essential to your story? If so, you can make your story take place prior to April 27, 1953.

b) Is a 1967 date absolutely essential to your story? If so, you can make your bus a single decker.

c) Are the double-decker bus and the 1967 date *both* absolutely essential to your story? If so, forget the whole thing. Instead of investing time and sweat in a story that can't succeed, start work on a new one.

Any way you slice it, research has paid off for you.

The myth of faraway places

Life for a writer, at least for this one, is a constant series of alarums and excursions, of self-pamperings and self-delusions. There is always some distant place, a thatched cottage in England, a hacienda in Mexico, where, if you could only be, you would turn out the lyric prose and deeply significant stories that you find you cannot do wherever you happen to find yourself.

This is, of course, sheer nonsense, but it is a good and harmless kind of nonsense. It keeps one hoping and helps one to get around. I managed to achieve the house in England, the villa in Mexico and many other places, and they were never the answer. One of the few stories that ever gave me any satisfaction was written in snatches on railroad trains and hotel rooms while I was batting around the country as a reporter.

I have written in furnished rooms, on boats, in the city, in the country and in planes. If I have something that I want to write, I know that I can do it anywhere and under any conditions. But I will not relinquish the cherished illusion of the need for far places. I don't even mind knowing that it is a fake. It is delightful window dressing. What one actually needs to write is an idea, a typewriter, a roof over one's head and three square meals a day, because writing is physical as well as mental work and therefore hungry-making. All one really gets out of the firm belief that ideas will burn and words flow three or four thousand miles away from the place where one is at is a pleasant and diverting way of living and the broadening that comes with travel. – Paul Gallico in *Confessions of a Story Writer*.

George Appell

Many readers – and writers as
well – believe tall tales about
the cowboy hero of fiction

Myths about Westerns

For more than a hundred years the American West in spirit and legend
has galloped across our continent and over the oceans and around the
world and into the receptive minds of millions. It's with us to stay, like
sunrise and sunset and the Space Age; no one of man's credos has been
proliferated to such a sustained extent as this timeless song of the frontier.

Yet facts alone don't support the avalanche of guns and spurs and dudes
and villains and redmen and saloons and cattle: myths have accumulated
as this adventure story's first century ends and the second begins – myths
that come with time, like barnacles on a hull, and which remain just as
durable. Let's rove the whole hundred years (the mystique of the frontier
wasn't apparent until after the Civil War), selecting some myths that have
withstood the passage of time if not the test of truth.

1. *A writer must know his subject intimately*. True enough – but only
to a certain extent. Owen Wister, whose fantastically successful novel *The
Virginian* established the genre for the Western, was a Philadelphian whose

primary interests were musicology and philosophy. Educated at Harvard, he lived in Paris as a young man, studying music before returning to his native Pennsylvania for a law degree. Admitted to the bar, he was known only as a musically minded attorney until 1902, when *The Virginian* first appeared. The following year he produced what he considered his most interesting work, a book the title of which speaks for itself: *Philosophy 4.* Only when *The Virginian* galloped away into history did the author finally consider himself a novelist.

Zane Grey, perhaps the most prolific of all Western writers, was also educated at the University of Pennsylvania (he was born in Ohio) and during his early years practiced dentistry in New York. Only when *Riders of the Purple Sage* made a hit in 1912 did he hang up his drills and strap on his spurs.

Clarence Mulford, creator of "Hopalong Cassidy," lived in Maine; James Warner Bellah, whose Western novels and short stories have been outstanding since the twenties, was a New Yorker who flew with the Royal Flying Corps in 1917, later lived in France, and finally became an advertising man residing in Connecticut. (He now lives in California, where he has translated many of his Westerns into successful Hollywood film scripts.)

2. *The Western story is popular only in America.* True as far as it goes, but let's take it further. Today, more than ever before, Westerns are going abroad not only as completed books and films but also to be written by foreign authors and to be filmed in foreign lands. For some reason which no computer can analyze, these novels are most popular in Denmark, and the films in Italy. In fact, Scandinavia as a whole buys more overseas rights from American authors than any other region, and at the same time Danish writers are fast-learning the techniques for themselves.

Italian producers of Western films (which they insist are "Eastern" Westerns as distinguished from Westerns from Hollywood) invariably have the Indians win. On the other hand, almost no one ends up alive in these films because, as one leading producer puts it: "There couldn't be any heroes in that epoch. Heroism is only a theory."

Actually, the Italians hadn't considered winning the West until a German Western, *The Treasure of Silver Lake,* grossed over 1.5 million dollars. Then the boots and Stetsons flourished the length of the Sunny Peninsula, and now in five weeks of shooting and for about 100,000 dollars, the "Eastern" Westerns are cranked out. However, Anglicized names remain in demand: Giuliano Gemma, a leading big star, became Montgomery Wood; director Marino Girolami is known as Fred Wilson; Franco Giraldo rides as Frank Garfield.

A recent "Eastern," *Per Un Pugno di Dollari* (*For a Fistful of Dollars*), was shot in seven weeks for 200,000 dollars and in its first year grossed four million dollars; another which cost about three times that is now racking up 10,000 dollars a day. Sergio Leone, a leading producer, explains that you need "a pinch of detachment" to succeed in this manner.

"I understand that the best American Westerns are made not by Americans," he says, "but by Ford, an Irishman, by Zinneman, an Austrian, and by Wyler, a Tyrolese. So I felt I could do a Western, too."

In France, which along with Western books and films imports such artifacts as boots, ten-gallon hats, and jeweled rodeo belts, there's been a translation problem in placing French visual titles on American film dialogue. One recent result was that when a Western movie villain in a saloon gruffly demanded, "A shotta redeye," the Parisian audience saw on the screen: *"Un Dubonnet, si'l vous plaît."*

In Japan, where for centuries women have occupied a position of virtual servitude, producers of Western movies are now casting stars like Shirley Yamaguchi in leading roles in order to appeal to this immense, newly emancipated female audience. And on Tokyo's Ginza, the main shopping artery, you can buy Western novels in both Japanese and English editions, you can attend a Japanese-made Western movie (including perfumed hot towels and popcorn); and you can purchase (along with pickled octopus and *balsa feruto* or clog sandals) such domestic items as lariats, imitation silver spurs, and plastic six-guns complete with holsters.

3. *The Western is not a woman writer's field.* Actually, the roster of successful women authors in this field rings like chimes: Edna Ferber's *Cimarron* in 1929 gave new scope to the Western, encompassing as it did a period extending from primitive Plains living to the new and glittering cities of today's Southwest; her more recent *Giant* is based upon Texas wealth in its modern sense. Dorothy M. Johnson's short stories about frontier life are noted for their incisive characterization and powerful theme (her *The Hanging Tree* stands as an example of both) and the novels of Helen Hull have for years entertained readers who want to know what the West and its people were really like – from the woman's viewpoint.

4. *The horse must be a strong emotional and moral force in the Western.* Well, Tom Mix always did hug his white stallion, Tony, at the end of each movie; but in reality the cowpuncher regarded his mount as a birdbrain (albeit a valuable one) who was only a little more important to the scheme of living than a taxicab is to a modern whodunit. The animal was a hay burner who had to earn that hay by transporting Tex from one place to another. Look at Fred Zinneman's classic film *High Noon:* it all takes place

on a horseless street; and think of *Stagecoach* (1939), John Ford's adaptation of Ernest Haycox's "Stage to Lordsburg," which most critics recall as one of the finest short stories and motion pictures. Its action was based in (a) a Concord coach; (b) a street jammed with people on foot; and (c) a buckboard.

As a matter of record, Print Olive, worst of the West's badmen and whose memory has been kept alive by Mari Sandoz (few will soon forget her *Old Jules*), once caused the killing of 2,000 horses in order to confound his enemies, the cattlemen, by depriving them of a means of getting around. No one at the time (the 1880s) thought it particularly remarkable.

5. *Woman characters are not necessary in a Western.* They certainly are necessary (though for the most part subordinate) and this is vividly evident in *The Oxbow Incident,* in which a secondary character known as Ma, a tough old plainswoman, eventually causes the deaths (by hanging, shooting, and by saber) of the principal people involved. That's only one example, of course, but author Walter van Tilburg Clark uses it so deftly and forcefully that it remains one of the most memorable pieces of characterization in this field.

Ma was no sex symbol, by any means, but her sisters of the fictional frontier excited three generations of aficionados with their demureness. The novelists of the day — and their outgrowths, the screen writers — kept the dames demure because that was the way the cowhand regarded them at all times.

No man was instinctively more gallant than the puncher when, dirty and smelly from work or frolic, he was confronted with a lady stepping from a thoroughbrace coach or entering a store or teaching school or simply standing with parasol raised against the incessant sun, awaiting husband or brother. At moments like this, the puncher's knees turned tallow and he dropped forward from the hips, like the cocking of a shotgun, and he swept off his hat and hoped in his inarticulate way that the lady might notice him briefly in passing.

There was no furtive desire in this hope; it was an attitude created in reaction to the puncher's faded memory of a mother long gone, or a sister; or of a more elegant existence never to be retrieved. And that's the way the Western authors drew the men and women of the period because that's the way they were, even though you may smile today at such lines as "daintily lifting her ruffled hems an inch, she descended from the folding step of the Wells Fargo stage to the plankwalk, studiously disregarding all those men who pretended not to watch."

The women in these novels were necessary as motivating characters: they provided a change, a contrast, from the prevalence of males; they gave the story a flare of romance and the salt of conflict. But the women of the period were essentially prudish and the men were essentially shy.

Though many professional writers avoid the myths just mentioned, many more go along with the myths because they're profitable. In fact, more money has been made by authors, publishers, actors, and producers than your average cowpoke ever heard of in his life. Two instances of this are former screen star Hoot Gibson, who earned 14,500 dollars a week for years; and the author of Westerns who takes in 1,000,000 dollars for book sales, movie rights, and TV residuals on a single property which might have taken less than six months to write.

The danger of self-criticism

Don't be too much of a critic of subject material or you may never write about anything. The critic that lives in all writers will question at once the seed of any idea. Criticism, particularly of self, is a good habit, but like all habits it will lead you into trouble if you use it to excess.

So take your time when you begin to play around with an idea of what to write about. Try to look at it from a variety of aspects over a period of days or even weeks before you reject it as stale, dull or impossible to convey by words to your anonymous reader.

Strange pathways to success

Famous writers did not all begin as writers. Some did (and still do) other things for a living, writing on the side when they had the time. Others became full-time writers, abandoning their original pursuits because fame and fortune came their way.

Zane Grey – a dentist and Western novelist.
A. J. Cronin – a doctor and novelist.
William Carlos Williams – a doctor and poet.
Jean Kerr – a housewife and writer.
Anthony Trollope – a civil servant and novelist.
Theodore Roosevelt – a President and naturalist.
Winston Churchill – a statesman and historian.
Lewis Carroll – a mathematician and satirist.
Louis Bromfield – a farmer and novelist.

Mignon G. Eberhart

The fictional people you write about must
seem plausible . . . or they won't be
convincing to your reader

Where do characters come from?

Stories are about people – people who are born, live, and breathe within your story. To all practical purposes their lives are lived within your story. Now we all know that authors get their material from observation, so this statement may seem inconsistent, but it is not. There are sound reasons why we rarely lift a character in its entirety from real life. The reasons are not scruples or a healthy respect for the laws of libel: the main reason is merely because the real-life character is, in a sense, limited to real life. He cannot take on the life required in relation to other characters and to your story.

A character in a story is usually a composite of characters you have known or observed with something extra added – the fictional breath of life which permits him to move and speak and live within the story, and to be highly interesting to your reader. However, a real-life character or a real-life incident does not necessarily make a story. What we want in fiction are characters and incidents that *seem* likely and are consequently convincing to that acute and sensitive judge, your reader.

In the process of writing a story, your situation, characters, plot, inci-

dents, and setting each give impetus to the other. They mesh together sometimes so spontaneously that it is hard to say which comes first. But certainly
when we are sowing the seeds of a story in our minds, we find we have
characters whom we have observed in daily life. We may take one trait
here, another trait there, add and subtract almost subconsciously until eventually a fictional character takes shape.

And certainly at some point we try to bring up this seedling in the way he
should go. He must be nurtured and his growth directed so that he
naturally takes his role in the story. Yet even when he begins to emerge, we
still don't quite know his complete potentialities: don't know exactly what
he will do and what he will say until he shows himself on paper.

He is born (or comes into flower if we want to continue our little simile)
when he emerges on your typewriter. He then takes on physical appearance
and begins to move and speak. His traits come out clearly. He becomes, in
short, a character living in your story.

I want to repeat that almost everything a writer writes derives in some
degree from observation. The author has made himself as sensitive a recorder
as he possibly can. He has dug into his storehouse of observations in the
hope of discovering each character. He has prowled through all his stored-up
memories and impressions. Sometimes a character seems already bursting
into life at the exact moment when the author requires him, which is a very
fortunate and happy experience for the author. But wherever characters
exist in that curious reservoir upon which the author draws, they begin to live
only when they enter the story.

Every author finds certain ways of writing which are helpful to him, even
though they may not be at all helpful to another writer. In encouraging the
birth and growth of my fictional characters, I have found it most helpful to
write a short biography of each, taking in the main facts of his life up to the
time he enters the story. This is for my information. I want to know his background, his family circumstances, brothers, sisters, cousins, where he went to
school, what he has done in the way of work or play, what has contributed
to his life – in short, a reasonably complete dossier. Much of this may not
appear specifically in the story, but it seeps through because I myself must
be fully informed.

Now the old saying about moderation applies to writing: do nothing too
much. When reading a story, I don't want to begin with a long-winded
biography of one character, to be followed by equally long-winded biographies of all the other characters. But I do want to be sure, as a reader, that
the author knows all this.

Bergen Evans has drawn an analogy worth underlining here: "A good

character is like an iceberg – seven-eights submerged in the creative imagination. Only a fraction of it appears above the surface of the action, yet the
rest is there. It must be."

To me, another helpful way of learning just what my characters are is
this: After I've put their short biographies on paper, I begin to put them
into the story. That is, I actually start the story, but usually at some point
before the story really starts. In other words, I simply begin to write. In the
process I find out something about my characters; I discover how they look
and what they say and do in relation to each other. When I have discovered
this, I may find that some character doesn't belong in the story – he has been
born, so to speak, in the wrong period. When this happens, out he goes.

There is another fringe benefit to this "prewriting": If I am lucky, I not
only find that the characters are beginning to come alive but also at what
exact point the story begins, at what exact moment in the lives of my
characters the curtain of drama and conflict should arise.

Once, when I believed this "prewriting" was in fact the beginning of the
story itself, a very wise editor enlightened me. "You have written this to
inform yourself," he said, "not to inform the reader." He was right. I put all
I had written aside to serve as notes and then suddenly I knew the moment
when the story as a story began.

There are many ways of delineating a character. Some main considerations
are his description, what he says and does, what other people say of him
(and whether the reader believes or does not believe the characters speaking),
and what the author permits the character to think (in words in the story)
to show his reactions or motivations. There was a time when a reader would
address himself patiently to pages of description of each character when that
character made his entrance. Today's reader is not inclined to make this
leisurely progress; he is more likely to say impatiently to himself:

"I've got the idea. This character is a good-looking man in, say, his
thirties, dressed according to his present occupation – now get on with the
story! What is going to happen to him? What is he going to say or do?"

We must know what the man looks like, we must be able to see him, we
must be able to guess something of his character from his appearance or
dress, especially *we must be able to distinguish him immediately from other
characters in the story*. Small bits of description, small gestures or mannerisms, may come out later and when the story permits: we needn't try to give
the reader a whole bottle of tonic at one time. As a reader, I like some description, but I want it to be fairly brief and, consequently, sharp and clear.
I am also more interested if that description is in some way provocative,
arousing my curiosity so that I want to know more about the character. I

mention description because description (as well as the character's name) usually must emerge at or near the beginning of the story.

It seems to me the writer must assume all of his readers come from Missouri: they want to be shown. They want to hear what a character says, they want to see what he does. For this reason, I believe the reading of plays is suggestive to a writer. When we read plays, we read only dialogue and action. When we see the play, of course, we see the characters, we see the settings, all of which the fiction writer must offer the reader in words. But for a practicing writer, the reading of plays is extremely revealing in suggesting how much of a story can be told solely in dialogue and action.

If I had my way, I would start every story with dialogue or with immediate action. Of course, the reader must know where this story is taking place, and at some time the author must give the reader a notion of exactly what events or what circumstances have led up to the situation which begins the story. But he must know or sense almost at once what the story is to be about. He must sense the gathering of the conflict.

Now, plot and incident come straight from character. There is no other way of developing a story. Fictional characters are people placed in some situation demanding decision and action on their part, and this decision and action must come directly from the posture these characters would normally and consistently take. They cannot be pushed around like checkers on the board of a plot. Instead, their actions must logically show cause and effect. The author must ask himself: *Why* does this character feel thus and so in this situation or this conflict? *What* would this character do?

If we find that a character refuses to do what we want him to do to further the plot, then we have made a mistake. Either we have not fully realized the character or we have permitted the wrong character to enter into the story or we have tried to make our characters follow a preconceived pattern which is faulty and full of holes. Characters are more than arbitrary names; they are people who live within the framework of your story and require understanding and respect on your part. A plot itself may be ingenious to a most remarkable degree, but if it requires actions on the part of your characters which they would not logically undertake, then it is no plot at all.

A frequent aid to characterization is to permit other characters to speak of the person you are presenting. This is a two-edged tool and must be handled carefully; the reader's credence is based upon the reliability of the characters who are speaking, who have presumably already been introduced by the author.

May a character be permitted to think in words in order to explain his motives, his feelings, his reactions? And if so, how much? Certainly there exist some brilliant examples of stories composed almost entirely of such thought processes, but they are rare. Also, there was a time when readers were willing to trace out some character's mental gyrations at length, but that time has passed.

My own feeling again is do nothing too much. I, as a reader, am frankly bored and impatient if a character requires several pages to arrive at some decision which might be accomplished in one or two telling lines. There are certainly times and places in a story which require thinking on the part of your characters, but I believe that too much of this thinking aloud may be a trap into which an author can fall far too easily.

In reading a story, we like to expect the unexpected. We like to see a character with whom the author has made us fully acquainted, faced with a situation which would put the character (and ourselves participating as readers) in a position so difficult that we ourselves can see no satisfactory way out. In broad terms, we want to hiss the villain – even though the villain is personified by a calamity, a storm, some inevitable turn of events which is hard to overcome. We want to cheer the hero – even if he can't win after a good fight. As readers, we want to participate in the story. And as authors, we want to enlist that participation on the part of the reader.

A definition for writers

Writing isn't just spelling; it's much more than spelling. Writing isn't just grammar; it's much more than grammar. Writing is grasping ideas, seeing images, harnessing words – giving shape and form to thoughts. What matters most in writing is not the rules and conventions for putting words on paper. What matters most in writing is the writer's mind. – Flesch and Lass in *The Way to Write*.

A lesson from rejection slips

The first rule for the beginning writer is constant practice. One lesson to be learned from early rejection slips is that the tyro-writer has not practiced long enough at his craft. In fact, the production of a good deal of unsalable writing is a necessary prelude to successful writing for publication. – Gorham Munson in *The Writer's Workshop Companion*.

Gordon Carroll

Unless your characters know how and
when to talk, your fiction
won't seem believable to your readers

Directions for dialogue

Dialogue is one of the most helpful and facile tools in the writer's work kit. Among other things, it brings light and air to your prose; allows you to make your characters natural and lifelike; gives depth to emotional scenes and acts; helps to establish physical background and setting; even enlightens the printed page because it calls for quotation marks – those little ditto-like symbols that bring your reader visual relief from a dull sameness of too much solid type. And, fortunately for all writers, dialogue is no longer the property of the fictioneer; in today's world of communications, dialogue is used in all sorts of non-fiction, from the free-lance's article for a popular magazine to the scientist's report on a nuclear discovery.

There are, however, a number of dangers implicit in using dialogue – dangers easy to recognize after your piece has been written but hard to forestall at the beginning. Dialogue can be overextended: that is, the writer may place too much reliance on it when he should be using exposition, description, or narration instead. Dialogue may over-characterize a person and thus create a false image in the reader's mind. Dialogue may become too folksy, too colloquial, and so confound its purpose. Indeed, some writers use dialogue as an all-purpose crutch and fall on their faces when the crutch crumples under the burden of superfluous chitchat.

Most of all, dialogue is dangerous because, more than any other ingredient in an article or a story, it can establish the time and place of what the writer is writing about. For example, if conversation between characters is reminiscent of the twenties while the writer is writing about the sixties, the damage is too obvious to mention (and this is not merely a matter of outdated slang and wisecracks). If anything about your dialogue doesn't ring true – doesn't convince the reader that he's reading about real people in real life – then it becomes a liability and you should avoid it. Always your characters must sound natural, always their words must carry the right tone and rhythm, always you must show that you have an accurate ear for human speech and know how to translate it from your mind or from your memory to the printed page.

Are there any mechanical rules for writing dialogue? Unhappily for the writer, dialogue is no more amenable to regulation than any other major ingredient of fiction or non-fiction. Some writers seem to have an instinctive talent for making characters talk true to life, others have consistent trouble in putting words into the mouths of people. Perhaps the best "rule" for the writer is this: Listen to real people as they talk. Jot down their words, develop your ear for conversation, translate what you hear to paper, then read it back to yourself – aloud.

Does it sound lifelike, is it convincing, is this the way "they" communicated while you were eavesdroping? If you are satisfied with your interpretation, then you're bound to write better dialogue in your story, your article, your book, or your novel.

Next to listening to people, the best thing is to read dialogue written by successful authors, since you'll find styles here as in other kinds of writing. Don't confine yourself to any one author – range as widely as you can, going back in time as well as keeping in touch with the present (and the future, too, if you want to write science fiction). As you read what others have written, and "see" the characters through what the characters say, you are learning about dialogue yourself; techniques are bound to brush off on you, however unconscious of the fact you may be.

Some things to be careful about in writing dialogue are:

1. Conversational tags. It's not necessary to overload your talk with "he said," "she said," "they said," and so on. A few "saids" will carry you a long way. The fact that your characters have to speak alternately (not all at the

same time as so often happens in real life) allows your reader to know who's talking and keeps the conversation going at the proper pace.

2. Stage-managing. When writing long passages of dialogue, you should move your characters around so they don't become lifeless or static to your reader. If you don't stage-manage the people, at least let your reader know something about their gestures, their frowns, their smiles, their mannerisms — in general, their physical reactions to what is being said. Don't write in too much of this, just enough to keep the reader oriented.

3. Adverbs. Often, a passage of good dialogue is weakened by what might be called the "ly" pattern. For instance: "He said quickly (or firmly or brusquely or harshly, etc.)." "She replied slowly (or rapidly or glumly or sorrowfully, etc.)." Too many adverbs tacked on where they're not needed weaken conversation and make it sound silly. Read over your own dialogue and if you find too many adverbs scattered around, remove them. Then read the dialogue again, and if it doesn't convey its meaning without the adverb, rewrite it so it does.

4. Synonyms. Many a writer who manages to avoid adverbs commits an even graver error by using too many synonyms for the plain "said." Everybody says something when he talks, but few people hiss their warnings, grunt their replies, voice their answers, smile their good-bys, grin their greetings, and so forth. Whenever you feel like writing that your heroine breathed some words, start over again with the old reliable "She said."

Now, let's look at some successful instances of dialogue, selected from modern fiction. How do these samples measure up to the "rules" of dialogue? And just how did each author make his characters talk so as to serve the purpose he obviously had in mind?

The first example is from that old master Booth Tarkington — a passage from his famous novelette *Monsieur Beaucaire:*

> M. le duc de Chateaurien handed Lady Carlisle down the steps, an achievement which had figured in the ambitions of seven other gentlemen during the evening.
>
> "Am I to be lef' in such onhappiness?" he said in a low voice.
> "Never!" said Lady Mary.
> "Ah, I do not deserve it, I know so well! But —"
> "Never!"
> "It is the greatness of my onworthiness that alone can claim your charity; let your kin' heart give this little red rose, this great alms to the poor beggar."
> "Never!"
> She was seated in the sedan chair. "Ah, give the rose," he whispered. Her beauty shone dazzlingly on him out of the darkness.

"Never!" she flashed defiantly as she was closed in. "Never!"
"Ah!"
"Never!"
The rose fell at his feet.

Among other things, we know from reading this passage that our French hero is much in love with his English beauty and will continue to pursue her until the story's happy ending. But the word Never is the key to this passage of dialogue. Note how cleverly Tarkington used it to sharply characterize his romantic couple, and how he continued to use it right up to the close of the scene.

In some author's hands, the word Never might have been used once or twice: in Tarkington's, it was used six times, and each time for increasing emphasis. Although no "rule" of dialogue may be established from this, the verbal trick is one you might want to experiment with some day.

In a literary generation next to Tarkington's is James Farrell, whose famous trilogy *Studs Lonigan* has become one of the classics of the century. The gap between the manners and times of M. Beaucaire and Studs Lonigan is almost immeasurable, but Farrell uses dialogue just as well as Tarkington in this passage from *The Young Manhood of Studs Lonigan:*

Martin Husk Lonigan poked Crabby Kentchy's books out of his arms.
"Pick 'em up?" Crabby commanded.
"What? Huh! I don't know what you're talking about."
"Well, you will know, if you don't pick up the books you knocked out of my arm."
"What's he sayin'?" Husk Lonigan said to his pal, Pete McFarland.
"What you say, Koney?" kidded McFarland.
"I said pick 'em up!"
"He said to pick something up," Pete said.
Husk Lonigan looked up and down the street.
"There ain't no girls around to pick up."
Pete laughed.
"Gonna pick 'em up?"
"Who was your servant last year?" asked Husk Lonigan.
"You knocked 'em out of my arm."
"What?"
"You did."
"You're a liar," Husk Lonigan said, sneering and looking quite like his brother Studs.
"Who's a liar?"
"You, if you said I knocked your books down."
"Aw, smack him, Husk," said Pete McFarland.
"Try it!"
"Oh, you want to fight?" said Husk, again sneering.

Crabby punched Husk's nose. They fought, and Crabby gave Husk a bloody nose and a shiner. Husk picked up the books.

With a minimum of stage-managing, Farrell has used dialogue to bring you a vivid scene from the sidewalks of Chicago during the era when Studs Lonigan, Husk's older brother, reigned supreme in a neighborhood of "tough guy" punks. The sentences are short, the talk is brisk and brusque, but the passage does just what the author wanted it to do. The reader quickly senses the braggadocio, the pathetic posturing, of these youngsters as they try to emulate the strutting of their local heroes. In short, dialogue in Farrell's hands combines description, narration, and exposition in one, since he makes every spoken word count.

In writing the best-selling *Fate Is the Hunter,* Ernest K. Gann was dealing with a subject he knows well, aviation. However, the subject can become too technical for the lay reader, so in many places throughout the book Gann cleverly used dialogue to put involved points across. Here is a passage from Chapter VII, "The Gypsies," in which Gann conveys in dialogue some details that might have become dull and distracting in expository prose.

Finally he said, still looking at the bay, "Where was the airplane on the night before this happened?"

I told him we had simply left it at the field.

"And you? Where were you and your co-pilot?"

"At the hotel."

"Who was guarding the airplane?"

"No one. Why?"

"It probably wouldn't have made any difference since the guard would only sleep under the wing anyway."

"Then?" This was a mechanical puzzle, a problem of metal and lubrication. I could not see how a guard asleep or awake could possibly provide an answer.

"The trouble with most pilots is that you are spoiled. And lazy. You have never taken the trouble to learn mechanics properly."

"There are times when there are things I would rather not worry about."

"If you were not so innocent you might have considered that if someone poured a cup of water into your oil tank the result would be exactly as you've described. It would take no more. As the oil heats, so does the water, until it becomes steam. Then as the process continues the pressure builds and something finally has to give. In your case it was the filler cap. Very fortunate for you."

"What about the other engine? It remained normal."

"But how much longer would it have done so? You said the temperature gauges stayed normal on both engines, which should prove even to you that the heat of the oil was only an accessory to the event. It was the temperature of the water that counted. It is possible that in another thirty minutes the same thing would have happened to your left engine. But I think it more likely someone bungled. Either they did not put enough water in your left engine or were interrupted before they could finish the job. It wouldn't have made a great deal of difference. If you had not actually seen the oil let go you would have had all the trouble you could handle and probably more."

And just then, like a child who has known his first brush with evil, my innocence departed.

Here is an example of two men talking about mechanical matters and yet conveying to the layman an understandable idea of the subject – in this case, aeronautical engines. The author wrote this dialogue to further a twist in his plot, and in the last sentence of the passage the reader understands that the narrator is about to walk into an area of possible danger.

Dialogue is most effective when a writer wants to use foreign-language words or phrases to give the prose a ring of authenticity. Just a touch here and there is all that is necessary, as witness this excerpt from a short story, "Far Enough," in Stuart Cloete's anthology, *The Soldiers' Peaches:*

John Allen pulled his horses up. "Good morning, Meneer!" he shouted.

"It is not good morning," Danie said. "It is bad morning that brings you back. It is a bad morning that brings any Englishman. They come before trouble. They are like the dust that comes before a storm, and no good ever comes of them." He spat between the spokes of the wheel and touched the safety catch of his rifle.

"So it is like that," Allen said. He laughed. "Then listen, Meneer. Yesterday you said this was a good farm?"

"I say it still. It is a good farm. There is no farm like it in these parts."

"Will you sell it?"

Here was his chance. Magtig, he would cure these Englishmen. "Ja, I will sell it," he said.

"What is your price?"

"It is a good farm."

"Yes, it is a good farm."

"And a good farm is worth a good price."

"It is also my home place; I like it here," he said.

"That also is worth something."

"Yes, it is worth something."

"It is a large farm and all of it is good. There is no wasteland here, Meneer. Not a single morgen of wasteland and the grazing is very fine. Have you seen my slaughter oxen?" he asked. "If you would like to see them, I will send a boy to fetch them in. If you see them, you will see what fine veld I have. Ja, it is a good farm. I think perhaps it is too good for an Englishman."

It so happens that Stuart Cloete is a South African himself and thus his judicious use of the words Meneer, Magtig, and Ja gives the right flavor to his conversation between a Boer farmer and an Englishman. However, any writer, irrespective of his nationality and antecedents, can make use of words from a foreign tongue to emphasize a scene or a setting or to delineate a character more sharply. Further, you will note that in Cloete's dialogue he has used more than just a Dutch word or two to identify his Boer: he has the farmer speaking throughout in the stiff and stilted fashion that a reader might expect in such a character.

For a final example of fiction dialogue that works well for an author, let's turn to the suspense novel – the kind of novel in which many characters have to be introduced with a minimum of words. In mystery stories, the author has neither time nor space to waste on the amenities: the reader wants action, not long passages of extraneous words.

The example taken from *Melora,* a best-selling suspense novel by Mignon G. Eberhart, shows how a major character can be introduced and explained through crisp dialogue, plus a few asides and a minimum of stage-managing. Had she not used dialogue, Mrs. Eberhart might have had to write quite a few hundred words of expository and descriptive prose to accomplish her same literary purpose.

> As she started downstairs, the telephone rang. Its imperative peal startled her. For a second she thought, perhaps it's Brent. The bad weather just might have delayed his flight; he might be returning home. She ran to the telephone extension in the library.
>
> "Hello, Anne." She knew the voice at once, hearty, warm, a little wheezy. "This is Gary Molloy. Is Brent at home?"
>
> Gary Molloy was a lawyer, too. He was not a partner of Brent's – Brent had no partners – but he was an old family friend.
>
> He sounded worried. "I phoned his office and they said he wasn't there and they couldn't tell me when he was expected."
>
> "He started for Paris this morning."
>
> "To settle the Cadell case?" There was dismay in Gary's rich, if husky, voice. "I thought he wasn't going until next month!"
>
> "He finished up another case sooner than he expected. So he had a chance to go now."
>
> "Look here, something's come up about the Cadell case. Brent should know about it. Will he be phoning to you from Paris?"
>
> "Yes, if he has time. What's wrong, Gary?" Dismay touched her, too. The Cadell case had dragged out for years; Brent had expected that his trip to France would at last end it.
>
> "I'd better come around to see you." There was a pause while Gary seemed to consult his desk calendar. "I can't make it until around six, or a little after. Is that all right with you?"
>
> "Yes, of course. I'll be here."

Remember – there are no formulas for writing dialogue. Like other ingredients in a piece of writing, the nature and quality of what characters say to each other depend on the nature and quality of the author's talent. The samples of dialogue offered in this article are neither definitive nor all-inclusive. They have merely been selected from a limitless library of fictional dialogue – the same library that is available to you if you will browse and read in the books of your choice.

Finding the time to write

Since I don't do anything else but write, my days are devoted entirely to my profession. I normally get to my desk about nine in the morning and stay there until four or five in the afternoon. During this time I take no phone calls and receive no visitors. I also don't go out to lunch but have a sandwich at the desk.

It is almost certain that your life doesn't allow you such a concentration of effort. My suggestion to you, then, is to do what I do in miniature. At the end of your regular day's work, closet yourself and start writing. Permit no interruptions. If you can manage a full day on weekends by all means grab it. Your social life will necessarily suffer, but you must make up your mind as to whether you want to be a writer or a hail-fellow-well-met. – Max Shulman

Practice, practice, practice!

There are certain basic principles of writing which every new writer learns, and every experienced writer *keeps on learning*. They may be expressed by different writers in different ways but all the definitions add up to much the same thing. First, there are the tools of your trade: words, grammar, syntax. They must become so much a part of you that you draw upon them unconsciously, as a carpenter reaches for the right tool without looking for it.

Also, the development of observation is essential. Self-discipline is essential. Thinking is essential. But nothing is written *until it is written*. So therefore a writer must write, write, write – practice, practice, practice! Beware of any writing that comes too easily; read it for the flaws that may have bubbled up. Don't be discouraged if it comes too hard; it may prove to be better writing than you think it is. But whatever happens, write and study, write and learn, write. – Mignon Eberhart

Janet Van Duyn

*There's a trick to using description so that
your readers will feel "right
there" with your fictional characters*

How to create settings

A well-known London pub recently created a tourist attraction – a replica of the lodgings of a world-famous detective, considered by his best friend to be "the very worst tenant in London." Details are startlingly authentic, even to a letter on the table addressed to "Sherlock Holmes, Esq., 221-b Baker St., London, W.1."

The visitor may observe the crowded little sitting room exactly as Conan Doyle visualized it: two armchairs pulled up by the grate near the coal scuttle and the Persian slipper containing tobacco; Holmes's pipe, a Stradivarius, a magnifying glass; Watson's watch and chain; a hat rack in the corner bearing greatcoats and the familiar deerstalker cap.

Doyle's use of setting to give plausibility to his stories and novels is well known. Long after he wearied of contriving strange adventures for his hero, his readers kept goading him to write more, simply because he had discovered the trick of creating settings that made you feel "right there."

How? Rarely by long paragraphs of description: the adventure tales were too short to bear elaboration. Even in a long story, "The Hound of the Baskervilles," where the author spends pages establishing the mood and setting of the lonely moor, it is one small, well-placed detail we remember with stunning clarity – the yew alley down which Sir Charles Baskerville strolled the last evening of his life.

Baskerville Hall remains in the flat landscape, remote, crenellated, vague. Grimpen Mire, by the very horrid connotation of its name, causes us an agreeable shudder or two. But the real sense of identification comes when the reader recalls that long avenue of yew trees, and just by the moor gate a pathetic clue – a dropped ash from Sir Charles's cigar.

Perhaps this is why, almost a century after these stories were written, we can stand with our noses pressed against a glass dividing us from the stuffy Victorian sitting room in Baker Street, half expecting to hear the clipped tones of its celebrated lodger: "Ha! I am glad to see that Mrs. Hudson has had the good sense to light the fire. Pray draw up to it . . . ."

One of the first things a fiction writer learns is that setting must "create a mood." It's an easy precept to explain but difficult to practice. Often a beginning writer will be tempted to go about it by drawing a plan or by cataloging details while the reader waits impatiently for the story to begin. In a short story, the background should be swiftly and unobtrusively sketched in, so that it not only provides a stage for the actors but also a subtle comment on their emotions.

In "Crazy Sunday," Scott Fitzgerald suggests the same room at three different times of day through the eyes of his main character. First is a cocktail party, as the young man, full of brash expectancy, surveys it:

> "The handsome, well-dressed people in the room, the lovely girls and the – well, lovely girls."

Later on he makes a fool of himself; the atmosphere abruptly changes:

> "The faces surrounding him in the gently molded light were intent and curious, but there was no glint of a smile anywhere."

Still later in the evening, with the guests gone, the party comes to a sad end, the room is empty:

> "Under the high ceilings the situation seemed dignified and tragic. It was an eerie bright night outside all the windows and Stella all rose-gold raging and crying around the room."

Thus a setting can come to life in a phrase or two, simply by the way someone looks at it. A dull day can look bright if we've just inherited a million dollars; sunshine can mock us if we've been crossed in love. The teacher in Katherine Mansfield's "The Singing Lesson" feels miserable in the bleak, chalky atmosphere of a classroom – but after a telegram comes from her young man, the room leaps into sunlight, each child is an angel, and the sentimental song they are learning magically acquires pitch.

In Stephen Vincent Benét's epic poem about the Civil War, *John Brown's Body,* the old Negro servant, Cudjo, polishes the silver for Christmas with his last scrap of chamois ṣkin and mourns the sad state of things in the Wingate mansion. He observes:

> "Grey hairs in Miss Mary's brush
>   And a whooin' wind in the berry-bush,"

and suddenly we get a deep and painful sense of this tragic period.

In one of Agatha Christie's crime thrillers, based in Baghdad, the narrator, a visiting nurse from England, tells us flatly that "there isn't going to be any local color in this story. Messing about with people and places that are buried and done with doesn't make sense for me."

She complains that "everyone hammering away at pots and pans" gives her a headache. "Such a smell," she protests fastidiously, "and everything ramshackle and tumbledown and mud and mess everywhere." After viewing the archaeologist's "digs," she writes to a friend in England: "Would you believe it . . . dirty mud walls about two feet high . . . no marble or gold or anything handsome . . ."

Bless the nurse! By her sublime lack of imagination, she's ushered us right into the story. How much better this way than if the author had painstakingly laid out the "digs" or handed us paragraphs of "colorful description."

Ian Fleming maintained that it was his habit of "venturing up back streets" that turned him into a writer of James Bond thrillers. As a young journalist, he often left the well-lighted boulevards in search of the obscure but eloquent detail which gave him a sense of the city. This curiosity about a new place is present to some extent in all writers, leading them to set forth to explore, to observe, to prowl. "What's beyond that fence? Who moved behind that shutter?"

Thomas Hardy, noted for his ability to write settings which are more than settings, is said to have created a virtual character out of Egdon Heath, the scene of many of the Wessex novels. The first chapter of *The Return of the Native* is a masterpiece of description through subtle observation of phenomena. Dusk:

> "The place became full of a watchful intentness now; for when other things sank brooding to sleep the heath appeared slowly to awake and listen."

In a short story, a writer is obligated to figure out a way to create an "instant setting," distilled from a detail so well placed and so apt that it tells the reader where he is and suggests what's likely to happen. It is only in the large scope of the novel that he can expand his impressions. Mary Stewart, whose novels of suspense are famous for atmosphere, is a master at putting the reader right into the middle of an unfamiliar place, a place he may never have seen but where he may long to go.

In one of her recent novels, *The Moonspinners,* she devotes a whole first chapter to the mountainous scenery of Crete. But she is too knowledgeable a writer to plunge into an orgy of description. Her reader will wait just so long, and she's well aware of it. So there's a girl in this picture, an English visitor with a rucksack on her back. She contemplates the ancient, brooding landscape, sniffs the air full of the scent of lemons. Suddenly an egret flies out of a lemon grove and wheels off into the mountains.

> "I looked upstream, where a path wound along the waterside under the willows."

A path! Who in his right mind could resist the temptation to follow it? Nothing's happened yet – but after four pages, the sense of expectancy is overwhelming. And so the chapter ends:

> "Here I was, alone under a lemon tree, with a path ahead of me, food in my bag, a day dropped out of time for me, and a white bird flying ahead."

A place and a person. An unbeatable combination.

Ever since ancient times, a sense of place has been strong in certain individuals. In fact, among primitive peoples it was probably much stronger than it is now. In the Old Testament there are frequent references to settings which have a sort of mystical ambience, making the observers fearful or filling them with awe. Jacob, after his dream of the ladder, could rise up and look about him at the forbidding landscape and say, "How dreadful is this place! This is none other than the house of God and the gate of heaven." Reverently he picks up the stone he has been using for a pillow, pours oil on it and sets it up for a pillar of the temple he will build there.

> "Nobody can paint the sun or the sunlight. He can only paint the tricks the shadows play with it, or what it does to forms . . . he can only paint the emotion they give him . . ."

So Willa Cather wrote in her essay, "Light on Adobe Walls." In other words, walls aren't enough; it's the way light strikes them, the way they confine, or shelter, or liberate, or depress, or cheer. A writer of fiction must have experienced this himself before he can expect his reader to feel it.

For this reason, he must often suppress the interior decorator in him, who wants to put a label on every stick of furniture; he must restrain the zealous property man who produces gadget after gadget until a scene is crammed with bric-a-brac. When the writer goes out of doors, he's got to keep a sharp eye out for the poetic muse who tempts him to rhapsodize over every rock and rill, or the map-maker who appears with charts and diagrams.

Granted there's some of the prop man in all of us, still the fact remains that the best descriptions are selective. All an author can put into his story is a special something he's seen or felt. Just as an artist must paint quickly to "catch the light," so a story writer must catch in his setting the emotion which reflects on the characters, theme, and action. All he can really give you, according to Miss Cather, is the "thrill of his poor little nerve."

Your words must be precise

One of the primary needs of the good writer is to be precise in word meaning. Mathematics is an exact science, and answers to mathematical problems can be proved. This isn't true of writing. Hence, the need for precision in words. The writer must pay just as great attention to word meaning as is required by the theorems of the mathematician. Samuel Butler said that definitions are the cross each writer must bear. "A definition," he wrote, "is a wall of words surrounding a chaos of ideas." – Gordon Carroll

Don't take spelling lightly

Bad spelling, the mark of an illiterate, is a terrible handicap to a writer. Writers often find they don't use words they can't spell, which seriously limits their range. In business, your bosses will spot you quickly as a person who can't spell and, hence, are less reliable than one who can. Poor spelling is tedious for the boss (or editor) and most bosses (and editors) won't stand for it long. It takes a lot of time to keep correcting words, and time's too precious at the boss's or editor's level. – Gordon Carroll

Elizabeth Lansing

There's more to success in the
juvenile field than meets the eye of the
would-be writer

Stories for young readers

I want to write for children."

My friend sat across from my study desk, her eyes bright with purpose. "You write for them," she added almost accusingly, "and I . . ."

"If I can, you can," I finished for her.

"Something like that." She laughed and settled back in her chair. "Ever since son Bill went off to college, George and I have been alone and I want something to do." She tried to speak lightly, but there was a note of genuine appeal as she added, "How do I begin?"

My fingers rested on my typewriter keys as she spoke, for Mary (as we shall call her) had interrupted me as I did my morning writing stint. Usually this is a sacred four-hour stretch when *no one* is allowed into the house and even the phone goes unanswered. But when Mary called after breakfast, saying she had something "really important" to talk about, I told her to come along.

"You've done some writing, haven't you?" I began, thinking as I touched my typewriter keys how many hours of tapping they'd done. "I mean, you aren't scared of the mechanical part of it – punctuation and that sort of thing?"

"Oh, I don't mean that!" She almost glared. "I'm not going to worry about quotation marks and . . ."

"Editors do," I said mildly. "They care a lot about what a manuscript looks like."

"There you go!" She was on the defensive. "You make such a mystery with all this talk about editors. They don't worry me. I know how to punctuate and I even know what I want to write. I've got a dozen stories in my head. I used to tell them to Bill and the others when they were little."

Mary was in full flight now. Bringing up five children, maintaining a home, and keeping George happy had made her a very confident woman. I listened as she outlined her writing plans. She had plenty of ideas and some of them seemed valid. I began to wonder why she'd come to me for advice.

". . . and so there's only one thing I'd like to know."

Mary's confident gaze wavered. She looked at her hands, now tensed in her lap. "It's . . . it's these kids today," she said. "They aren't the way mine were. I used to have some idea of what made them tick; but the ones you hear about today . . ." She looked up. "How do you know who you're writing for?"

I drew a breath of relief. I might have known that Mary was smart enough to realize that in writing for young people, it's vitally important to know your reader and she was honest enough to admit she'd lost track of the Younger Generation.

Thinking of all the little faces that float before my typewriter as I "compose" my stories, I began rummaging in a drawer of my desk. Only the day before I'd read an article in a writer's magazine that touched on a part of Mary's question.

"Listen to this." I read from the article: "The trouble with most juvenile writers is that they don't really get the child's point of view. You can't talk *to* them or *at* them. You have to talk *with* them, *feel* with them."

"That's all very well," said Mary, "but has anyone ever . . ."

I held up my hand. "Let me finish. 'Where most writers of juveniles fail is that they don't really *understand* children.'"

"That's it exactly," said Mary. "How do I go about understanding them?"

"Try *remembering*," I suggested, closing the desk drawer.

"You mean, what it's like to be . . . say, six years old?"

"That's a good place to start. It might also help to think about some of the books you once loved. Have you ever read a book called *Books, Children and Men,* by Paul Hazard? It was written more than thirty years ago but it tells more about the *way* young people feel about books and *why* they like certain ones than anything I've ever read."

"I'll get it at the library," said Mary hastily, for she was anxious to get back to her problem.

"Hazard tells a great deal about the history of children's literature, too," I said relentlessly. "You've read the wonderful old books he talks about and many of them are popular today — *Robinson Crusoe, Gulliver's Travels,* and the fairy tales."

"I remember them, all right, but how can they help me now?"

"They illustrate a point. Young people today like those books as well as they ever did — and for a special reason. They are *not written down* to their supposed level. In fact, they're adult books that children have adopted because they tell good stories."

"That's what I want to write!" said Mary. "Stories and perhaps biographies."

"Start at the library, then. In fact, you should live in the children's room of the library for the next few weeks. Talk to the librarian. There's no one who knows more about children's books."

"I *did* go to the library," Mary confessed, "but I got a little scared by all those shelves of science and information books. There's a 'How-to' or 'Why' book on every subject and for every age level."

"Indeed there is," I said cheerfully. "They've increased by the thousands since Sputnik and today's kids have dozens of wonderful ways to learn things."

"But what about the kind of stories I want to write about people? Are kids today really interested in anything but facts?"

"Of course! Study the fiction shelves, too. Ask the librarian which books are taken out most often. You'll find that many of the successful ones appeal to the kids' imagination, their sense of fun or their special hopes and problems. Now . . . I'd like to talk about something a little more fundamental."

Mary listened intently.

"Children hate to be talked down to, as I've already said. Old-fashioned stories used to have a moral that the author hammered home on every page. Even *Little Women,* still a favorite, makes certain of each point by having Marmee give a periodic little lecture on it. Today's children tune out on a sermon. A story must have a special meaning, a theme if you like, but it's got to be buried in the characters' activities."

"Give me an example," said Mary.

"Charlotte's Web," I replied. "Everything that anyone, young or old, needs to know about loyalty and friendship is inherent in all that Charlotte does. The book is really a perfect example of conveying a 'message' in a delightful *and* interesting way. Young readers have a sixth sense of the phony. They know that Charlotte is a 'good friend and a good writer' as that last line says. No one can ask for more than that."

Mary frowned. "But what about TV and its influence on today's kids and their reading habits."

I paused for a moment, remembering how I had once battled with my own children over watching time and choice of programs. Why had I worried so much about the "ill effects" of television? None of my children are bug-eyed and all of them read with voracity.

"I suppose it's all part of the adult habit of 'viewing with alarm,'" I said. "and I don't mean a pun. I read somewhere that the average child has been exposed to 3,000 hours of TV before he enters the first grade. Most children are just 'with it,' absorbing this extraordinary new world. Do you realize that this same first-grader has already made a trip to the moon – by TV at least. How far had *we* gone at that age?"

"I went to Schenectady when I was five to visit my grandmother," said Mary.

"Exactly," I said. "We lived in a narrow world. Today's kids have all five senses sharpened and want to use them to find out, explore, and discover. Go visit an elementary school and see what's being done with audio-visual aids. Try watching what children look at on TV; see what they see. Otherwise, writers are in danger of talking into a void."

"I begin to get your point," said Mary. "It's better to appreciate than depreciate, isn't it?"

I nodded. "You can't preach, that's for sure," I said. "Personally, I think today's young people are a remarkably fine group." I leaned toward her over my typewriter. "If you don't believe that, you haven't any right to write for them."

"Now who's preaching?"

"Perhaps the best way to say it is that you must respect them and never, *never* write down to your reader, no matter what his age."

"I suppose choosing the age group really depends on the story you have in mind," said Mary, scribbling in her notebook.

"That's something else you can best learn about in that favorite place of mine – the library. And while we're on the subject of age levels, let me warn you it's a mistake to think that writing for young people is somehow easier than writing an adult book."

"Who said that?" demanded Mary.

"You didn't. But I suspect a great many would-be writers for the young hope that writing a children's book is easier. Someone once said that when a writer has learned enough to write for an adult, he can hope to interest a child. But any sort of watering down of adult material will fail. I've had too many well-meaning friends ask me when I'm going to stop writing for children — implying that I'm fiddling away my time — and start writing what they call 'something worthwhile,' meaning an adult book."

"I get the point," said Mary. "But — with all those hours at TV, all those factual books on every subject, what has a child left to find out on his own? Where can he really explore and discover for himself?" She hesitated, then said, "Where has the wonder gone?"

For a long moment I looked at her, caught by a stab of the same concern. Then I remembered the small boy I had seen from my window that morning. About seven, he was careening past the house on his way to school. A patch of flaunting crocus blooms, growing by my steps, caught his eye. Getting down from his bicycle, he knelt beside the steps and stared into the heart of a large purple crocus. He stayed perfectly still for several minutes, then jumped on his bike and pedaled away whistling.

I told Mary what I'd seen.

"I know what you're trying to tell me," she said. "But you know perfectly well this boy had seen a crocus on television and had had it explained to him, too."

"I suppose so," I answered. "But you see, this was *his* crocus!"

Let your feeling guide you

The new writer can probably write best about that which he knows from personal experience. He's still functioning on a new level. He's unsure of his tools and will be unsure for a few years to come. Under those circumstances, it's best that he doesn't take on the added pressure of research into alien fields.

But this rule can never be hard and fast. If in the beginning you have something to say about a subject which is not a part of your own experience and yet you have a strong feeling about it and interest in it, you should write about it. There is nothing that begets better writing than the process of writing. It's as simple as that. — Rod Serling

George Lowther

Putting aside a little time each day, and
sticking to the schedule, works wonders
for the man or woman who wants to write a
novel – or anything else

Writing a novel in half hours

Many men and women could write a salable novel and perhaps (who knows?) a best seller if, in their words, they "only had the time." Without knowing it, each one of them, no matter how busy, has at his disposal two full months a year – sixty days – of uninterrupted leisure in which to write whatever he pleases.

Half an hour a day, 365 days a year, equals 182½ hours. Few "full-time" writers spend more than three hours a day actually writing. Divide 182½ by 3 and you wind up with more than 60 full working days you can devote to writing alone. However occupied a business executive may be, whatever hours a housewife must put in per diem, each can afford to put aside an "hour-day" for writing.

But writing, you say, simply isn't done that way: novels – and short stories and articles and plays and whatever – aren't written in bits and pieces of time. The writer must seek inspiration, must compose his thoughts before beginning the task of writing. Here is Mary Roberts Rinehart's answer:

I trained myself to pick up a pen and start writing the moment I sat down at my desk. This is one way to do it. The word "inspiration" means, I suppose, writing above your head. I have written above my head on occasion, but usually I build my stories by plugging. It's the only way I know.

And Louis Bromfield:

I can only give two or three days a week to writing, so when I write I don't fiddle around. When I have two hours for work, I write every minute of the two hours, simply because I know what I want to say before I start writing.

And again, Somerset Maugham:

No professional writer can afford to write only when he feels like it. If he waits until he is in the mood, till he has the inspiration as he says, he waits indefinitely and ends up by producing little or nothing. The professional writer creates the mood. He has his inspiration, too, but he controls and subdues it to his bidding by setting himself regular hours of work.

Maugham's normal writing stint, it may be added, rarely exceeded three hours a day. Nor did Hemingway's or Fitzgerald's or almost any author you can name. Granted there were days when, spurred by a deadline, they worked longer, the fact remains that their normal typewriter time was three hours. (You can match the longer periods during weekends, if you like.)

Quite obviously, the accomplishment of writing in half-hour sections demands a bit of discipline. A regular time must be set aside each day and strictly adhered to, come what may. But it would be a frenetically busy man or woman who didn't have that half-hour — or couldn't find it. Arnold Bennett, one of the most prolific and successful writers of his time, suggests in *How to Live on Twenty-Four Hours a Day* that, if necessary, you can rise earlier. In his words, "the proper, wise balancing of one's whole life may depend upon the feasibility of a cup of tea at an unusual hour." A practitioner of what he preached, Bennett often wrote his thousand words a day in half-hour snatches.

The importance of this regular schedule — this same half hour each day — is vital; a definite rhythm is created both mentally and physically, and the writer automatically goes to his desk at that certain time, drawn by habit. The brain, too, being a creature of habit, quickly learns to operate efficiently at such times and, though the first few attempts will almost surely prove disappointing, adherence to the schedule soon brings surprising and gratifying results. These in turn act as a spur to further effort.

Once the pattern of a daily half hour at a stated time is set, nothing short of disaster will keep you from writing. All writers attest to this, but perhaps the fact is best illustrated by Robert Louis Stevenson, who had so disciplined himself that even grave illness could not keep him from his daily task. In 1893, he wrote to George Meredith:

> For fourteen years I have not had a day's real health: I have wakened sick and gone to bed weary; and I have done my work. I have written in bed and written out of it, written in hemorrhages, written in sickness, written torn by coughing, written when my head swam for weakness . . .

"That's all very well," you protest, "but I simply don't have a definite half hour I can set aside each day. My day is too mixed up, because if it isn't one interruption it's another." Barbara Tuchman, author of the best-selling *Guns of August,* answers thus:

> All the while you're writing, there's the pull of household duties. I'd like to suggest to writing students who are wives and mothers that they set aside a specific time each day to write. Neighbors phone you to gossip, to fetch the children. You must *insist* on being left alone on certain hours of the day.

The objection may be raised that writers must have time to think before they write, and not much thinking can be done in half an hour. True enough, but in connection with Bromfield's remark that he knew what he wanted to say before he sat down to say it, the following from Maugham is revealing:

> The author does not only write when he's at his desk, he writes all day long, when he is thinking, when he is reading, when he is experiencing; everything he sees and feels is significant to his purpose and, consciously or unconsciously, he is forever storing and making over his impressions.

On the same subject, Clarence Buddington Kelland, unquestionably one of the long-time greats in the field of magazine fiction, says this:

> Too many people let six months pass while they wait for an idea. If they'd sit down at a typewriter and simply start to write about a fellow named Joe Jones in the lumber business, ideas on Joe and his job would come fast. It is work, and that is, of course, harder than just waiting. But it is effective.

William Carlos Williams, the physician-poet, scarcely had time in which to write, so busy was he with his medical practice, yet he turned out a large body of work during office hours by writing *single lines of poetry between patients*. Williams kept pad and pencil in his desk drawer and between the time one patient left his office and the next entered, he would scribble a line — and sometimes two or more!

Curiously, the busier some authors are on outside matters, the more they seem to produce. As a young reporter for *The Chronicle,* Charles Dickens could scarcely have had a daily half hour to call his own, yet he produced *Sketches by Boz* and *The Pickwick Papers* during this period. Charles Lamb's entire working life was spent in the offices of the East India Company in London, but he still found time to write his famous *Essays of Elia* as well as, with his sister Mary, *Tales from Shakespeare* for children – classics that will live forever.

Anthony Trollope's job as a postal inspector occupied his every hour riding from town to town on horseback – and so he wrote in the saddle, letting the horse pick its way while he busied himself with such novels as *Barchester Towers*. Mary Wollstonecraft Shelley in the midst of chores (to say nothing of other problems!) certainly had little time for writing, yet she wrote *Frankenstein*. No man's life has ever been busier than that of John Buchan, Lord Tweedsmuir, one-time governor general of Canada, but he found time to turn out novels like *The 39 Steps* and biographies on the order of *Sir Walter Scott*. Sir Walter himself was occupied each day of his life from dawn to dark with the demands of his law practice, the managing of his farm, and his duties as sheriff, yet he wrote prodigiously.

Bennett Cerf runs a publishing business, goes on extensive time-consuming lecture tours, acts as panelist on TV shows, yet turns out columns and has many a book to his credit.

In an interview with Faith Baldwin, Robert van Gelder had this to say:

> She had recently left a hospital where she had spent nearly two months and undergone two operations, but though she had not yet gone to her home in Connecticut and taken up her regular working schedule, she already was turning out 2,000 words a day.

In *The Art of Authorship,* Edwin Valentine Mitchell says:

> One often wonders how busy men with jobs which occupy them during the day find time to write books. The secret seems to be that they systematically write a certain number of words a week. If a person writes 1,000 or 1,500 words a week, at the end of the year he has a book. Even if the work has to be shoved into the tag ends of time when one is tired, it is not much of a chore to produce that amount of writing.

Clearly, then, anyone who wants to write a novel can turn out at least one a year, writing only half an hour each day. Remember, those half hours add up to two months of three-hour writing days. It really works, for using this method, the present author has turned out a great number of TV scripts and radio plays. In fact, this article was written in six such half-hour sessions.

Section IV   Special markets

John Mack Carter

The editor of Ladies' Home Journal
talks about a special kind of piece
that is becoming highly salable

Writing regional articles

It is not true that Julius Caesar was the first regional writer. But as a writer, Caesar showed he was alert to the possibilities when he observed that all Gaul was divided into three parts. Unfortunately for his health, he chose to pursue other lines of work.

Now it is magazines that are divided into parts. The number of consumer magazines now producing regional editions or regional inserts is impressive – 205. Although these special inserts offer very limited opportunities to free-lance writers today, the situation is changing rapidly. What can you do to take advantage of this development? You can start by understanding what this fractioning has done to national magazines and what problems it has produced for editors that you may help solve if you are trained as a writer.

Let's look at it from my point of view as an editor. I have been editing regional inserts for magazines since 1955, when *Household* magazine began accepting advertising in four different regions. That was simple compared to today's problems. For the staff of *Ladies' Home Journal,* the regional insert program means, in effect, twenty-six miniature magazines within its regular "national" edition. (You can identify these sections in most magazines because the pages usually are keyed a, b, c, or R1, R2, R3. For mechanical and other reasons, these pages cannot be included in the regular pagination of a magazine.)

Each of these twenty-six miniature magazines has an identity all its own — they vary in size in both editorial and advertising content. The regional that goes to the Chicago area, for instance, may contain thirty-two pages a month and the New England regional only four. The problem for the editor scheduling copy flow is that he must always be prepared for the largest region.

What is the ideal regional "filler" to handle these mechanical problems? It's several things. It's short, it has no specific period in time, it is of national interest, and it is noncontroversial in nature. A strange list of requirements, I agree.

By short, I mean 1,200 words or less. Even better, it should be flexible in length, so that the editor can cut it or pad it to fit different positions. This is sometimes accomplished by using boxes or lists within the text. Here, the writer is servant to mechanical requirements. Ideally, editorial content on each regional page is self-contained, and as the size of an ad varies from region to region, so must the length of the adjacent editorial.

Since there are so many different-sized ads, there must always be available a heavy inventory of short, flexible articles to drop in, like a jigsaw puzzle. In fact, this need for flexibility usually prohibits any extensive use of pictures or illustrations — still another factor to consider when preparing a regional article.

The reason a "filler" should have no special period in time is that it may be used in different regions over a period of several months. A two-column article may fit neatly into the Chicago region for February, but because there may not be need for a two-column article in the Texas region, it won't be used there until March or April. Multiply this by twenty or more regions and you have an idea of how an article is used. To be of maximum use, a regional filler should have a life expectancy of at least six months.

But so far we've explained only the limitations of regional pages, and authors and editors who stop at this point are settling for less than the best. Let's get on to the real opportunity for writers. Let's look at the true regional article as it is beginning to develop in national magazines. Most of the examples I cite here are taken from the New York metropolitan regions of various magazines, which other regions will follow.

A suitable subject for a regional article was Marion Javits, the effervescent, fun-loving wife of the New York senator. Mrs. Javits was a perfectly acceptable national subject but an even stronger regional subject for her New York audience because the city is "her scene." Although she was an obvious choice, I had never singled her out for treatment until free-lance writer Judith Krantz suggested her as a profile for regional treatment. Judy won the assignment by submitting the name, not waiting for me to take the first step.

A study of regional pages will show that many top free-lance writers accept regional assignments, even at one-third their usual rates, because they find the assignments easy to do. I have carried regional pieces by Hildegarde Dolson, Harriet Van Horne, Eugenia Sheppard, Jimmy Breslin, Barbara Walters, Martin Mayer, Gloria Steinem, and Liz Smith, among others. Thomas Meehan was persuaded to depart from his regular *New Yorker* assignments to do a witty report on the making of the movie *The Group*. Even best-seller author Harry Golden accepted a regional assignment, "Only in New York: A Valentine to a City."

Celebrities who might make good regional features are waiting for the assist of a writer. An example is Andrew J. Varuchek, who was special assistant on nationalities to Mayor Robert Wagner. Mr. Varuchek's byline appeared on a spread story on the colorful clusters of nationalities living within New York. Of course, there was a writer in the background, and this could have been you.

In regional articles, polished prose is not valued as highly as indefatigable legwork (although the telephone does most of the walking for magazine writers these days). This was what sold me on Seena Hamilton, a young mother who worked so hard at exploring her "region" for her own children that she wrote regularly for publication on private schools, restaurants for families, weekend activities, etc. The same technique worked for Barbara Lang on local tipping habits for the Christmas season, and for Kate Simon on "What's Open in the City on Sunday."

A fairly obvious regional story – though not yet exploited by editors in many regions – is the list of choice restaurants. This is the kind of job that a staff shuns doing because it requires so much time on the telephone and at the table. When *McCall's* did it, the editors assembled a long list of favorite restaurants and a writer was assigned to eat his way through them, then reduce them to a list of forty-one. It was the most envied assignment of the month, but not one for the faint at table.

Regular reviews of new restaurants, have been done regionally in the *Journal* by Poppy Cannon and in *McCall's* by Selma Robinson, and might well be extended across the country. One big drawback is that experts and writers in other regions are unknown to most editors and must take the first step if they hope to be on the receiving end of assignments later.

Surely the most unusual *Journal* assignment ever handed a young lady was one given Gael Greene for regional use. Obviously, it was one that could appear only in regional because it had to be written as a service piece, full of useful directions. The title: "Where to Powder Your Nose in New York." It was a revealing guide to Manhattan's ladies' rooms, and an article the author terms the most demanding she ever wrote.

She accepted the assignment with a straight face and, by her own admission, did more research than for any national piece of the same 3,000-word length. She investigated dozens of ladies' rooms from Tiffany's to the private rest room in Bennett Cerf's office, and then proceeded to rate each with her own star system. It's a classic worthy of study, even by men.

Regionals frequently lend themselves to use of the tape recorder because so many can be interview features. One entire regional series was developed by author Bill Adler on reminiscences of famous persons, including Richard Rodgers, Quentin Reynolds, Leonard Spigelgass, and Fannie Hurst.

Because they are effective locally, where things eventually have to happen, regional articles sometimes can have even more effect on readers than editors realize. For example, in an impressive ceremony, Mayor Lindsay dedicated a million-dollar addition to New York's Gracie Mansion. This was the culmination of three years' work by volunteers and fund raisers but it had its start, interestingly enough, in the regional magazine article by Lenore Hershey which called attention to the inadequacy of New York's "White House" and stirred the public to form a committee to solve the need with private funds.

What makes a regional approach? Take a good national story: the growing problem of shoplifting among teen-agers. Take a top free-lancer—Alice Lake in this instance—and put her to work doing this in regional form, and she can concentrate on the specific stores and communities the readers know. It has even more identification because children of the readers may well be involved.

Even the shops themselves can make good regional copy. New York readers were treated to a series about their favorite stores in *McCall's* and taken behind the scenes to meet designers, sales clerks, and management at Tiffany's, Hammacher Schlemmer, Saks Fifth Avenue, Bergdorf Goodman, and other stores. This series was staff-written only because no enterprising free-lancer came up with the idea. Remember, editors view regionals as a headache and would happily free lance every word of them.

What about selling fiction for regional editions? In general, forget it. About the only way to sell fiction for regionals is to do a piece specifically on assignment, as Sherwood Kohn did to dramatize New York City's drastic water shortage by concocting a bit of science fiction based on solid fact: "The Day New York Ran Out of Water."

Better yet, stand the editor on his ear and *think big* about regionals, such as picking a single subject for the entire section. Judy Krantz won this assignment when she suggested doing a special section devoted to the life of a very rich girl: "Susan Stein's New York—Life at the Top." Judy made contact with Miss Stein, won her confidence, and worked with her for two months of interviews and observation. Then she returned to supervise a photographer in illustrating the story.

Also a major effort and one of the most helpful local stories in any magazine was "The Exclusive World of New York's Private Schools," a special report by Grace and Fred M. Hechinger that appeared in the *Journal*. The result—a complete section of some 8,500 words—was as long (and rewarded its authors as well) as any feature in the national edition.

It may not be only the writer who proves himself to an editor through regionals. Sometimes the story itself soars from regional to national by publication time. I remember in early 1964 making an assignment to Judy Krantz for a regional story on a then relatively unpublicized Sybil Burton. Judy got the story, the first magazine interview given by Sybil, and turned in a sparkling manuscript full of the magic names Burton and Taylor.

With scarcely a change, I rescheduled the piece for the full national edition, gave it a prominent cover blurb, and sent the writer a check for $1,500, three times the agreed-upon price.

So visit your friendly neighborhood editor. Tell him you understand his regional problems. Both of you could do worse.

Words are dead until used

Take a piece of good English writing—from Swift or Hazlitt or H. M. Tomlinson—and ask *why* the meaning is so clear and the pleasure in reading so great. The answer lies wholly in the color and arrangement of the words. A word is dead until it is used. Only when it is used in conjunction with other words has it any chance of living. And the real argument for good writing is that it enables the reader to experience something of the author's authentic emotion. The purpose of writing is not just that the literal meaning should be clear: words should be used to convey feeling. They are so used by all prose writers of merit, and in the order of their use lies all the difference between tedium and vivid interest.—Frank Swinnerton in *Modern Writers at Work*.

George Rinehart

*Some helpful pointers about translating
technical information into good reading
for the layman*

Wanted: science writers

A visitor from a few decades ago would be astounded at the technical vocabulary of today's citizen and his curiosity about the events taking place around him. This world of surprises is the kind of world in which the popular-science author thrives. Armed only with a notebook and an inquisitive mind (a college degree is not necessary) he moves in to translate scientific jargon for the layman. He is, in effect, the "pipeline" between the scientist expert and the general public. Editors of popular magazines, of trade magazines and house organs, and of special-interest magazines are constantly looking for people who can write clearly about technical subjects.

Who are these people? Those, naturally, who like to keep up with modern life. It's the woman who reports on flavors and quantities in "A Tomato Sauce Sampler" for the restaurant-trade magazine, *Cooking for Profit;* or the author of "Computers Count the Cars," a piece on traffic problems in *Lamp,* publication of the Standard Oil Company of New Jersey. And if you wonder why an article, "Great Wines Start in the Vineyard," should appear in *Du Pont Magazine,* think about how the weed killer Karmex has influenced the lives of grape growers in New York State.

One thing is certain; no popular technical publication will print head-spinning jargon directed solely to Ph.D.s; instead, they look for a combination of common sense, solid research, and plain talk. And, since the practicing writer does some of his best work when he throws out what he can't use, let's see what a popular-technical article is *not* – and how it should *not* be approached. For example:

Today, the human heart is undergoing study with a daring that would make a nineteenth-century medico gasp in disbelief. Unlike research in, say, defective hearing, the heart captures the attention of young and old – and for a simple reason: if it stops, you do, too. Many devices, such as plastic valves, pumps, oxygenators, have been developed – and the man-in-the-street wants to know more.

Where can he turn? Logically, the first stop would be the library. Here's a sample of what he'd find in the journal of *Surgery, Gynecology and Obstetrics:*

> ". . . the oxygenator . . . developed as a result of these studies . . . is a large bubble oxygenator composed of five essential elements: mixing column, bubbling chamber, helix reservoir, arterial filters, and the cardiotomy aspiration chamber."

As the reader plunges on, the going gets even tougher, and it's soon apparent that the doctor-author is talking to his own trade. Overpowered by specialized jargon, our average citizen swings the other way – to the newspapers. Surely, news reportage will be factual, accurate, and written in understandable language. But look at this copy from the Associated Press:

> Artificial Heart
> Gets First Test
> A team of surgeons began placing a plastic artificial heart in the chest of a patient at Texas Medical Center today. The patient was identified as Marcel DeRudder, 65, of Westville, Illinois. He has been unemployed because of his heart condition. . . . His wife, Edna, was identified as a grocery store cashier.

The technical information which follows is skimpy. The AP, aware of its obligation to stress the human-interest side of reportage, has shifted emphasis to the personal background of the patient and his family. The subject of heart-aids remains a mystery.

Home again, our puzzled seeker-after-knowledge chances upon an issue of *Popular Science* and catches the title, "Booster Pump Gives New Life to Failing Hearts." Quickly he turns to page forty-eight, and learns much from the subtitle (sometimes called, in magazine parlance, the "blurb"):

"Auxiliary heart boosters will soon be saving thousands of lives – and many more will be lengthened by amazing new pumps that replace the heart itself."

The lead or opening paragraph? A fine example of vivid, nuts-and-bolts writing:

On the table, a knackwurst-size plastic bulb jerked sharply in time to bursts of escaping air – once each second. Blood-colored liquid sluiced through a net-work of glass tubes attached to the odd apparatus.

For more than a year this weird mechanical ballet has moved through its monotonous routine. . . . Soon an identical pump will be buried in the chest of a human patient because his heart can't pump enough blood to keep his body alive. The plastic pump – a heart booster – will take over half the natural heart's job, giving the failing organ desperately needed help.

Following hard on this dramatic opening, the popular-technical article next resorts to that reliable device, dialogue.

"We have two or three patients a week who die of cardiac deficiency," says Dr. Adrian Kantrowitz, chief of surgical research at Brooklyn's Maimonides Hospital and co-developer of the heart booster, "and thousands of others die elsewhere. With the booster we can give hearts more pumping power. Many of these people won't have to die."

Pursuing the dialogue technique even further, the author demonstrates graphically the reason why heart research is important to you. He ties scientific matters directly into our daily lives with a picture of what you or I almost inevitably experience – weakening of the heart muscle.

"Sometimes a patient will get to where his heart has maybe a 10-percent reserve," says Kantrowitz. "He gets dizzy when he walks up a flight of stairs. Then his reserve drops to 5 percent. Finally he's got no reserve. His heart can barely keep him alive. Then heart capacity drops to 99 percent of what he needs. That day he dies."

The person who'd like to write popular-technical articles can learn some very valuable lessons here. The author has used a grim but very effective device – he has related the ultimate catastrophe, before he gives chapter and verse on the "new hope" – the progress of DeBakey in Houston, Kolff in Cleveland, the progress of heart research in general. For a clincher, he ties his story into the mainstream of our lives:

But whether these advanced schemes or some yet unknown plan proves best, the artificial heart is on its way. Improvements will come over the years. Already the first tentative steps have been taken toward conquering one of man's most dreaded killers.

This is a good closing; it resounds and maintains the same tone of urgency set at the beginning. And since openings are so important in setting the tone of an article, let's examine a few more ways to fascinate your reader from the first word. Here are some recently published examples:

Dramatic Narrative: The American Telephone & Telegraph Company, concerned over the damage being done to its underground cables by construction crews, now operates a helicopter surveillance system. AT&T's magazine, *Long Lines,* starts its article "Sentinel in the Sky" with a panoramic scene:

> From 500 feet up the excavation looked like a red scar on the soft green fields. Pilot Skip Staudt banked his helicopter and descended in a series of wide circles. . . . He waved to the curious men below and nudged the copter to the ground.

Direct Quote: Eileen Burke, writing "Stain Repellents Gain Acceptance" for *Furniture Design and Manufacturing* magazine, decided on the horse's mouth angle. She begins:

> "Within five years any furniture manufacturer who doesn't offer stain- and dirt-resistant fabrics will be out of business," asserted Donald Sturtz, upholstery division merchandising manager, Baumritter Corp.

Flavor-of-the-Land: The author of "Great Wines Start in the Vineyard" was faced with the problem of making an agricultural weed killer interesting. His solution – choose an area of the country where the product is in use, and appeal to the nature-loving element in all of us:

> Hammondsport, N.Y.
> Autumn comes early to this hill country, where original settlers described the lakes they found as the fingerprints left when the Creator's hand was extended in benediction.

The Teaser: Lamp magazine wanted to dramatize the subject of traffic control, so it ran the article beginning:

> Why would two cars be driven through the busy New York-New Jersey Holland tunnel connected by a strand of piano wire?

There's one common element in all these leads – enthusiasm. Once you begin to investigate your topic, you'll love every minute it takes to research your facts, and you'll find yourself increasingly absorbed by the material you uncover.

Who is the popular-technical writer anyway? He (or she) is nothing special—not an engineer or a technician. This writer combines a reasonable degree of writing skill with the ability to recognize the drama in any given development—whether it's a new kind of soap or the recent discovery that smoking causes emphysema in beagles. No matter what your interest, you should strive to cultivate the quality which Hal Borland describes in his book *How to Write and Sell Non-Fiction:*

> . . . That something is a combination of curiosity and what I call for want of a better term, *constructive imagination.* He is an inquisitive fellow, but he is also a speculative person. He wants to know why something happens, how it happens, what its effects are. He also speculates about the thing that has aroused his curiosity, about its meaning, about its causes, about what would happen if other factors were added or if known factors were subtracted. He thinks all around his topic. . . . He not only dissects it; he puts the pieces together in ways other than they were originally. And he doesn't necessarily do this consciously or for a purpose; it is simply his way of thinking, his approach.

Thinking? Approach? Take one example—a widely distributed product known in various guises as hexachlorophene, pHisoHex, or G-11. It's a crackerjack remover of germs and many of us use compounds of it in our homes for sanitation, skin cleansing, and personal deodorant. Hospitals use a solution of the chemical to wash down the walls of a room recently occupied by a patient with communicable disease.

Simple enough—on the surface. But the thinking technical writer moves in on this subject with a two-pronged question: does the stuff kill germs directly, or does it starve them out by creating an area where they cannot live? Once you've developed this distinction in your mind, you're well on your way to surprising and intriguing your reader, who'll say to himself, "Golly! I never thought of it *that* way."

While medicine and health are two of the most popular science topics today, many others of equal importance are available to the writer. Electronics, mechanics, and allied fields give you the opportunity to spring welcome and fascinating surprises on your readers. Your discovery of new areas can include boating, art, agriculture, photography, music, pets, foods, nature, theater—in fact, almost any subject affected by new developments.

Out of this intriguing list of subjects, what should the beginning writer choose? Here's one answer from Robert O'Brien, consultant to the *Life Science Library* and a regular contributor to *Reader's Digest, Esquire,* and other national magazines:

> The beginning popular-technical writer *must* start writing about a subject

with which he or she is familiar. Don't be tempted, early in the game, by the glamour of, say, space technology or recently developed drugs. Start with something you know about and work from there.

For instance: you're interested in nineteenth-century dolls; how were the ceramic heads painted and fired? Where? In what respects does the doll industry of today differ from the past?

If you follow this trail you'll soon disocover that you're an expert in your field – and this is important, because the editors to whom you submit your manuscripts will gain increasing confidence in your output. What you become, actually, is a reporter – a *spotter* – who dramatizes a development that's taking place under our noses, but which you alone recognize for its importance.

Virtually all popular-technical editors will agree with this point of view; but these editors often have an even greater problem. Many times the writer of a highly competent piece will submit it to the wrong publication.

"We read everything that comes to us," says Art Mikesell, editor of photography, boating, and general science for *Popular Mechanics,* "and we're always looking for new writers who can become regular contributors. But too many 'over-the-transom' manuscripts betray a lack of knowledge about the subjects we cover and the readership we're trying to reach.

"Whether the writer is gunning for us or another magazine in the same field, he's *got* to read what's selling – discover for himself where the market is for his material. Otherwise, he's liable to send a perfectly good piece to the wrong publication and suffer an undeserved rejection."

Once you've decided on your subject area and the type of publication you're aiming at, there are a few simple rules to follow – and your editors will love you for observing them:

1. *Emphasize a new slant or approach.* Like the inventor of striped toothpaste, you don't have to discover something radically new – just find a way to present your idea differently and urgently. Not too long ago a newsstand magazine ran an article on centuries' old ways of finishing furniture, and it was so popular that the readers demanded a follow-up!

2. *Research and organize carefully.* Gather all the material you can, but build that all-important outline in keeping with the special approach you've adopted. For example, an industry near your home has added a railroad siding because a new product is a tremendous success. Stick to the product – but keep the material you've gathered on the new tracks. One day you might want to do a piece under the title, "Railroad Spurs Keep Business Going." Never throw out "useless" research; it can come in handy at a later date.

3. *Create strong openings and endings.* Your opening can be one of

several kinds; we've already seen an example of the "strong word picture" – the heart pump compared to the knackwurst, the bursts of escaping air. But "visual" openings don't always make your point effectively. Sometimes the "gee-whiz" fact does it better.

Popular Science writer Bill Taylor kicks off a piece on the dilemma of the new-car buyer with this attention-getting statement: "The man who wouldn't think of buying a 60-dollar suit without trying it on often shells out fifty times as much for a car he's never driven."

Your ending must be equally resounding; it must tie up the loose ends. If your reader doesn't hear the door slam behind him, he'll soon forget that he's been to your house. Here's how Jacques-Ives Cousteau concludes a *National Geographic* article on life – human, sustained life – under the sea:

> We are now planning Conshelf Four. . . . We are confident that within a few years, we will entirely eliminate ties to the world above. Then, for the first time, oceanauts will have true freedom of the deep.

The depths of the ocean, the reaches of outer space – your kitchen, your garden, your street. Where will the next wonder occur? Under your very eyes, if you're looking for it!

Many write but few think

I spent some years as editor of a publishing house. I remember one of those crank letters that all publishers receive, this one concerning a manuscript from an author who wanted to know how much it would cost to have it "published into a book." That comic-pathetic phrase has stayed with me ever since. There are many items on the market, fiction and nonfiction, that are books only because literally they have been "published into books."

So far as writing is concerned, there are a good many men and women around who can write a novel in the sense of producing something sufficiently articulate, and with enough story fabric, to induce a publisher to put it on the market. But there are relatively few who are able to *think* a novel. It is in the area of concept that contemporary fiction is anemic. Only a minority of our novelists have something clear to say, and of these a dismaying number have emphatic things to say of a virulently destructive and antisocial character.

That our age will so readily accept certain superficial glibnesses in literary production is a corollary of the fact that it will accept the same superficialities and glibnesses in the human personality. In the long run, the work is the artist and the artist is the work. It is possible for the artist's work to represent considerably less than his potential, but it is not possible for it to represent more than he is. – Edmund Fuller in *Man in Modern Fiction.*

Robert E. Hood

*The editor of a leading juvenile magazine
tells what he wants . . . and how he wants
to present it*

How to write for boys

Visitors to my office spot the following sign on the wall:

> *Mit der Dummheit kämpfen Götter selbst
> vergebens.* – Friedrich von Schiller.

A friend gave me the plaque, framed under glass, the day I became editor
of *Boys' Life*. And I'm grateful. The quotation – "Against stupidity even
the gods fight in vain" – sustains me when depression threatens to drown the
creative process. I recommend it as a talisman for all writers who inevitably
must face stupid, inexplicable acts by editors.

Accept stupidity in others, but don't tolerate it in yourself. With a certain
amount of talent and the energy to develop it, you can become a successful
professional – *but only if you act intelligently.*

In other words, don't be stupid. Don't call up or write the editor of a
magazine and say: "My name is Joe Gump. I'm going to Africa next month.
Anything I can do for you?"

Several writers who ought to know better have done this to me. My immediate inclination is to tell them to go to the South Pole. Instead, I say, "What *can* you do for us, Mac?"

Remember, you're in business to supply ideas to hard-pressed editors; you're an idea man. And how we editors love ideas! Sparkling ideas, clearly expressed in simple English, presented with flair and enthusiasm. In my book there can never be a surplus of ideas; demand always outstrips supply.

All our fiction and 90 percent of our non-fiction is free-lanced. Some of this is bought from "name" authors such as Gene Caesar, Leonard Wibberly, Isaac Asimov, Margaret Coit, Paul Darcy Boles, Jack Schaefer, Pearl Buck, and Jesse Stuart. Although we commission most of our material, we would publish more unsolicited features, particularly fiction, if they were up to our standards.

Fiction offers the best possibility for new writers, but the problem is that our short stories run only 3,500 to 4,000 words. A writer has to be able to sketch characterization in a few strokes, handle background and atmosphere briskly, plot solidly – in short, distill material with great skill. Our fiction editor, Fran Smith, insists that stories arouse feeling, laughter, tears, love, hate, suspense, or some other definite emotion. She advises new contributors to think a story all the way through before putting a word to paper.

Once written, the short story should be "seasoned" – put aside for several weeks – before you submit it to the magazine. After this cooling-off period, an author can tell if his material has true emotional impact or if he was only deluding himself.

The point of view of *Boys' Life* fiction invariably is masculine, even though women often play strong roles in the stories. Some short-story writers – highly skilled pros and shaky amateurs – make a curious mistake when writing for us the first time. They think that because we have a magazine for boys, the central character must be a boy; and thus they have boys doing things not quite believable, e.g., capturing bank robbers or swimming the English Channel.

Although our heroes usually are teen-agers or young men, they can be mature men if the situation demands a man for plausibility. Our heroes shouldn't be cute or kittenish in behavior; nor should they be too folksy. These errors come from adult nostalgia, a disease boys suffer lightly. I can't count the number of short stories I've read over the years which began, "When I was a boy growing up in, etc." We have never bought one of these; our readers would laugh us out of business.

What kind of stories are boys reading? The most popular fiction subjects in *Boys' Life* today are outdoor adventure, mystery, sports, and broad humor.

A vocal minority screams constantly for science fiction (which we give them), but the majority of readers can either take it or leave it.

At present we are looking for strong, sharp mystery stories, but they cannot be Mickey Spillaneish, bloody, tough, or violent. They have to be superbly plotted and strong on ratiocination. Stories of spying and espionage are in demand, too, but you'd better know the trade or you'll come on like a square to our readers. Tales with historical background are welcome now. These need a strong, significant theme.

Writing short stories for boys differs only in degree from writing for men. The distinction is subtle, a matter of sophistication. Sex is taboo; violence is toned down; brutality is deleted. Believe it or not, we still manage to come up with strong, exciting fiction, but we are always crying "more, more" because our requirements are demanding.

A general tip on writing fiction or non-fiction for boys: youngsters have a smaller reservoir of experience and understanding than do adults. Therefore, you can't depend on nuance to sustain a narrative – the nuance, say, of unrequited love, or of things that might have been, or of a life unlived or unfulfilled. What I'm saying is that you must know what a boy is capable of feeling or understanding at ages twelve to fourteen.

He is capable of experiencing affection, fear, hunger, dread, anger, laughter, jealousy, pride, humiliation, and other "simple" clear-cut emotions or longings. He responds to these emotions most quickly when they're vividly presented.

Here are some examples of good fiction leads:

From "Opening Day" by Jim Brosnan:

> On a late-winter day in an old Southern town the Bruins opened their 45th camp for hopeful pros. At noon the air was warm as a Northern-city summer. Tommy James took a deep breath, sniffed the orange-blossomed air and sat back to enjoy the ride to the camp. Pulling the taxi to a stop, the cabbie said, "Here's where the Bruins play."
>
> Work you mean, fella. Pros don't play baseball. Didn't everybody know that?
>
> Johnny Story, the scout who had signed Tommy James to a contract, had told him, "First thing Giff will do is run your legs off. You like to run, don't you, Tommy?"
>
> Tommy had nodded, moronic smile on his face. That's what his father thought anyway.
>
> "You're running away, son. From yourself. From your family, from responsibility. You know that, don't you? Baseball's just a game!"
>
> Well, nuts to that noise, Tommy thought. He hefted his suitcase and walked into the camp.

From "The Big Fight" by Pearl S. Buck:

"Come out of the cage!" Ranjit heard his father's voice clearly but he did not move. He curled himself behind the tiger; he made himself small so that he could not be seen from the dusty road.

"Raj," he breathed into the left ear of his huge pet. "Say nothing, Raj! Do not turn your head. Hide me, Raj! Remember that I am your darling."

Understanding or not, the tiger did not move. He crouched upon the wooden floor, his forepaws stretched straight before him. Even his tail was motionless.

"Ranjit!" his father bellowed. "Come out before I enter the cage myself and drag you forth! Your silence does not hide you. I know you are there. Wicked boy to teach an honest beast how to lie and deceive his master!"

From "The Samaritan" by Richard Harper:

The ship was in deep space, traveling with sleek mechanical precision at nearly the speed of light, its computers and drives all functioning smoothly, efficiently, automatically. . . .

. . . Yet they were beginning to feel the remoteness of their situation, the complete and utter isolation that was sometimes frightening. Landin had noticed the strain first in Haverson.

From "Flight of the Jungle Bird" by Hugh B. Cave:

Johnny Bannon awoke at four in the morning with every nerve tingling. The house was quiet. The sound which had disturbed him, if any had, was not repeated. No breeze jostled the palms. The frogs were not talking.

The frogs. They should be talking. In the islands of the West Indies the frogs always talked unless something frightened them. Johnny slid from his bed and glided to the door, past the painting propped against the wall.

To write articles for *Boys' Life,* you must be alert and accurate, for the readers are filled with curiosity and critical of errors. Our articles either are entertaining or educational (both at best) and are of two types: major features of 2,500 to 3,000 words and short pieces of 500 to 1,250. The shorts deal mostly with ways to do or build things, and depend more on subject know-how than writing technique. The long articles use the standard techniques of adult non-fiction—anecdotes, narration, description, dialogue, and the various other tricks of fiction. They cover a wide range of subjects— sports, history, biography, war, general interest, science, adventure, and so on.

Please query the articles editor, Lou Sabin, before submitting any long article. Short-feature queries should go to Dick Pryce, senior editor.

Warning: Don't patronize! "Writing down" is the deadliest sin of all when aiming at juveniles. Here's a special tip: Learn how to write an intelligent *short* query. If a writer can't do that, I doubt he can write a 2,500-word article.

Here are some leads that attracted our editors and readers:

From "The Navy That Crossed Mountains" by James Norman:

> He was a wiry, spade-bearded young adventurer, as skilled with the sword as he was with the saw. Partly because of his sword, but mostly because of proficiency with carpenter's tools, Spain conquered the New World when she did—yet, today, the name of this man who had so much to do with the success of the conquest is hardly known.

From "Tumbling Georgians" by Tom MacPherson:

> The roads that lead to Rome, Georgia, are well-traveled by Explorers of that city who have become adept at getting their feet off the ground. The daring young men of the flying techniques have been riding high since the day in 1955 when Post 17 elected to throw together a tumbling act for a PTA program during Scout Week. The Post had just been organized in January, but the show they put on in February became the first highlight of a high-wire career that has since taken them in and out of Rome to gymnastic competitions, television programs, and other community programs such as the PTA affair at which they tumbled into tumbling.

From "The Biggest Texan" by Margaret Coit:

> The man stood tall: nearly six-feet-six in his high-heeled cowboy boots. Beneath a domed forehead his deep gray eyes blazed with fire and indignation, and his voice rolled majestically from his barrel-like chest. Around him a teeming, sullen crowd shifted and muttered and cried out finally that he should not speak from their courthouse steps. Suddenly the man's voice cracked over their heads. He would speak from the hillside then; he had a right to speak on the soil of Texas, he shouted, "because I have watered it with my blood."

Writing for boys is a stiff challenge. I have written more than 100 articles for *Boys' Life* and also two juvenile books. It has been a satisfying experience, richly rewarding because when you are successful, when you touch the reader, his praise is quick and exuberant. When writing for youngsters I keep in mind the touchstone of Catherine Drinker Bowen: "Will he turn the page?" This is my way of reminding myself *not* to be stupid.

Dorothy Kostka

*The answer, says this author, is yes,
provided you follow some sound rules
and truly know your subject*

Can you write a column?

Nearly every writer cherishes a secret longing to be a columnist. It looks so ridiculously easy. All the columnist does is sit at his typewriter and knock out a few hundred words of personal opinion. Not for him the painstaking research involved in article writing or the exhausting struggle with a stubborn fiction plot. He's syndicated, he reaches an audience of millions – *and* he makes pots of money!

We may forget, as we read a columnist, that behind this writing lies special knowledge and competence in some field or experience acquired over years of living. This is why he's qualified to write a column. He has something substantial to say concerning a subject about which he knows quite a lot.

Perhaps this is true of you, too, and if you can bring to your special knowledge a fresh slant and an engaging style, you have a good chance to break into the column-writing field. This market is close at hand, right outside your front door where the boy drops the weekly or the daily newspaper.

If you live in a small town, it's probably a weekly and you know the editor personally. These weeklies (6,315 of them in our country) offer a splendid opportunity to the new writer who hasn't made a name for himself. Your hopeful goal is syndication, but you must be published first, and your best bet is a local editor who can be persuaded to give your column a trial.

Let's consider your qualifications for column writing. For your own sake, you should be a facile writer. Words must come to you fairly easily or the agony you'll undergo as you try to keep your column going won't be worth it. You should write thoughtfully, responsibly, and as well as you can, but with an awareness that you're not writing for the ages. For the editor's sake, you should be a disciplined writer. He's saving space for you and he has a deadline he expects you to meet. If you fail him, you'll shortly be an ex-columnist.

I'm now in the third year of writing a column called "Freedom after Fifty" for the Denver *Post*. It's published on Sunday in "Contemporary" – the women's magazine section. My columns are longish, 500 words or a little more, and are more suitable for weekly use.

During the first week of each month I write my columns for the following month. I write two, sometimes three in one day from ideas I've tucked away in my file. As I begin each column, I jot down the points I want to make in their logical sequence. Then I think for a while about the style I should use in this particular column.

I write for the middle-aged and the elderly from an optimistic, buoyant, "let's-enjoy-these-years" viewpoint. Some columns are factual, dealing with such subjects as retirement, health, recreation, employment. These are usually written in a straight article style.

However, people over fifty are, or should be, still involved in the world. We have relationships with younger people. We have personal problems and personal needs. We hope, we doubt, we suffer, we make mistakes. In these areas, my column offers my own philosophy on how to remain loving and lovable human beings all our lives. I sometimes present this philosophy in a fictional form, using characters, setting, and conversation. These changes in technique help to keep my column varied and alive. In all my columns, I permit my personality, my experiences, and my opinions to flavor my writing.

We'll assume that you're facile and disciplined but can you *communicate?* In our big and indifferent world, people are increasingly hungry for warm contact with others. You must "come alive" to your readers as a real person. Often I meet a stranger who will say, "Oh, you're Dorothy Kostka! I feel as though I *know* you."

Sometimes I achieve reader-identification. Not long ago a friend said: "You write the things I've always thought and didn't know how to say." This quality is essential in a personal column and it's useful even in factual writing. If someone feels that he "knows" you and is interested in your ideas, you've acquired a loyal reader.

The subject matter of your column will depend on what you know and what you feel is important to communicate to others. This list is almost endless. In factual writing: household hints, cooking, sewing, knitting, hobbies, pets, etiquette, gardening, health, finance, politics, bridge, beauty tips, literature, music, art. Personal columns include: marriage problems, child care, parent-child relationships, the teen-ager, older people, religion, humor, the kind of column that began with "Dear Dorothy Dix" and now is flourishing as "Dear Abby," and the general "this-is-what-I-think" column.

Consider your own experiences in living, which may qualify you to help others with your hard-won knowledge. If you're well known in a small community, people may want to read your column simply because you're *you*.

I chose to write a personal advice column for people over fifty for two reasons. I'd reached that age myself and discovered that the later years hold many rich rewards. Surely, I reasoned, there were others like myself who'd welcome a reinforcement of their feelings of personal worth and their zest for living. I might also be helpful to some who had bogged down in self-pity and useless longing for the past.

The second reason concerned my writing career. Although I'm primarily a fiction writer, I began to write "art-of-living" articles a long time ago. So long ago, in fact, that my first such piece dealt with the etiquette of pregnancy and was titled, "Don't Make Him Have That Baby!" Articles on family relationships and social problems followed, so I was accustomed to reaching my reader on a personal basis and in a counseling role.

Now, let's sell your column. You don't begin by approaching an editor with the bare bones of your idea. Outline what you plan to do and then write about a dozen sample columns. My own sample columns were written on the general subjects of the health, personality, and opportunities for personal fulfillment of the woman over fifty. I called it "Women after Fifty" but the editor changed it to "Freedom after Fifty." This was wise, because my column is read by many men. Hold your column to 500 words at a maximum. Newspapers never have enough space – except for ads.

Prepare a sales talk about your audience and what you can offer them. I knew how many people over fifty were living in our country and something about their interests and their problems. Gardening? Look into your local garden clubs, their activities and membership. Children? Cooking? Everyone has children and everyone cooks, but you might want to know about school dropouts and juvenile delinquency in your area or the circulation of cookbooks at your library and the status of home economics instruction in your schools. You must exercise your own ingenuity.

Take your sample columns and your sales talk to the newspaper that you think offers you the best chance to break into print. As I suggested before, a weekly newspaper can be a good springboard. However, there's no reason to shy away from a daily – big or small. Your problem here may be competition from a syndicated column in your field. Don't let that frighten you. If you can write a better column, he's out and you're in.

I live in a suburb of Denver, with two weekly newspapers, but I didn't submit my column to those outlets because I'd written many articles for the Denver *Post* and had contacts on that newspaper. The *Post* was using at the time a syndicated retirement column that seemed to me to be stale and repetitious. It was dropped a few weeks after my column started.

After your column has taken hold, you will want to extend its publication. If you're being published in a weekly or daily that circulates in a limited area, you can reach out to other newspapers in the state. Send them half a dozen tear sheets, with a covering letter. In the case of a large daily, such as the Denver *Post,* I'm not free to do this because it's circulated all over the state of Colorado and in half a dozen neighboring states.

Syndication is a beautiful goal and one worth striving for. I must be honest and explain that it's crowded. The syndicate directory issued by *Editor and Publisher* lists over forty syndicates that carry about 1,600 columns on every imaginable subject. They're busy, they're rushed, they have a backlog of columns waiting to be launched.

I wasn't daunted by these facts, nor should you be. I selected eight top syndicates and sent them tear sheets with a covering letter. They all read my columns, I'm convinced, and a writer can't ask for more. Their letters were flattering but that blasted backlog kept cropping up. I haven't given up hope of syndication. Sometime the lightning may strike me – or *you!*

Now your column's launched and you must keep it going. When I first started writing "Freedom after Fifty," my husband observed: "You're going to be the Abby Van Buren of the wheelchair set."

I wasn't a bit ruffled. "That'll be fine," I said, but I was speaking from the depths of ignorance. I was visualizing all those people over fifty writing in to ask me to solve their problems. All that would be required were a few sage words of advice.

I failed to realize that people over fifty are like *me*. We don't ask for advice. We give it. My fan mail consists principally of comments on my column, written as one friend would write to another. I acknowledge every one. The elderly are often lonely people. Sometimes they phone me, just to chat. As I was working on this article, an elderly man called. I listened to him patiently and my reward was his remark, "You write as though it comes from your heart."

Sometimes a reader wants to share with me a sorrow or a joy. A woman wrote me about her daughter-in-law who seemed to "slam the door" on her, and this germinated a column on this often-difficult relationship. Another letter described happy retirement in a mobile home and I used an excerpt in a column on this subject. Occasionally there are questions such as: "How can three generations live in harmony under one roof?" and "Should I marry a middle-aged bachelor with a possessive mother?"

My experiences in living account for some columns. Examples are my thoughts on what we owe our adult children and what we shouldn't give them; the fears of the later years; the folly of regret; the bad habits of the "middle-aged marriage"; the problems of loneliness.

Reading and research are often required. For a two-part piece on jobs for older women, I took a three-hour vocational aptitude test and interviewed job counselors. I researched my facts for columns on Social Security, Medicare, the different kinds of retirement facilities, the technique of will-making, inheritance taxes, financial facts for wives. I took a hearing test and wrote columns on deafness and hearing aids. I interviewed three older women who had returned to college, and wrote about this new trend.

My best source of all is what I hear, see, and read. Once you're in the groove with your column, you become highly sensitive to everything that's related to your subject. For instance, I heard two grandmothers talking on a bus. One said to her friend, "I adore having our grandchildren visit us but I'm glad to see them go, too. That's natural, I hope." Her friend assured her it was, but I detected a guilty note in their voices. I wrote a column on "the new breed of grandmothers" as opposed to the "cookie-jar grandma."

A friend in his sixties fell off a stepladder while cleaning rain gutters, broke his arm and shattered his knee. This inspired a column on the foolish things older men do, including pushing stalled cars and shoveling snow. I heard a woman say, "I won't let Jim retire. He'd drive me crazy, sitting around the house all day." I came up with some ideas on happy (or at least tolerable) twenty-four-hour togetherness for the retired couple.

"She's crawled in a shell and won't come out for anyone," a woman observed about her widowed sister-in-law. I talked to several widowed friends and wrote a column suggesting practical ways of adjusting to the loss of a husband. A beautiful woman in her fifties, who tells her age without the quiver of an eyelash, talked to me about "the richness of the past" and how much it adds to our enjoyment of the present, if we don't deny it. I used her thoughts in a column.

I wrote in short-story form the experience of a retired couple who pulled up their lifelong roots and went to California to be near their only child. In three months they were back, admitting it had been a mistake. Watching a TV interview with a cosmetic surgeon spawned a column on the desperate means to which some women resort to keep their youth.

I have a file of newspaper and magazine clippings and one-sentence notes I've written to myself under the headings of appearance, finances, health, jobs, personality, recreation, relatives, retirement. In planning each month's column, I try to keep a balance between fact and philosophy.

Unless you're capable of this sustained effort, your column may be short-lived. During my time on the Denver *Post,* I've seen this happen to several promising new columns. One was called "You and Your Child" and was written by a psychiatrist. He invited questions from readers and while waiting for them wrote an erudite, rather dull column on this lively and provocative subject. The letters didn't materialize and the column soon disappeared.

If you fail to become syndicated, the financial return for writing a column won't be large. I had an amusing hassle with the woman's editor of the *Post* (who happens to be a man) when we came to the sticky subject of payment. He pointed out plaintively that the paper pays an average of $7.50 for a syndicated column. I pointed out, also plaintively, that my column was exclusive with the *Post.* We reached a figure that doesn't compensate me for the time involved but I still have those syndication stars in my eyes.

If you can syndicate your column and sell it to 75 or 100 papers at $7.50 each per week, less the syndicate commission, you'll have a tidy income. There's also the possibility of publishing your columns in book form. I've now written about 90,000 words on the subject of successful living in the later years and I plan to select, edit, and rearrange this material for book publication.

Personal rewards that won't show in your bank balance will come your way. Column writing is a marvelous ego-builder and every writer, even the most successful, needs constant reassurance that he can write something worthy of publication and payment. You'll also have the satisfaction of knowing that you are reaching other people with your knowledge and your values, advising or influencing them, clarifying their thinking or helping them in practical ways to live more happily and fully.

You'll be given many opportunities to speak to groups. Readers of your column will be curious about you, eager to meet you in person and see for themselves what you're "really like." I feel an obligation to do this and I find it's great fun. The subject of your talk, of course, depends on the nature of your column.

My present talk, which is on the light side, is called "The Seven Ages of Woman." It expresses my sincere belief that women are the fortunate sex, should realize this and stop pushing. Both men and women seem to enjoy my talk. And don't be too hasty in saying, "I don't charge anything." Many small groups can't pay, but others will if you hesitate long enough for them to make an offer.

If you want to try a column, dig deep into your mind, identify your interests and capabilities, evaluate your knowledge and experience. Then choose the subject that you'll enjoy writing about.

Don't be intimidated by that long vista of future columns waiting to be written. I didn't expect to last longer than six months!

Should you talk about your work?

Without question there is value in discussing your work with your friends, your family and other writers. But there is also a great danger — especially for a beginning writer. Writing is a private affair — it is not done in committee. Gathering a large number of uninformed opinions can only compound your confusion. The blind cannot lead the blind. Find one or two people whose taste you trust. They do not necessarily have to be professional writers or editors — just people with sound judgment. Show your manuscripts only to them and nobody else.

A word of warning: don't show your manuscript to anyone at frequent intervals during its composition. You cannot expect a baby to be born if you pull it out every few hours and pass it around. There may come a point in the composition of a story when you are stuck and need help — but try your best to lick your problems by yourself. As a general rule it's wise not to show a story until it is completed. — Max Shulman

Getting the right attitude

When you are writing you are a writer, no matter how fumbling or poor your work may be. If you assume an attitude seriously enough and often enough and intelligently enough, it is likely that the attitude will become a part of you. — Roger H. Garrison in *A Guide to Creative Writing*.

Joseph Callanan

*In today's growing market, there's room for
writers of many different tastes, backgrounds,
and talents*

Writing travel articles

Not long ago I ran into a free-lancer friend at Kennedy Airport. He was
carrying a suitcase, a portable typewriter, and a Leica over one shoulder. I
asked if he were going on vacation.

"I'm too busy for vacations," he said with a grin. "I may never *take*
another vacation. I'm having too much fun in my new job."

"What's that?" I asked warily, expecting a gag.

"I'm a jet-age travel writer," he said. "An instant Magellan. Last week
Paris. Today Mexico City. Next week, who knows?"

He told me that for the past year or so he'd written nothing but travel
pieces, and was doing very well because of the demand for them from the
magazines.

"The whole country's on the great Go Now – Pay Later kick," he said.
"Swoosh, you're in Madrid! Swoosh-swoosh, you're in Hawaii! And swoosh-
swoosh-*swoosh*, you're in Bangkok! So naturally travel articles are in demand. People want to know where to go, what to see. And they want to
read all about it again when they get back."

Today, as always, travel writing has a prominent niche in literature and journalism, and the niche is getting bigger. Most established magazines, even the women's service magazines, have increased space devoted to travel articles, and so have the newspapers. Guidebooks of all kinds – Poor Man's, Rich Man's, Gourmet's, Wine Drinker's, to mention only four out of many – come off the presses in a flood.

After years of stately growth, the *National Geographic* has calmly but firmly pushed above four million circulation. And *Holiday* has achieved a reputation for quality, wit, and maturity far beyond its somewhat brief span of life.

This vast and growing market is supplied by writers of many different tastes and talents. It would almost seem there is room somewhere for any writer who studies the market and knows the editorial preferences of the publications he's aiming for. Literary standards and policies vary widely, and what's just wrong for one may be just right for another. To catch a glimpse of such variance in editorial taste, let's look at the openings of two stories in *Holiday* and the *Geographic*.

The first is the lead paragraphs of Part II of "A Stranger in New York" by V. S. Pritchett, the prominent British novelist, short-story writer, and critic. Judging from the frequency of his appearance in its pages, Pritchett is a *Holiday* favorite.

> There is a strong case to be made against New York, and particularly against Manhattan. In many respects it is the case against all great modern cities and the life they offer. Architects like le Corbusier and Frank Lloyd Wright have attacked Manhattan's buildings and its lack of design; for with the exception of Central Park, little has been planned as a whole. Hardly a building is situated – the Seagram being one of the few "placed" buildings in the city, along with those of Rockefeller Center.
>
> The skyscrapers were described by Gorki in 1909 as a jaw load of rotting teeth and mere stumps. The world has, however, gradually come to admire them through a trick of the eye; we rarely see them individually but only as an aggregation. But the inhabitant knows that the more the city soars the worse the stink and confusion at the foot. Architects have turned into engineers, bewitched by function.

The famous Australian author, Alan Villiers, has written many articles about his seafaring adventures for the *National Geographic*. Here's how he began a piece titled "Fabled Mount of St. Michael":

> Suddenly the sea mist lifted in just one place over the land to the north of us. A ray of sunlight broke through, like a floodlight. Silhouetted against the gray was the most fantastic castle I had ever seen, a fairy-tale place of shining white upon a perfect plinth of its pyramidal hill.
>
> Spired and turreted, the fortress rose with such symmetry and grace that

it was difficult to see where man's work began and nature's ended. For the castle blended into the hill, and the hill carried the castle as if it had grown there, right out of the tumbling sea.

"St. Michael's Mount!" shouted the seaman beside me.

Though the two pieces differ widely in subject matter the style and tone of each represent the magazine in which it appears. Pritchett's piece is amazingly critical by any standards of travel writing. Villiers, by contrast, is boyishly enthusiastic. Pritchett's style is sophisticated, personal, subjective. Villiers concentrates completely on evoking a vivid picture of the scene before him.

Incidentally, the photographs accompanying Pritchett's article were chosen to highlight certain aspects of the scene. In the Villiers piece, photographs are more for page decoration.

Other well-established magazines in the field have different approaches. There's *Travel,* for instance, a magazine published for many years and directed not so much at the armchair adventurer as at the person about to take off on a trip. It's full of specific tips about things to do and places to go. The lead paragraph of an article by Dick Momsen, Jr., called "Portugal's Mondogo Valley," is a fair example of its feature-article style:

> Probably the most picturesque, varied and yet most overlooked region in Portugal is the valley of the Mondogo River. Starting high in the Serra da Estrela, whose 5,000-foot crest supports the country's only organized ski resort, the river winds through a narrow gorge until a 180° bend takes it out among the jumbled hills that reach nearly to the Atlantic. These widen out below Coimbra to accommodate a broad flood of plain, presided over by a brooding Moorish Castle. At the fishing village of Figueira da Foz, the Mondogo empties into a sea over a shallow bar marked by long, rolling breakers.

This is good, colorful reporting, but the author's own feelings and impressions scarcely intrude upon the scene.

Arizona Highways, a magazine published monthly by the Arizona Highway Department but widely known for its pictorial and editorial excellence, manages to strike a note of general interest while confining its subject matter to Arizona. Typical of its direct and simple style is this lead by Rosalie Goldman in an article, "The Wrinkled Pink Walls of Kanab Canyon":

> Arizona has a lost canyon. If not lost, it is overlooked. Yet it is a major canyon, over one hundred miles long. It is Kanab. Only a handful of people have been in it since a Powell survey quit the Colorado River at Kanab canyon in 1872. The gold rush may have brought a few prospectors in it before that. U.S. survey maps on the larger scale are not even available for its lower end. Kanab fills its many roles unknown, unspoiled, unvisited.

Simplicity is certainly the keynote here, but there's also a kind of poetic feeling in the final lines.

Many of the flourishing men's magazines publish travel articles, often in connection with an international sporting event or with a strong topical angle. "Canoe Racing's Drop Dead Derby" by Robert Warner in *Saga* begins in a terse, reportorial style fairly typical of that magazine's tone:

> On September 5, on an inside page of a small town weekly newspaper, the *St. Maurice Valley Chronicle* of Three Rivers, Quebec, there appeared a short account of the toughest and most important canoe race on earth — the annual 125-mile sprint down the St. Maurice River from La Tuque to Three Rivers. Even though Three Rivers is less than 100 miles from Montreal, that big city's two leading newspapers, the *Gazette* and the *Star*, ignored the race completely. There was no radio coverage outside of a small local Three Rivers station and no prerace advertising.
>
> Despite the lack of publicity, the Three Rivers police estimated that a crowd of 100,000 spectators turned out, while the Provincial police pegged the attendance at 125,000. Both explained that the turnout was much smaller than usual because of very bad weather the first day. The year before the crowd exceeded 150,000.

As exemplified here, *Saga* likes the drama of little-known events as a peg on which to hang a story. The writing is brisk, forthright, not much concerned with local color or stylistic niceties.

It's a good idea for the aspiring travel writer to make such comparisons of the magazines he hopes to write for, because each is sure to have certain quirks of policy and taste that a little study will reveal.

Except in the straight "Baedeker" kind of article, which simply reports the principal places of interest, hotels, restaurants, and so on, a writer must try to capture the spirit and feeling of a place in order to make the reader know what it's like to be there. There are countless ways of doing this, but beginners often make the mistake of thinking that description alone is enough. It almost never is, simply because description is usually static. Telling the story in narrative form helps, because the reader then anticipates what will happen next as he travels from place to place.

A travel writer must search constantly for anecdotes that will dramatize, illustrate, or simply inject a human note into his piece. He can't get enough of them. They're likely to pop up anywhere, often unexpectedly. I once did a story about hurricanes on the Gulf coast of Louisiana. I talked to meteorologists, ships' captains, airline pilots, town officials, old residents. I got much information and some startling facts, but few really good anecdotes.

When I finally gave up and went to dinner in a small village café, the waitress couldn't stop talking about the experiences she and her neighbors had had with hurricanes. She told me story after story, and some of these contained the best anecdotes I'd found in days of searching.

A good writer will do as much research as possible before making a trip: he should know what to look for before he gets there. But you never know completely what information you're after because some of the best material will come as a surprise. It's always the odd fact, the unexpected anecdote, the little-known place that provides the best material.

There are times, though, when it is better *not* to be full of information. I once was assigned to do a story on "The Changing Caribbean." I read a half dozen or more books before I started out, and I traveled around the islands for three weeks taking notes. When I got back, the editor told me that the art department had made changes in the layout for the story. Now only 1,800 words were needed. I had enough material for a couple of books – and he wanted 1,800 words!

It was the toughest assignment I ever had; I really sweated blood because I seemed to have much too much to say, no matter from what angle I approached it. Finally, in desperation, I went for a long walk, and when I came back to the typewriter I somehow seemed to have the proper angle. The words came, and the article turned out to be a good one.

More often than not, a writer on a trip will have more than one assignment. Perhaps one week he'll do a story in Paris, the next in Brussels, the third in Amsterdam. I once had nine stories to do throughout Europe on one trip, and I was bothered by the idea of coming back with all those notes and trying to make stories of them a long time after I'd done the research and interviews. So I decided to write each story on the spot, no matter how badly it seemed to be turning out. I'd simply hole up for a day or two in a hotel room and keep hammering away at the typewriter until I finished. Then I'd shamelessly send the rough manuscript to New York.

As it turned out, this was the best thing I ever did. The stories, when I got back to them, were rough, but not half as bad as I had thought them to be. It was a simple matter to revise them. The funny thing is, if I'd written those stories in New York it would have taken me more than twice as long, and I doubt if they would have been as good.

All writing methods are personal but I suggest that beginning writers, whose habits may not be firmly fixed, try writing their stories as rapidly as possible, then coming back to them. It's a way of catching fresh first impressions.

Trying to convey their feelings about an experience, beginning writers sometimes get carried away – and their writing shows it. Here's how a novice might describe a trip through British Columbia's Inside Passage:

> The Inside Passage is probably not really a wilderness, I suppose, but its vast, stark, almost frightening magnificence makes it seem like the Land that Time Forgot. There are hundreds of wild animals you can see from the deck of the ship. Huge eagles, for instance, that fly overhead among the weirdly shaped clouds. Porpoises swim right up to the ship to say hello as you lean against the rail breathing in the dazzling beauty of the natural surroundings.
>
> Once in a while you see a huge, fearless bear standing like a statue on a rocky promontory, staring daggers at you. Every now and then you shiver when you hear the funny whistling sound that means a loon is calling for its mate. It sounds strange in the solemn silence of nature's solitude.
>
> As the mighty ship makes its lonely way northward, the atmosphere becomes even more rugged in its natural grandeur. You pass myriad islands where nobody lives. After a while these islands seem to be all around you, they're so close together. In terror, you think you're going to be shipwrecked! And your heart leaps into your mouth when you hear the third mate utter a sharp, terse warning to the quartermaster steering the ship. The vigilant mate stares grimly into the gathering gloom, and you're sure the ship is headed for some terrible disaster. What a relief when you finally see a narrow channel, and once again gaze upon the heady and spine-tingling beauty of sea and mountain and sky! What a trip that was!

Now let's see how the same trip was described by a more experienced hand:

> The Inside Passage is hardly a wilderness, and yet you have a sense of wilderness all around you. Eagles wheel under fat, low-hanging clouds; porpoises scratch themselves against the ship's hull; bears, bold as terriers, stare at you from the rocky shore; and every now and then, in the distance, you hear the mournful cry of the loon.
>
> This sense of wilderness is heightened as you sail on. Uninhabited islands, with trees growing out of the cracks in rocks, seem to draw closer and closer together, crowding the ship into a narrow channel. Presently, a wall of green looms ahead. "Watch it, Wallace!" the third mate says to the quartermaster behind the wheel. "Or we'll have Christmas trees in the wheelhouse."
>
> But his eyes never leave the water as the ship pushes toward what appears to be an inevitable wreck. Suddenly, at the last moment, there's a sharp bend in the channel, and you're looking, with relief, at a new vista of sea, mountain, and sky.

Traveling is fun, and so, usually, is writing about it. There's something less restricted, less formal about travel stories than about other kinds of nonfiction. It also can be more of a personal expression, for the travel article admits to almost any kind of writing, as long as it's effective. *Holiday*'s essays, for instance, are the reflections of strong personalities and intelligent, inquiring minds who bring wit and perception and grace of style to their articles. *Holiday* has, in fact, considerably raised the standards of travel writing by insisting on high literary quality.

Years ago, *Holiday* editors discovered that some of their best pieces came not from professional travel writers but from good novelists. Since then, the magazine has published nearly every major English and American author, including Joyce Cary, Ernest Hemingway, John O'Hara, Frank O'Connor, John Steinbeck, Seán O'Faoláin, and William Faulkner.

Such a roster seems to indicate that fiction and travel writing are closely allied. The excellence of both lies more in the writer, the reflection of his mind and heart, his interpretation of life, than in the things he perceives. All good travel writing nowadays has a personal quality, a kind of poetry and analysis, that lifts it above the simple reporting of facts.

It would probably be more helpful for the beginning travel writer of today to read contemporary books of travel, such as Alan Morehead's *The White Nile* and *The Blue Nile,* Leigh Fermor's *The Traveler's Tree,* Lawrence Durrell's *Bitter Lemons,* to name just a few, than to struggle through the "classics" of travel literature. I don't mean to deprecate the classics, but they simply aim at a different target.

Until the jet age, travel writers often addressed an audience they knew would never see what they were describing. They emphasized the marvels they came upon. Some of them – Marco Polo, Richard Burton, Charles Doughty, and Lafcadio Hearn – were even great reporters. Today's highly skilled travel writer knows well that he's talking about things his audience may see for themselves. So his aim is to interpret, to make his audience feel as he does, to share his experiences and his insights. Instead of wonder, we now get analysis.

Nevertheless there's a classic model for the travel writer of today – a little book by Robert Louis Stevenson called *Travels with a Donkey.* Stevenson here captures, in style and viewpoint, just what the modern travel writer strives for: a simple narrative style that evokes by the unerring choice of detail the essence of the travel experience. Here's how he describes waking in a sleeping bag in a pine forest in southern France.

> When that hour came to me among the pines, I wakened thirsty. My tin was standing by me half full of water. I emptied it at a draught; and feeling broad awake after this internal cold aspersion, sat upright to make a cigarette. The stars were clear, colored, and jewel-like, but not frosty. A faint silvery vapour stood for the Milky Way. All around me the black fir-

points stood upright and stock-still. By the whiteness of the pack-saddle, I could see Modestine walking round and round at the length of her tether; I could hear her steadily munching at the sward; but there was not another sound, save the indescribable quiet talk of the runnel over the stones. I lay lazily smoking and studying the colour of the sky, as we call the void of space, from where it showed a reddish gray behind the pines to where it showed a glossy blue-black between the stars. As if to be more like a pedlar, I wear a silver ring. This I could see faintly shining as I raised or lowered the cigarette; and at each whiff the inside of my hand was illuminated, and became for a second the highest light on the landscape.

Of course, in the broad spectrum of travel, there's a definite place for the purely factual report. Often the lead of such a piece has some news value. The announcement of the fiesta in Trinidad, for example, would be followed by a rundown on the places a visitor should see, a list of hotels and restaurants, possibly with prices. Such stories are the bread and butter of travel writing, and many newspapers – magazines, too – often welcome articles of this kind, if they are newsworthy.

Personal travel experiences that aren't especially startling but contain information about trips others might take are also good material for stories. The New York *Times,* which now has one and sometimes two complete travel sections in its Sunday edition, often runs such stories. It's a good idea to look around your own neighborhood for material. Your hometown might be, after all, a tourist spot for someone who lives fifty or more miles away.

With imagination, you may well find travel stories in your own back yard – or close to it. In fact, you might even make enough money from them to go to Europe or the Orient next year.

No compromise with quality

Any first-rate novel or story must have in it the strength of a dozen fairly good stories that have been sacrificed to it. A good workman can't be a cheap workman; he can't be stingy about wasting material, and he can't compromise. Writing ought either to be the manufacture of stories for which there is a market demand – a business as safe and commendable as making soap or breakfast foods – or it should be an art, which is always a search for something for which there is no market demand, something new and untried, where the values are intrinsic and have nothing to do with standardized values. The courage to go on without compromise does not come to a writer all at once – nor, for that matter, does the ability. Both are phases of natural development. – Willa Cather in *On Writing.*

Bennett Cerf

The light touch in writing is what publishers are always looking for, according to one who is a humorist himself

How's your humor?

On a vacation trip to Barbados I was asked by the editor of the local magazine, *The Bajan,* what advice I had for the new writer. The question hardly surprised me, even coming, as it did, in that idyllic environment so far removed from Publisher's Row. It proved – if, indeed, the point needed proving – that despite the differences on the surface, a beach front in Barbados, a beatnik pad in San Francisco, and an elegant sitting room in Sutton Place are basically the selfsame setting so far as literary aspiration is concerned.

My reply to the Barbadian editor was the same I would have given to the San Francisco hipster and the Sutton Place matron: "The greatest opportunity for a new writer today lies in the field of humor."

There's an urgent need for humor in the world today – and I'm speaking now not only from the literary point of view but from the philosophical as well. We must have laughter, much more laughter, to balance the unrelieved diet of grave, disturbing problems that make up the daily fare of people everywhere. We need more than a sprinkling of laughter; we need a heavy seasoning of it – laughter at outside, objective things, and even more important, at ourselves.

I don't want to make light of current problems – Lord knows, they're weighty – but nevertheless I feel strongly that we don't laugh at ourselves anymore. That goes not only for our personal foibles but for the foibles of our government and all those sacred institutions which might well profit by a little kidding. There's nothing like laughter for ventilating the dark recesses of gloom or pomposity.

But, in my opinion, it should merely ventilate; it should not blow its target apart in a cyclonic rage of fury. I'm totally out of sympathy with that particular kind of humor – exemplified by the so-called "sick" joke – which is offensive and seeks only to wound. If a new writer hasn't got good taste, he's wasting his time trying to get anywhere in the literary field. There's nothing less palatable than clumsy humor, awkward humor – humor equipped with barbs designed to hurt people or to make them uncomfortable.

Beyond these few strictures, I feel only one rule applies as to what sort of humor should be written: namely, *funny* humor.

I'll try now to come back to the opening question and offer some advice to the young writer who wants to crack the humor market. To begin with, it's happily a wide-open market. There's a lot more demand for humor by book and magazine publishers than the meager supply can satisfy. This fact alone makes it an admirable field for the new writer to venture into; he doesn't have to buck the stiff competition and glutted market of other forms of writing.

The beginning writer wants to know, sensibly enough, where to begin. The answer, I think, lies in a commonsense assessment of the situation. If you were a new prizefighter, you wouldn't inaugurate your career by issuing a challenge to the champion. No, you'd start in a modest way and gradually gather your experience against less awesome opponents. In much the same sense, I'd recommend starting out in the humor field by writing shorter pieces, by working against the "prelim boys" of the literary ring. Once you've mastered the short form you can expand with confidence.

Very well. You've decided to write short humor pieces. What, then, is your market? Interestingly enough, it's a rather good – in terms of literary quality – and well-paying one. Heading the list is the *New Yorker,* which buys many short pieces with a humorous slant. Admittedly, the *New Yorker*'s standards are very high; but if your piece is right, they will buy it, even though you're just plain old Elmer Smith from Pawpaw.

Although the *New Yorker* represents a vast degree of prestige to the writer who's published in its elegant pages, there are other publications nearly as good. *Esquire* is one. Then there are a number of the so-called men's magazines like *Playboy, Rogue, Cavalier,* and others.

The difference between the photographs and the text in this group of magazines is quite marked. The *former* depend for effect on the rather uncomplicated attractions of undraped females; the *latter* is frequently of good to excellent literary quality.

Apart from the money and the delight of seeing yourself in print, publishing in a magazine – particularly the ones I've named here – offers another advantage. Book publishers scour these magazines each month in their never-ending search for talent. A promising magazine piece is almost certain to bring its author offers or inquiries from half a dozen or more book publishers. And no matter how exciting it is to see one's name in a widely circulated magazine (particularly for the first time), I think there's little doubt the El Dorado of the writer is book publication.

Let me mention a few of the novelists who have won fame and fortune on the wings of comedy: Max Shulman, my fellow faculty member at the Famous Writers School; Peter De Vries, like Max (and like the School) a Westporter; Richard Bissell, author of *Say, Darling* and *7½ Cents,* a pair of best sellers that also became Broadway musical hits; William Brinkley, who found material for humor in the Navy and wrote the highly successful *Don't Go Near the Water;* and the late Mac Hyman, who hit the jackpot with his uproarious *No Time for Sergeants.*

These are all established authors, but it was not always thus. And what about the current crop of aspirants? What – assuming he has served his novitiate in the magazines – are the new writer's chances of marketing a humorous novel? The answer is an unequivocal "excellent."

The reason is not – certainly not – that humor is easier to write than anything else, but that the submission of humorous novels is no more than a tiny fraction of the fiction manuscripts that come into a publisher's office. The first novel dealing with a youth seeking to find himself, the first novel of family life, the first novel dealing with the problem of a special ethnic group – each of these must compete with hundreds of others dealing with the same themes. Only a few of them – the most outstanding – can be accepted; the rest, despite their excellence, must regretfully be sent back to their authors.

Obviously, a publisher must have a varied list. This is one of the reasons why most publishers are desperately on the lookout for humorous books. It goes without saying, therefore, that the reception accorded such a book would come under the heading of preferential treatment. I'm risking little when I say that, although numbers of good straight novels are declined, very few good humorous novels are. It's very simply a matter of supply and demand.

Yes, the market for humor is wide open. There's hardly a publisher in town who isn't looking eagerly (and usually in vain) for a funny novel. And if you're wondering why I'm so serious about such a light subject, may I remind my readers that, among other things, I happen to be a publisher?

Where style must come from

People constantly ask me whether the student of writing should confine himself to the style of any given period or branch out on his own and experiment as freely as he wants. If he wants to experiment with the style of any period, it would just be an exercise. It might help him to try to write one story in the Victorian style of George Meredith and try to write another in the Faulknerian style. Or he might try the style of Scott Fitzgerald or the people who came after him – people like Thomas Wolfe or even J. D. Salinger. But this would only be exercise.

Young writers should never model themselves faithfully and slavishly after another writer. They should be themselves. When you sit down to write, express yourself the way that comes easiest and most naturally, without deliberately aping somebody else's style. – Bennett Cerf

Giving pleasure to others

Do you realize what a writer can contribute to the world in which he lives? He can contribute a thousand things: amusement, relaxation, escape; he can contribute the springboard for serious thought, ideals and standards; he can contribute pleasure and pondering; he can evoke happiness or pain, both of which every reader has experienced. And more than that, he can give of himself. For all writing in fiction and non-fiction must, to be valid, contain something of the writer – experience, principles, desires and belief.

Writing does much for the writer in an inward, even a spiritual sense. As you write of people, as you share their misery or joy, their insecurities and fortitude, their hesitancies (for you must share in order to communicate to the reader), you are learning more and more about people; the good, the evil, the in-between (which most of us are) and what's more, you are giving to others an immeasurable gift of entertainment and pleasure. – Faith Baldwin

Rudolf Flesch

The growth of gobbledygook, says this
expert, is a by-product of modern
civilization and growing bureaucracy

Why business can't write

For the past twenty years I've worked with industry and government, trying to improve their writing. It's been an uphill job. It has led me to the disappointing conclusion that all the efforts of lecturing, classroom teaching, consulting, and advising are useless against the tremendous social forces that make for gobbledygook and jargon.

Of course I can't produce any statistics to show that business writing has deteriorated by so-and-so-many percent. But after twenty years at my observation post, there's no doubt in my mind that things have gotten steadily worse. Let me give you a few examples:

About fifteen years ago I drafted a series of three short form letters for one of our largest corporations, to be used in a frequently recurring standard situation. Naturally I tried to make the letters as simple, practical, and effective as I could.

Not long ago I ran across the set of letters used by the same corporation today. I could hardly recognize my handiwork. The basic structure and some of the original phrases were still there, but they seemed to be affected by an insidious disease. Sentences had become bloated, pseudo-formal prepositional phrases had crept in, "want" had become "wish," "close" had become "terminate," "help" had become "assistance." What had been friendly, human little letters had changed into stiff, cold business communications.

Or take the writing that goes on in a large publishing house offering information services on taxes and government regulations. I've been working with their editors for many years. Still, I haven't been able to prevent publication of routine items such as this one:

> Fiduciary custody account: Section 45–88, Connecticut General Statutes, permits fiduciaries, unless the governing instrument or a court order provides otherwise, to entrust the custody of securities of the fiduciary estate to New York, Massachusetts or Pennsylvania banks or trust companies, which are members of the Federal Reserve System, and whose capital, surplus and undivided profits in the aggregate are not less than fifty million dollars.

As you can see, this sentence uses sixty-two words and bristling grammatical armor to convey the rather simple thought that Connecticut trustees can keep securities in large New York, Massachusetts, and Pennsylvania banks.

For a third example, let's look at a world-famous monstrosity – U. S. Army prose. Back in the early fifties, I served a tour of duty conducting seminars in writing for high officers in the Pentagon. You'd think that this experience had inured me thoroughly to the prose style customary among our warriors. Not so. A recent specimen, passed on to me by one of my disciples, goes considerably beyond anything I ever ran into. Here it is:

> A feature that needs to be added is improved procedures to assure that each decision with respect to the Army program is transmitted on a timely basis to all agencies whose activities will be affected following translation into terms appropriate to the responsibilities of those agencies.
>
> (English translation: "When we make a decision about this program, we must pass it on promptly to the people affected and show how it applies to them.")

Somehow, in the last decade, the spirit of gobbledygook has come up with a brand-new set of military circumlocutions, replacing such unsightly English words as "promptly" or "fast" by the stately expression "on a timely basis."

I could go on with examples like these, illustrating the progressive decay of corporate and governmental prose. The question is Can this trend be stopped or reversed? I wonder.

What we're up against here is something that goes very deep — much deeper than sentence structure, vocabulary, or the use of personal pronouns. Gobbledygook and business jargon stem from the same roots as air pollution, traffic jams, slums, and organized crime. They're by-products of modern civilization.

Consider my first example of the three form letters. When I drafted them, the corporation was already large, but probably only half as large as it is today. Its capital has vastly increased since then, as has the number of its customers and employees, the scope of its business, and the number of times those three little letters are being sent out. The number of persons who have to clear a form letter has gone up from, say, five to ten. Naturally everything gets more complex in the process.

Every one of those hypothetical ten people feels he has to contribute something to show he's on the job, and everyone on the lower rungs of the ladder has more eyes watching what he's doing and more supervisors to be afraid of. What inducement is there for him to say "help" instead of "assistance"? All he knows is that "assistance" is safe, whereas "help" may be frowned upon by someone higher up as too undignified or something. He can't go to his boss and argue out the question because there are many people sitting on top of his boss and no one can go up the line to the forty-third floor to fight for the decencies of English prose. And so the little letters get covered with ugly barnacles and the money paid to consultants like me is thrown out the window.

Or consider my sample sentence about Connecticut trustees and their securities. The trouble here is not so much that the writer or editor was caught in an expanding organizational web, but that his subject matter is growing more complex year after year after year. Once upon a time it may have been enough to talk about large banks; then the fifty-million-dollar cutoff definition was introduced by law; and finally this fifty million dollars had to be further defined by spelling out "capital, surplus and undivided profits in the aggregate."

How could the poor editor have simplified that expression? Only by punching a legal loophole into it somewhere and giving the reader incomplete and less useful information. The result of all this ever-rising complexity of laws, regulations, technical subject matter? An ever-rising tide of gobbledygook.

Finally, let's look at our precious bit of army prose. Now of course there's no defensible reason or excuse for writing "on a timely basis" when you mean "fast." What causes these monstrosities is something akin to the famous Parkinson's Law dealing with the problem of all large organizations.

You may remember that Parkinson's Law goes like this: "Work expands so as to fill the time available for its completion." Applied to the problem of corporate prose, this becomes: "Language expands so as to fill the time available for paperwork."

In other words, once you have an organization like the U. S. Army with millions of men in uniform and an unlimited supply of man hours available for paperwork of every conceivable kind, it's virtually inevitable that you wind up with language containing such expressions as "on a timely basis." Language expands so as to fill the time. . . . Professor Parkinson was – and – is a very wise man.

After all, this problem has been with us ever since human organization began. Schopenhauer fulminated against the ugliness of "paper German" 150 years ago; so did dozens and hundreds of other sensitive people in all countries that developed a bureaucracy. Of course, until the twentieth century, this bureaucratic language was mainly confined to each country's army, police, and civil service; it wasn't until our own times that the disease spread to such semi-governmental bodies as the corporate giants.

In the late 1940s a little movement got under way, trying to counteract the trend. Readability was studied, conferences were held, pamphlets were issued, and civil servants and business employees were told ad nauseam that they should do this, that, and the other to improve their writing. Well here we are twenty years later and things have gone from bad to worse.

Is it all inevitable? Can anything be done about it at all?

My disenchanted answer is that conventional tactics are no longer any good. The effect of lectures has a way of dissipating; seminars become routine exercises in exhortation; classroom training of personnel sooner or later is ground under by the pressures of the corporate machine.

I do think that an enlightened corporation could improve its language if it took the problem seriously enough to invest some money and effort in it. As it is today, letter writing is considered as something on the order of the shrubbery outside the building or the trimmings in the halls and offices around Christmastime. (Memo and report writing don't even have that modest status.) If a corporation recognized the enormous expense and waste caused by poor, ineffective communication and went about it in a planned and businesslike manner, there'd be no reason why it couldn't set an acceptable standard of English vocabulary and syntax, charge a vice-president with the responsibility for enforcing it, and make this a matter of permanent supervision and control.

But in all my years as a consultant, I have never found an organization interested in doing just that.

Meanwhile, there is a splendid opportunity for a young man looking for a way up the organizational ladder. All he has to do is learn the art of writing (which after all can be taught – and taught well) and put his acquired skill to work where it can and will be seen. There's no easier way to be noticed in a large organization than by writing a letter, memo, or report in ordinary decent English. It will stick out and immediately catch the eye of someone upstairs.

Unless, of course, the man upstairs no longer recognizes decent English when he sees it!

Illustrate your article

Business papers use more illustrations today than ever before. Why? There are several reasons: (1) Illustrations – photos or drawings – convey a message or idea faster than the printed word. (2) Many complex machines and circuits can't be adequately described in words – illustration is necessary. (3) Readers usually find illustrated articles easier to read and give them more attention. (4) Good illustrations improve the appearance of a published article. (5) Editors have greater flexibility in planning the article layout when the author supplies good illustrations.

You can use almost any kind of illustrations for your article. Photos, line drawings, graphs, charts, maps, business forms and cartoons are frequently used in modern business papers. The choice rests with you. At times the editor may suggest what kinds of illustrations he thinks are best. Follow his suggestions if possible.

To get the best return from the time you devote to illustrations for your article:

1. Get the best illustrations possible.
2. Use a professional photographer or draftsman.
3. Use only those illustrations that help your story – reject others.
4. Send "atmosphere" shots as extras.
5. Follow the editor's instructions when preparing illustrations.

Reading helps your writing

Reading for profit (or for pleasure) is a habit most successful, ambitious men discover to their advantage early in life. People who get ahead in most businesses and professions consciously take time out for reading. The most successful ones instinctively knew early in their lives that to get the better of their competition, they would have to use high-powered mental ammunition. They got it largely by reading. Having developed the reading habit early in life, they used it to become successful.

Joseph Callanan

Hundreds of industrial editors
are looking for material . . . and
are willing to pay well for it

How to write for house organs

Most free-lancers are well aware of the demand for feature articles among newsstand magazines, but few know much about another big market for their output – the house organs. Here are a few cold statistics calculated to warm the hearts of all writers in search of new markets:

1. There are, by conservative estimates, more than 10,000 regularly published house organs in the United States.

2. Their combined circulation exceeds 200 million per issue.

3. The combined cost of a single issue of every house organ in this country amounts to more than 75 million dollars. It's a billion-dollar-a-year business.

Now, what is a house organ? The following definition comes from the International Council of Industrial Editors, so it's as official as you can get:

> The term . . . refers to many types of communications . . . issued periodically by private sponsors: business and industrial companies and various associations. They include magazines, newspapers, newsletters and

mimeographed bulletins. In almost all cases they are free-circulation media, and in very few cases do they carry paid advertising.

They fall into three general classifications: internal, for circulation primarily or only among employees of the sponsor; external, for circulation among the sponsor's customers, prospects, dealers, salesmen, stockholders, among so-called thought leaders and other interested persons; and combinations of the two.

Most giant corporations are in the publishing business in a big way, producing many different periodicals. In Standard Oil of New Jersey's international network of affiliates, for instance, there are more than 300 magazines and newspapers. General Electric, which publishes a number of plant newspapers as well as magazines, runs a company-wide news service, modeled after the AP and UP, with teletype bulletins and flashes from the home office.

Every major automobile manufacturer publishes a number of flossy magazines, of which *Ford Times,* with its excellent artwork and professional travel articles, is probably the best known. Nearly all leading companies in the fields of pharmaceuticals, insurance, oil, and chemicals produce first-rate magazines with high editorial and artistic standards.

Most of the big magazines regularly buy free-lance material, and often their rates of payment rival those of slick newsstand publications. They also tend to like impressive by-lines. Nevertheless hundreds of less elaborate house publications welcome free-lance material and are excellent markets for beginners.

Today, the editors are striving mightily for greater recognition and higher editorial standards; they shy away from chitchat about babies and bowling scores, so characteristic of earlier house organs. Recently I phoned ten house organ editors in New York and asked how they felt about getting free-lance material. With varying degrees of enthusiasm, each said that he'd be happy to look at whatever was sent, provided the writers knew the magazines and had made a reasonably intelligent estimate of requirements.

Knowing the magazine is, in fact, as important in this field as it is in the slicks. This is often forgotten, even by pros who should know better. When I was on the staff of Standard Oil's *The Lamp,* a well-known magazine writer submitted an article which the editor tossed back for revision with the comment that it was dull.

"Good heavens," the writer said in surprise. "I thought you wanted it dull!"

Heavy policy statements and statistics-laden articles on economics have long made many house organs seem dull indeed, but you can be sure that the editor didn't plan for dullness; he had it thrust upon him by company executives, who sometimes appear as though they have to say something but would prefer that no one read it. However, there's a trend toward livelier and more professional editing among house organs these days; as a matter of fact, a number of former national magazine editors are now in the field as house organ editors. At a recent International Council of Industrial Editors' annual conference, two of the most popular speakers were Herbert R. Mayes, former editor and publisher of *McCall's,* and Edward Barrett, dean of the Columbia School of Journalism, both of whom emphasized the growth of professional standards among house organs.

By far the largest number of house organs are internal—they're employee publications. What kinds of articles do they publish? Tastes differ, of course, and so do fundamental aims, but one editor recently summed up what his magazine tried to accomplish in words that should give free-lancers a clue to the requirements of many employee publications.

"The themes we have to hit year after year," he said, "are 'Work safely, play safely'; 'profits are essential to the health of business'; 'new products are evidence of progress.'"

Such themes are basic to the employee publication, though each magazine has its own technique and approach. I once met a free-lancer who told me he had a long list of titles for articles that he could always sell to one employee magazine or another. Here are a few that I remember: "The Need for Profits," "How Big Business Helps the Community," "Is Bigness Badness?" "The History of the Corporation," "Let's Cut Taxes." Never missed, he said. The demand from editors of employee magazines was insatiable.

For free-lancers, though, the "externals," which go to a wider audience, offer the best and most interesting opportunities. The editors of many externals feel they're in competition with *Life, Look,* and *Reader's Digest.* So they strive for wide appeal, and tend to look toward free-lance writers to help them out. Among the best-known externals are IBM's *Think,* which publishes articles on subjects of general interest to businessmen, and usually unrelated to business machines; *The Du Pont Magazine,* a slick, four-color magazine with articles about Du Pont's products; Chevrolet's *Friends,* a lively professional magazine with a circulation of more than 1.5 million.

According to Dr. Russel J. Jandoll, head of the department of journalism at St. Bonaventure University, who made a study of house organs, the average editor of an external prefers the material of each issue to be one-third about his company, one-third of indirect company interest, and the remainder general subjects, such as travel, food, fashion, world affairs, books, sports, hobbies, and general science.

In general, though, the articles with the best chance of being accepted are those combining some aspect of a company's activities with material of general interest. Often, free-lancers make the mistake of thinking that all house organs want a direct, drumbeating approach, and their articles tend to sound like publicity releases rather than professional magazine pieces. While I was with *The Lamp,* a story about one of Standard Oil's marketing affiliates was submitted in typical news-release form:

> The Carter Oil Company, an affiliate of Standard Oil (N.J.), is expanding its marketing operations in the Pacific Northwest, especially in the Columbia River Basin, where the desert is being reclaimed by irrigation from the Grand Coulee Dam. Six new service stations have been erected, and more are in the planning stages. . . .

In an effort to interest a wide audience *The Lamp* linked Carter's expansion with the dramatic changes taking place in the area. Here's how the story's lead was rewritten:

> Dust devils whirl like ghosts through the parched sagebrush east of the Columbia River, and rainfall, when it comes at all, is merely a soft spattering upon the unquenchable soil.

After vividly describing the desert before the irrigation project and the upsurge in growth after the land had been reclaimed, the piece introduced the company angle in this way:

> Attracted by the exciting promise of the irrigation project, people from all over the country are coming to eastern Washington. New companies are moving in, too. Among them is the Carter Oil Company, a Jersey affiliate.

With all the talk about "public images" and such, business now makes an effort to be less stuffy and self-conscious. Even insurance companies have turned away from traditional solemnity. Time was when an insurance company talked to its policyholders in words of this sort:

> It behooves every policyholder to become well acquainted with the terms of his contract . . .

In its lively magazine *Minutes,* however, the Nationwide Insurance Company takes a more lighthearted view:

> They're not exactly what the book publishers call "hammock literature," but – believe it or not – your insurance policies can give you hours of profitable reading.

The trend reflected in many house organs is toward an easy, natural style – a more human approach to the business of business.

For writers who have a knack of describing technical or scientific developments, there's a great opportunity among the house organs. Industrial research laboratories are forever coming up with new developments and new products. The important thing to remember about such technical pieces is that most readers are more interested in what the product or development will do for them than in the ways and wherefores of it. In other words, it's almost always best not to be too technical – just technical enough to be convincing.

Here's how an amateur in the pop-technical field might go astray in a story about research into turbine-powered automobiles:

> Scientists in white smocks are scurrying around Detroit's automobile research laboratories looking for a way to adapt the gas turbine wheel that will withstand 2000° Fahrenheit in the compressor where heat and energy provide the power to turn a second turbine, which in turn turns the rear wheels.

Here's a more appropriate lead for the same story:

> In the research laboratories of Detroit's car manufacturers an eerie, whistling sound, as of cyclonic winds rushing through a tunnel, issues from behind doors closed to all but the engineers and technicians who work there. This strange sound may be heralding the start of a new era in the history of the automobile.

Personality stories are always a good bet, and an almost sure sale if the man you portray has some direct connection with the company. Most editors, for instance, favor stories about employees who participate in community affairs and local politics, or who have achieved some distinction with unusual hobbies. The guy on the production line who's a mayor or an alderman in his spare time is almost a sure idea.

Company magazines these days are also trying to treat executives in somewhat less stilted and formalistic terms than they used to. The old way was to be coldly objective and remote:

> Mr. Frank Thompson, after forty-five years' service with American Co-Ordinates, Inc., has retired as executive vice-president, a position which he assumed in 1952, after having served as Plant Manager in the Newark Co-Ordinates Works since 1941. He was president of the Co-Ordinates Association in 1945, and associate director of the Blue Feather Drive in 1957. He was a well-known statesman of free enterprise.

Editors nowadays try for a less wooden approach:

> It's characteristic of Frank Thompson that, in his farewell talk to his associates at a party in his honor, he should mention the novel *Candy,*

Homer's *Iliad,* the statistics of sewage disposal in Laredo, Texas, in 1924, and the "Song of Solomon" to make a point about the future of Ameri-can Co-Ordinates, Inc. He brought a wide-ranging and active mind to his post of executive vice-president. He was also a great, free-wheeling story-teller, and an unbeatable poker player.

Of course, house organs vary widely, as companies do, and it's extremely difficult to generalize about them. Every house organ editor faces the specter of the executives above him, and usually it's their judgment and taste that prevail. House organs shy away from controversy. Editors are eager to cram articles full of color and anecdote, but it's always well for a free-lancer to keep in mind that the house organ is part – and probably a very expensive part – of the company's public relations program; it has nothing to do with "fearless journalism."

In fact, executives often seem unduly skittish about what appears in their company's magazine, and this sometimes leads to a certain amount of frus-tration for the writer. I encountered this years ago when doing a story about Milton Berle, who said during the interview: Television is like sex. When it's good it's wonderful, and when it's bad, it's not so bad."

This struck me as being a pretty quotable quote, but the company for whom I wrote the story was shocked that I should even consider mentioning the word "sex" in their magazine. It was one of any number of words that didn't exist for them.

Such restrictions are a minor part of writing for house magazines, and all writers encounter similar frustrations. The important point to remember is that the whole house organ field does offer a large and challenging area for free-lance writers, and many beginners will surely first see their work in print there. They offer a wide variety of subject matter and approach from the very simple to the highly sophisticated. It's mainly a matter of looking around and seeing where you might fit in.

One great advantage is that the house organ market isn't concentrated in the East, as is most general publishing. The chances are good that there are several house organs published within visiting distance of your home, and these are probably the best to focus on, at least at first. The advantage of being able to talk over your story ideas with an editor can scarcely be over-estimated. Also, if you live close by, the editor welcomes the fact that you're available for last-minute revisions. Soon, he may feel that he can call upon you for help during the inevitable crises that arise with predictable regularity.

I've heard of several free-lancers who've attacked the house organ field from another angle. They've looked around their town or city and sought out companies who didn't have house organs, and then offered to edit one on a free-lance, part-time basis. It's safe to assume that any company with 100 or more employees has some kind of a "communications problem" which a regularly published paper or magazine would help to alleviate.

If such a suggestion doesn't ring the bell, you might follow it with another: Let the company buy a page or two in the local newspaper at regular intervals for company news and policy statements. This is done frequently, and would provide you with an interesting spare-time job, one that would help prepare you for any kind of writing you plan to do.

Such editorial work sometimes leads a free-lancer into other and more lucrative assignments for the company. There's much demand for editorial help in modern business: the manual for new employees, product brochures, executive speeches, annual reports. In a relatively short time, you may find yourself a pro in a field that is certainly growing in importance and stature.

> Since the end of World War II, the quality of house organs has steadily improved, until today quite a few maintain standards rivaling those of the best newsstand publications. The work of well-known writers often appears in their pages. Some examples: Nobel Prize winner John Steinbeck in *Ford Times;* novelist John Dos Passos and former Secretary of State Dean Acheson in IBM's *Think;* Famous Writers School faculty member J. D. Ratcliff in *Steelways; Harper's* editor-in-chief John Fischer in the *API Quarterly;* "inside" reporter John Gunther in a special publication of the Pfizer Pharmaceutical Company; *Reader's Digest* editor and book author Stuart Chase in *The Lamp.* Though house organs generally don't pay as much for articles as newsstand magazines, some equal or surpass the top publications in rates of payment for important pieces.

John J. Green

The world outside your window
or your door offers countless
subjects for salable manuscripts

Nature stories are naturals

One day recently I sat fascinated in my office as I watched a bit of nature in the raw. On a sand bar in the Saugatuck River, which runs back of the Famous Writers School, two sea gulls were trying to eat a large eel they had dragged out at low tide. However, the creature was too tough for them to rip apart and too large to swallow. So they gave up and went on to other business.

Within moments, another gull, not quite so ambitious, settled on the same sand bar with a small eel. This gull must have come from a long line of swallowers for it maneuvered the captive into its beak and worked the wriggling creature down the hatch. As I watched this little drama, it occurred to me that many aspiring writers probably overlook nature as they seek material for articles. Just stop for a moment and consider the possibilities.

Nature in its various forms is all around you—in the green of spring grass, the burgeoning trees and shrubs, the insect, animal, and bird life, the clouds. And each season has its own activities and interests. There are countless untold stories close at hand, just waiting for the observant eye to see them and the imaginative mind to run them through the typewriter for others to enjoy.

An example of what *you* might see in your own back yard was printed in an issue of *Famous Writers Magazine.* A student, Fred J. Weaver, submitted an assignment in the Non-Fiction Course in which he recounted some of the things he'd observed without ever leaving home. Simply written and augmented by some of his reactions, it told of amusing and tragic happenings among nature's creatures.

On a more ambitious scale, the best-selling author Edwin Way Teale wrote of "wild life" in his back yard and an adjoining apple orchard. He studied the insects that abounded there, photographed them, learned all he could about them. The result was one of his first major books, *Grassroot Jungles.*

Five years later, he followed with *Near Horizons,* subtitled *The Story of an Insect Garden.* The material for both these books, which did much to establish him as one of the world's foremost nature writers, literally came from his own back yard.

Going further afield, Teale came up with a series of four books, each dealing with one season. Each volume required extensive research, since this author is no armchair naturalist. With his wife he drove to the southernmost tip of Florida; then they worked their way *North with the Spring,* the title of this first volume in *The American Seasons* series. Published in 1951, some nine years after Teale first broached the idea to his publisher, it included material gleaned from 17,000 miles of driving, the taking of thousands of photographs, and the keeping of voluminous notes which he completed at the end of each day.

The series was completed in 1965 – some 22 years after inception – with *Wandering Through Winter,* which won the Pulitzer Prize for general nonfiction. And between these volumes Teale researched and wrote *Autumn Across America* and *Journey Into Summer,* along with several lesser projects. The *Seasons* books, the distillation of his research, represent more than 100,000 miles of driving.

Not many writers are situated so they can devote years to such a project, but Teale's experience points up what can be done by a dedicated naturalist who also is an accomplished writer. When I asked him recently for a few words of advice to aspiring nature writers, he said: "It's easy to be interesting and inaccurate. It's easy to be accurate and dull. But to be both interesting *and* accurate is the great goal. And that is a goal that takes a considerable amount of work to achieve."

No discussion of nature writing would be complete without mention of Henry David Thoreau (1817–1862) and John Muir (1838–1914). Stalwart pioneers in the nature writing field, their works are classics. Though Thoreau died more than a century ago, the latest edition of *Books in Print* lists almost a column of his titles in various editions.

In characterizing this great naturalist-writer and his work, Brooks Atkinson, in the introduction to the Modern Library edition of *Walden,* wrote:

> . . . There is no better prose in American literature than the clear, sinewy, fragrant writing in *Walden* which discusses the homely details of house-building and kitchen economy and rejoices in the romantic loveliness of sounds at night and bird images and simple phrases that do not change the pace with the change of subject. Although his writing looks easy, only a man of keen mind and remarkable skill could have made a sentence carry so much baggage and have given form to impulses of the imagination.

And in the same introduction, Atkinson added:

> . . . Thoreau did not merely write verses to the evanescent beauties of the out-of-doors and stroll placidly through the fields after a stuffy day in the study; he made it his business to know everything that he could about nature from personal observation. He wanted to know the cold by the tingle in his finger-tips and the darkness by stumbling through the woods at night, and he felt most elated when his senses were alert as those of the woodchuck and the loon. He felt that his whole life was on the most solid footing when his boots were deep in the riverbank muck in the springtime.

Two points stand out in Atkinson's comments on Thoreau – the importance of sound knowledge of your subject and the use of imagination in presenting it.

As for John Muir, his works live as a literary monument to his efforts to make America aware of the importance of conservation. He spent most of his life getting close to nature and his field trips on foot led him on treks of as much as a thousand miles. No outburst of nature could keep him from enjoying the beauties and the strengths of the elements. This is how he described an experience in *The Mountains of California:*

> One of the most beautiful and exhilarating storms I ever enjoyed in the Sierra occurred in December, 1874, when I happened to be exploring one of the tributary valleys of the Yuba River. The sky and the ground and the trees had been thoroughly rain-washed and were dry again. The day was intensely pure, one of those incomparable bits of California winter, warm and balmy and full of white sparkling sunshine, redolent of all the purest influences of the spring, and at the same time enlivened with one of the most bracing wind-storms conceivable. Instead of camping out,

as I usually do, I then chanced to be stopping at the house of a friend. But when the storm began to sound, I lost no time in pushing out into the woods to enjoy it. For on such occasions Nature has always something rare to show us, and the danger to life and limb is hardly greater than one would experience crouching deprecatingly beneath a roof. . . .

I heard trees falling for hours at the rate of one every two or three minutes; some uprooted, partly on account of the loose, water-soaked condition of the ground; others broken straight across, where some weakness caused by fire had determined the spot. The gestures of the trees made a delightful study. Young Sugar Pines, light and feathery as squirrel-tails, were bowing almost to the ground; while the grand old patriarchs, whose massive boles had been tried in a hundred storms, waved solemnly above them, their long, arching branches streaming fluently in the gale, and every needle thrilling and ringing and shedding off keen lances of light like a diamond. . . . But the Silver Pines were now the most impressively beautiful of all. Colossal spires 200 feet in height waved like supple goldenrods chanting and bowing as if in worship, while the whole mass of their long, tremulous foliage was kindled into one continuous blaze of white sun-fire. The force of the gale was such that the steadfast monarch of them all rocked down to its roots with a motion plainly perceptible when one leaned against it. Nature was holding high festival, and every fiber of the most rigid giants thrilled with glad excitement.

Any reader will agree that there's imagination in Muir's writing and, while imagination is stressed as one of the prime requisites of fiction, it's equally important in non-fiction. This doesn't mean fictionalizing facts — nature students would be quick to catch you up on inaccuracies. But you can make imagination work for you in the way you present your material. An excellent example is the way Hal Borland characterized a month in "March Is a Promise," condensed in *Reader's Digest* from books he has written:

March is a tomboy with tousled hair, a mischievous smile, mud on her shoes and a laugh in her voice. She knows when the first shadbush will blow, where the first violet will bloom, and she isn't afraid of a salamander. She has whims and winning ways. She's exasperating, lovable, a terror-on-wheels, too young to be reasoned with, too old to be spanked.

March is a rain, drenching as June and cold as January. It is mud and slush and the first green grass down by the brook. March is pussy willows. March is hepatica in bloom, and often arbutus. March is a sleet storm pelting out of the north the day after you find the first violet bud. March is boys playing marbles and girls playing jacks and hopscotch. But most of all March — here in New England anyhow — is a promise. March is when it all begins anew.

As a further example of using imagination to present a nature subject, consider how Paul and Myriam Friggens introduced their experiences in

America's newest national park, Canyonlands. Here's their lead as it appeared in *Reader's Digest* under the title "Standing-up Country":

> Halting our pack outfit on a canyon rim, we gazed in awe at America's newest national park. Before us towered battlements resembling some medieval fortress or fairy-tale castle; sandstone skyscrapers that might have been the Manhattan skyline; spires and needles higher than the Washington Monument. Here the Colorado River and the Green, while slicing through stair-stepped plateaus and down-plunging canyons, had laid bare 200 million years of geologic history in colorful 3-D.
>
> It's "standing-up country" ("There's more of it standing up than laying down!" an old-time cowpuncher described it) and probably the greatest red-rock fantasy on earth. Officially, the new park is called "Canyonlands."

Immediately the reader can visualize this colorful country and is eager to learn more about it. Why? Because the writers brought a bit of imagination to the subject.

Beginning non-fiction writers, taking material close at hand, often write about their pets. One trouble here is that many people aren't able to distinguish between material interesting to them and that which has wide general appeal. Our own pets are something special to us, but they're a good deal like our children—other folks don't always think they're cute.

Sterling North, however, wrote a book about his boyhood experiences with a young raccoon and the volume became a best seller. Though it is a simple story of a boy and his pet, it has universal appeal. *Rascal,* the name of the coon and the book, was a real character and the account is full of interesting happenings, complete with suspense and drama. So, as you consider nature writing, be sure your material has broad human interest. If it doesn't, no editor will consider it.

You never know when or where you'll come upon a nature subject worth at least a newspaper feature. New York newspapers not long ago had stories about a porcupine strolling along a busy street in lower Manhattan. Finally it was captured and hustled off to a shelter by men from the SPCA.

In another part of the country, a California park ranger found a bear with a face full of porcupine quills. He shot the animal with a tranquilizer gun but as he was removing the quills, the bear's heart began to fail. The ranger administered artificial respiration; after forty-five minutes bruin regained consciousness and ambled off, a bit groggy but on the way to recovery. This story had so much human interest it made the press association wires.

Another area frequently overlooked by beginning writers is conservation of wildlife, forests, streams, and lakes. Many states have publications devoted to conserving natural resources and it's a subject often used by many of the general magazines. The material should be timely, of course, and written with a fresh angle.

Not long ago, an FWS student wrote a story of a cow in his herd on the ranch. Fresh with calf, she had too much milk for her own offspring so they gave her an orphan calf that needed nursing. While she mothered the two youngsters, the rancher kept her in a feed pen near the barns and gave her special care and extra rations. But when the calves were weaned and they turned the cow out on the open range, she grieved and refused to forage for herself.

Later, they found her body. She literally had starved herself to death. That human-interest story based on an unusual situation in nature found a ready sale to a stockmen's magazine.

The publications that use nature stories are many and varied. They range all the way from the *Reader's Digest* to magazines devoted to pets, and include livestock journals, outdoor magazines, and even children's magazines. And don't overlook the Sunday newspaper supplements and the travel sections. Just keep in mind that the story you tackle must have strong human interest and that it must be told well.

If you aren't familiar with it, study a copy of *Natural History* at your library. Published by the American Association of Natural History, it is devoted entirely to nature subjects. Though some of the articles are quite scholarly, many of them hold interest for the general reader. A recent issue included "Flood History Told by Tree Growth," "Rock Carvings at Chalcingo," "Control Systems in Bird Reproduction," and "Summers in Penobscot Country."

The aspiring writer of nature stories who lives in the country or in a small town may have an advantage over the city dweller, for there's more to see. However, this didn't deter John Kieran. A long-time resident of New York, a sports writer and a radio and television personality, he is also a student of nature. Realizing that few New Yorkers were aware of the great variety of wildlife to be found within the city limits, he decided to inform them. The result was *A Natural History of New York*. Through the years his other nature books, including *Footnotes on Nature, An Introduction to Wild Flowers,* and *An Introduction to Nature,* have entertained and informed countless readers.

So, if you have an observing eye and a receptive ear, a keen interest in the subject, and the ability to use a little imagination in presenting your material, nature provides an inexhaustible source for articles and books, regardless of where you live. What are you waiting for?

Some thoughts on best sellers

When a book by a new writer becomes a best-seller, a body of legend grows about it. It appears that it was declined by a dozen stupid publishers until some genius saw its worth and brought the author from his garret into the daylight. It is not explained that the genius who discovered Author A, the week before let Author B's manuscript slide through his fingers to another genius who may, indeed, be the very oaf who originally saw no prospects in Author A, but now is acclaimed as the discoverer of B's masterpiece. Nor is it told how long and patiently both these publishers have labored with the beautiful lost words of Authors X and Y, upon whom, year after year, the public has inscrutably turned its back.

To those who know the facts beneath the legend, therefore, it is not surprising that good publishers waste so few tears over mistaken judgments of manuscripts. Over a long career any publisher can find in his record dozens of declinations of books which later brought fame and profit to someone else. If, in that career, he has built up a solid body of good authors who enjoy working with him and bring him a steady income, year after year, and if, besides, he has laid a backlog of departments producing steady-selling, religious, educational, juvenile, subscription or technical books, he has spent his energies more wisely than in the restless search for big sellers.

The proof of this is in his survival. Those publishers who have approached their job in this way have lived the longest, and the wisest young publishers in the field today are those who are steadily building, regardless of brilliant, quick and sporadic successes. – Roger Burlingame in *On Making Many Books*.

Time to start all over again

I would be upset if every writer with whom I have exchanged shoptalk had not confessed to instances of illusion and insecurity which expressed themselves in one form or another. And we were all agreed that nothing was quite so shattering as a rejection or a sour notice or criticism from an editor, and the further along we went in our profession, the more damaging were the results of such a rejection.

The first thought that arises to harass every writer when a piece is bounced, for whatever reason, is: "I'm through. I'm all washed up. This is the end. I can never write again. I've lost the touch." One feels as helpless, dejected and amateurish as the veriest tyro or beginner, as though one had to start learning all over again.

Of course it is sheer nonsense, of course one writes again because one must, and if the subsequent piece is accepted with hosannahs, or merely accepted and paid for, all one's confidence comes flooding back again and one rides atop the world – until the next fall. – Paul Gallico in *Confessions of a Story Writer*.

Section V

Revising and editing

Gordon Carroll

*To prove that a good writer is
generally a good reviser, here is
a group of celebrated manuscripts*

Authors as editors

Publishers, editors, and printers are usually the only people to see a manuscript after an author has worked over it with pen or pencil. The ordinary reader of a published book, article, or story has no way of telling whether the finished product represents a writer's first draft that was well-nigh perfect (a rare occurrence) or whether what appears on the printed page is the end result of a dozen editings and rewritings. Only rarely does an author's corrected manuscript appear in public, and then during a temporary exhibit of rare and selected manuscripts.

In this chapter are pages of manuscript that show you how five celebrated authors have worked, or do work, on their copy after it leaves their typewriters. As you will note in these pages, some of the authors are busy editors: they go over their work with great care; they weigh every paragraph, every sentence, sometimes every phrase with an eye to improving their prose. Others are not so thorough: their pencil does a first draft – and didn't surrender to an impulse to change just for change's sake.

The manuscript facsimiles on the following pages are quite representative of the contemporary author as editor. My selection, made from a wide range of samples in the Beinecke Library, Yale University, is designed not only to show different authors at work but also to show the variance in their editorial labors. Along with each page of manuscript I have supplied a caption on the author, his work, and his editorial corrections. But do not expect me to supply more than comment. The reason is self-evident: I can't.

No one (the author excepted) can tell you just why certain changes were made at a certain time and place in his working day. For me to attempt to explain his inner motivations would be as futile as attempting to explain the nature of talent or genius. All anyone can be certain of is this: that at the particular time the author used his pen or pencil, he had good reason for doing what he did, and when finished, he was satisfied that the change was worthwhile. If you will keep such imponderables of editing in mind, I think you will enjoy (and profit from) reading these pages.

Conrad was a man who shaped his prose with meticulous attention to detail. His sentences, his paragraphs, were structured so precisely that occasionally, according to some critics, he deprived his writing of a certain richness that his dramatic themes may have deserved.

These three consecutive pages of Conrad manuscript, taken from his distinguished novel *Chance,* show that his revising was just as scrupulously done as was the first draft of his writing. Some of his editorial efforts were ruthless: note the penciled excisions which removed more than a full page from the 750 words represented here.

Oddly enough, these sample pages show that Conrad, when editing or revising, used both a pen and a pencil, although he is best remembered for unusually clear calligraphy in which he used a stub pen and black India ink to make his revisions stand out boldly from the lines of typescript.

rumble.   It was as if the whole world existed only for selling

and buying and those who had nothing to do with the movement of

merchandise were of no account.

"You must be tired," I said.   One had to say something

if only to assert oneself against that wearisome, passionless

and crushing uproar.   She raised her eyes for a moment.   No,

she was not.   Not very.   She had not walked all the way.   She

came by train as far as ~~thu~~ Whitechapel Station and had only

walked from there.

She had had an ugly pilgrimage;   but whether of love

or of necessity who could tell?   And this precisely was what I

should have liked to get at.   ~~This~~ It was not however a question

to be asked point-blank, and I could not think of any effective

circumlocution.   It occurred to me too that she might conceivably

know nothing of it herself - I mean by reflection.   That young

woman had been obviously considering death.   She had gone the

length of forming some conception of it.   But as to its com-

panion fatality - love, she, I was certain, had never reflected

upon its meaning.

~~You may say that feelings are~~ outside the scope of re-

~~flection.   But the profoundest~~ and least controllable of our

emotions becomes in its consequences a fruitful subject of medita-

tion.   I am not alluding here to the everyday matches of this

world. I suppose there isn't a minute passes of the legal
hours, (whatever they are) but somebody is getting married. A
if these were all acts of passion fraught with the direst possi
bilities the thought would be too awful to contemplate. But
you know that it isn't so. For most people the pages of life
are ruled like the pages of a copybook headed with some sound
moral maxim at the top. They can turn them over with the
certitude that the very catastrophes shall keep to the traced
lines. And it is comforting, in a way, to one's friends and
even to oneself to think that one's very misfortunes, if any,
will be of the foreseen type.

     With that man in the hotel, whom I did not know, and
this girl standing before me in the street I felt that it was an
exceptional case. He had broken away
from his surroundings; she stood without the pale. One
aspect of conventions which people who declaim against them
lose sight of is that conventions make both joy and suffering
easier to bear in a becoming manner. But those two were outsi
all conventions. They would be as untrammelled in a sense
as the first man and the first woman. union
you will see the truth of this statement which may seem to you
absurd at first view. For conventions exist only as embodied

~~in the people who, so to speak, stand around to watch the game.~~
~~And they would have no one to watch them. I am not alluding~~
~~here to their life at sea. I mean that they would have nobody~~
~~outside their two selves to whom they need refer any~~
~~consequences that may arise from love — and even from a~~
mere marriage. ~~Do you see now why I was interested in the~~
~~whole thing with its touch of romance and its possibility of~~
~~being an idyll? Why not an idyll? Must an idyll necessarily~~
have rustic surroundings - the green fields, the murmuring
stream, the leafy shade of sheltered nooks? Or is the freshness
of unsophisticated hearts enough to create an idyllic atmosphere
about two lives exposed to the rough salt winds of the open sea?
You shake your head. You don't know? But if we may believe
sundry story-tellers there have been idylls of the slums. And
I am not altogether incredulous as to the bare possibility.
A drawing-room idyll is more difficult to manage, a drawing-room
being a more ~~artificial locality~~ than a slum, though I daresay
less tempestuous. ~~A certain mental serenity is one of the~~
~~necessary conditions of an idyll.~~ A certain primitive fineness,
too, ~~rather unlike our modern notion of refinement which so often~~
~~is but the grossest materialism turned inside out~~ The trouble
was that I could not imagine anything about Flora de Barral
and the brother of Mrs. Fyne. Or if you like I could imagine

John O'Hara

There is quite a difference between O'Hara's copy and Conrad's, and the difference is far more than visual. O'Hara has rightfully been called a master of dialogue, and most of his manuscript pages are devoted to talk and quotation marks. In this particular sample from his best-selling novel *Butterfield 8,* the author has used his pencil only five times; and the corrections are minor indeed. However, do not be misled by this. Like any other topflight professional, John O'Hara reads his draft copy with a keen eye and a capable pencil. That is one reason why his stories and novels are popular classics of our time.

this minute in that beautiful big chariot. I'd rather know a girl that
yells out of a taxi, 'Spit in their eye,' and than two polite people
that can't wait to be alone before they're at each other's throats."

"Well, that's the difference between you and me.
I'd rather live ~~up here~~ in this part of town, where the people at
least---"

"I didn't say anything about living with them, or
having them for neighbors. All I said was I'drather know that kind
of girl---that girl---than those people. That's all I said."

"Still stick to my statement. I'd rather know the
man and his wife. As a matter of fact I happen to know who they are."

"And I don't really give a damn who they are, but
I do give a damn who the girl is."

"A girl who would wear a mink coat on a day like
this. She'scheap."

"Well, with a mink coat she must have come high at
some time."

He was silent a few seconds before ~~answering~~. "You
know what I'm thinking don't you? No, you don't. But I'd like to say
it if you'd promise not to get sore? . . . I was just thinking what a
powerful sexual attraction there is between us, otherwise why do we go
on seeing each other when we quarrel so much?"

"We only quarrel, if you'll look back on it, we only
quarrel for one reason, really, and that's the way you talk to me."

He said nothing, and they walked on in silence for
~~many~~ blocks.

William Faulkner

Faulkner's work is remarkable for its visual aspects. From the beginning of his career to the end, he wrote with pen and ink in a singularly neat hand, leaving to his editors and publishers the problem of converting the handwriting into typescript for the printer. In these two sample pages, you will see that his corrections are as carefully inscribed as the original prose. The author's title, written at the top of page one, was "Never Done No Weeping When She Wanted to Laugh." Even though he changed *She* to *You,* no improvement resulted; and it's no wonder that the story was finally titled, "That Evening Sun." This phrase, of course, comes from the famous *St. Louis Blues,* and is part of the line: "I hate to see that evenin' sun go down."

That was how she lost her teeth, and all that night in the jail house she sang and yelled, until just before day she tried to hang herself. She didn't have on but her garment when they arrested her, and so [...] they heard a jerking and scraping noise on the wall and went up there and found Nancy stark naked, hanging from the jailed window. She had herself [tied?] all night, but she hadn't had her [...] and so she couldn't make her hands let go. That was how they [found?] it was cocaine and not whiskey, like [...] thought.

That was how she lost her teeth, and all that night the ones that passed the jail house could hear her singing and yelling behind the barred window, and a lot of them stopped and stood along the fence, listen to her and to the jailer hollering at her to shut up. But she didn't shut up until just before daylight, when the jailer began to hear a kind of thumping and scraping upstairs and so went and found Nancy hanging from the window bars. She hung herself with her dress. She had [tied?] herself all right, but when they arrested her she hadn't had on [...] but the dress so she now had only to tie her hands with. On maybe she [tried?] to. But anyway she couldn't make her hands let go. So the jailer heard the jerking and scraping and he came up and found Nancy hanging there, stark naked, with the place where she had got fat swelling out and [...] a little on the [...] swelling like a [...] colored balloon does.

One day her apron was swelled out over it. Jesus said,

"Look how fat Nancy is." and ~~Caddy said~~ ~~Caddy said.~~ Jesus said.

~~Nancy's not fat You're got too~~   dress

"Nancy got something hid under her apron." It was silk behind the stove.   dress

"You have?" Caddy said. "What you got under your apron, Nancy?"

"What you want to tell these children things like that for?" Nancy said.

"What you got under your apron dress, Nancy?" Caddy said.

"It's a watermelon." Jesus said.

"It never come off of your vine." Nancy said.

~~"That's what I knows." Jesus said.~~

"I can cut the one down it did come off of." Jesus said.

"Yes, you can." Nancy said.

hully named will childel.

[...] how they found not if [...] came and not where, [...] the jailer said that no [...] could commit suicide unless [...] fully cocaine, because a [...] fully cocaine was no less a

F. Scott Fitzgerald

When he wanted to be, Scott Fitzgerald was a careful editor and reviser, as evidenced by this page from one of his short stories, "Crazy Sunday." His changes here are well worth studying: you will observe how a celebrated writer goes about improving and refining what is already first-rate prose. Line six offers an interesting revision. In the draft, Fitzgerald had Stella "absorbed in her story . . ." He changed this to "emptying out her story" – a vast improvement. Elsewhere on this page you will see other intriguing revisions, all of them aimed at getting the most out of every sentence the author had created.

Still quivering with the shock of her discovery, ~~she~~ *Stella*
found ~~the~~ unbearable the spectacle of a new girl hovering over **482**
Miles so she led Joel into a bedroom, and seated at either end of
a big bed they went on talking. *emptying out*

People on their way to the washroom glanced in and made
wisecracks, but Stella ~~absorbed in~~ her story paid no attention. *After
a while* ~~Finally~~ Miles stuck his head in the door and said ~~forcefully~~, "There's
no use trying to explain something in half an hour (to Joel) *w*that I
don't understand myself and the psychoanalyst says will take a whole
year to understand."

She talked on as if ~~he~~ *Miles* were not there.   She loved Miles,
she said -- under considerable difficulties she had always been
faithful to him.

"The psychoanalyst told Miles that he had a mother complex.   In his first marriage he transferred his mother complex to
his wife, you see -- and then his emotions turned to me.   But when
we married the thing repeated itself -- he transferred his mother
complex to me and all his romantic side turned toward this other
woman."

Joel knew that this probably wasn't gibberish and yet
it ~~didn't~~ *ed like gibberish.* sound ~~right~~.   He ~~had met~~ *knew* Eva Goebel; she was a motherly
person, older and probably wiser than Stella who was a golden child.

Miles now suggested impatiently that Joel come back with
them ~~for dinner if~~ *since* Stella had so much to say ~~to him~~, so they drove
out to the mansion in Beverly Hills.   Under the high ceilings the
situation ~~appeared~~ *seemed* more dignified, *and* *tragic* ~~even took on a certain air of~~ *The* ~~It was an~~
~~tragedy.~~ *remembered* ~~He long afterwards that~~ eerie bright night with the
dark very clear outside of all the windows and Stella all rose-
gold raging and crying around the room. *Joel* ~~He~~ did not quite believe

No author could be a more careful or effective editor than Marquand in this page from his classic novel *H. M. Pulham, Esq.* Almost every line of the manuscript sample deserves scrutiny and evaluation, since the changes are not only numerous but most significant. The first thing to note is that the author, as he went over his copy, changed a major character's name from *Dee* to *Jo-Jo*. But much more interesting are the changes by which John Marquand consistently sharpened and polished his already well-chosen words. The moral for the beginning writer is clear: revision – and more revision – is generally the secret to professional prose.

(I have wondered sometimes why *it was,* ~~everybody didn't like him, because, as a mat-~~ ~~ter of fact, a good many of us didn't, and)~~ as time went on, *this* there seemed to be quite

a clique that didn't like him, ~~perhaps because he was so sure about everything and~~ ~~perhaps because his type was not as fashionable as it used to be, (or because we were~~ ~~all getting older.)~~ It certainly is a fact that when *Jo-Jo* ~~Dee~~ used to come around five or

six of us would always get into a corner and say things about him, ~~probably out of~~ ~~sheer envy and out of the definite knowledge that we were not effectual.~~ Bill King,

for instance, always used to say that *Jo-Jo* ~~Dee~~ Brown was a bastard, a big bastard, ~~and~~ there was something ~~descriptive in the expression as he used it,~~ (for you could tell ~~exactly what he meant.~~ *Perhaps* ~~I think~~ he meant that *Jo-Jo* ~~Dee~~ was not kindly and that he *Sometimes* ~~was al-~~ *threw* ~~ways throwing~~ his weight around.

"Some day," Bill said, "someone is going to stop that bastard." But then

Bill never did like *Jo-Jo* ~~Dee~~ *and* ~~and Bill was clever enough so that~~ *Jo-Jo* ~~Dee~~ never liked him either.

I remember *when* ~~how~~ Bill *discussed* ~~looked at~~ him once, *not so long ago.* It was at a big dinner party that

Joe Eustis gave where everybody got swept together from odd corners and all the men

were in the library *and didn't seem anxious to S/2 T* ~~trying to put off the minute when we should~~ *they* join the ladies. It

was in the autumn and *Jo-Jo* ~~Dee~~ was telling what was the matter with the ~~Harvard~~ football

team and what was going to happen to Electric Bond & Share, so you can guess the date,

and I was sitting next to Bill, listening to *Jojo's* ~~Dee's~~ voice.

"My God," said Bill, "I don't see how you stand him."

"*Jo-Jo* ~~Dee~~ is all right," I said.

"Well," Bill said, "it's my personal opinion he's a bastard."

Revising on the typewriter

On the preceding pages are facsimiles of manuscript as edited with pen or pencil by five celebrated authors. Now I should like to present a remarkable example of editing on the typewriter, done by Bruce Catton while he was writing Volume III of his distinguished Centennial History of the Civil War.

In Chapter Two of *Never Call Retreat,* Catton reached the point where he wanted to describe the results of Lincoln's Emancipation Proclamation. As it happens, the author is known for the care and precision with which he prepares his manuscripts. He is also known for the painstaking lengths to which he will go to achieve the exact effect he desires. But in so doing, he does not depend on pen or pencil; on the contrary, Bruce Catton does most of his revising on the typewriter, despite the fact that to many writers this method seemingly involves too much extra effort and diligence. Nevertheless, it is the method which Catton uses consistently and which has proved –for him– to be the most effective and the most rewarding.

The sample script pages of *Never Call Retreat* are reproduced here just as they came from the Catton typewriter. They deserve the most thoughtful study by anyone interested in improving the quality of his writing. Beyond dispute, they reveal the importance of revising to an author who is not satisfied with his copy until "it says exactly what I want to say in exactly the way I want to say it."

You will note that the first three pages of manuscript are folioed "132" and then, in pencil, are marked "1," "2," and "3." The remainder of the pages are not folioed but are again numbered "1," "2," and "3" so that the author could keep track of revisions in the pile of manuscript constantly growing on his desk. By reading each page through and then comparing it to the draft immediately following, you may appreciate the techniques used by Catton to create his superb prose.

Catton begins this segment of his book by–simply beginning. Using his own working methods, he starts the paragraph, knowing quite well that once under way, he will keep going. After typing twelve lines he decides to revise, and this occurs where the phrase "take place" appears. Note how he paused, thought about his wording, then changed "took place in" to "took place with." Then he veers off again, this time starting the thought all over again with "suddenly it was something people were living with . . ."

/

The trouble was that emancipation came in with such a surprising rush. The
Proclamation had been an approach to the problem rather than a solution, and it had
been written by a man who supposed that once the government's intent had been stated
there would be time to make the delicate adjustments that were necessary. What was
happening in Missouri was a case in point; spurred by the President's warning, the
 people of this slave state were trying to work out xxxxxx some arrangement that
would provide a slow transition, and the President was willing to allow a good deal
of margin for trial-and-error expedients in the hope that other slave states would
fall in line. But events were moving too fast. Emancipation was an accomplished
fact long before andone had done any planning, and the innumerable problems that
it brought were ////   and the greatest single change that ever took place in
the United States came in

                    took place with

                    suddenly it was something people were living with, even though no
one had had time to

Most writers would be content to carry on from the point reached by Catton on the previous page. But he was dissatisfied, as is clearly apparent in version 2 of page 132. He commences again with "The trouble was"—but here he talks first about "events" rather than "emancipation." If you read this page of copy slowly, comparing it with the first version, you will detect the way in which Catton's thoughts precede his placement of words on paper. Always he's seeking a better way to express what is in his mind.

2

The trouble was that events were moving too fast. The Emancipation Proclamation had been nothing more than a statement of intent, written by a man who
supposed that there would be time to make the necessary adjustments. What was happening in Missouri was a case in point: the people of this slave state were trying
to work out a slow transition, and the President was willing to allow a margin for
trial-and-error expedients in the hope that other slave states would fall in line.
But emancipation came with a rush and there was x no time to adjust anything. The
greatest single change that ever took place in American life arrived with no advance planning at all. Men found that they were living with it while they were
still wondering whether it ought to happen at all.

In his notable speech Congressman Vallandigham had warned that nothing of
occur.
the kind could possibly happenxxhexdaxex The institution had too many roots and
the roots went too deep. Sudden change was out of the question.

"You cannot abolish slavery by the sword", he declared, "still less by
proclamations, though the President were to 'proclaim' every month. . . Neither,
sir, can you abolish slavery by argument. As well attempt to abolish marriage or
the relation of paternity."

This was a perfectly logical statement, robbed of its logic only by the
dismaying   xhatxVallandighamxcalledximpossiblexwasxactuallyxbeingxdonex
astoundixg fact that slaveryxwasxbeingxabolishedxbyxthexswordxandxbyxproclamationx
the impossible was actually being done.
Slavery was being abolished by the sword, and by proclamation; perhaps because
by sudden fire and by uprising of the spirit,
there was no other way to do it, or perhaps because in time of war incomprehensible

things do happen.

It's hard to believe, but here is a *third* version of the Catton type-script in which the author stays with the opening sentence of version 2 but decides that another run-through on his typewriter will produce a still better page of copy. At the bottom of the page he has begun to elaborate on the lines contained in the previous ver-sion. Note that in the first paragraph, Catton has crossed out a sentence with his pencil instead of the "x" on his typewriter.

3

The trouble was that events were moving too fast. The Emancipation Pro-clamation had been nothing more than a statement of intent, written by a man who supposed that there would be time to make the necessary adjustments. What was happening in Missouri was a case in point: the people of this slave state were trying to work out a slow transition, and the President was willing to allow a mar-gin for trial-and-error expedien**ts** in the hope that other slave states would fall in line. But emancipation came with such a rush that there was no time to adjust anything. ~~The greatest single change that ever took place in American life arrived without benefit of advance planning.~~ Men found that they were living with it while they were still wondering whether it ought to happen at all.

In his notable speech Congressman Vallandigham warned that nothing of the kind could possibly occur. The institution had too many roots, and the roots went down too far in too many hearts. Sudden change was out of the question.

"You cannot abolish slavery by the sword; still less by proclamations, though the President were to 'proclaim' every month," he cried. "Neither, sir, can you abolisy slavery by argument. As well attempt to abolish marriage or the relation of paternity."

This was a perfectly logical statement, robbed of its logic by the dis-maying fact that ~~the~~ what Vallandigham considered impossible was actually being done. Slavery _was_ being abol-ished by the sword and by proclamation, by fire and by sudden uprising of the spir-it; perhaps because there was no other way to do it, perhaps because in time of war incomprehensible things do happen. And so the greatest single change that ever took place in American life arrived without the benefit of advance planning.

After typing the three script versions presented here, Catton went another step before the printed page took shape. Here is the ultimate version, just as it appears in *Never Call Retreat*. By comparing the printed page with version 3 of the typescript, you will find that in lines 3, 4, 21, and 22 of the copy, Catton continued to revise until he felt that the book passage represented the final distillation of his thoughts.

The trouble was that events were moving too fast. The Emancipation Proclamation had been nothing more than a statement of intent, written by a man who supposed that there would be time to make all necessary adjustments. What was happening in Missouri was a case in point: the people of this state were trying to work out a slow transition, and the President was willing to allow a margin for trial-and-error expedients in the hope that other slave states would fall in line. But emancipation came with such a rush that there was no time to adjust anything. Men found that they were living with it while they still wondered whether it ought to happen at all.

In his notable speech Congressman Vallandigham warned that nothing of the kind could possibly occur. The institution had too many roots and the roots went down too far in too many hearts. Sudden change was out of the question.

"You cannot abolish slavery by the sword; still less by proclamations, though the President were to 'proclaim' every month," he cried. "Neither, sir, can you abolish slavery by argument. As well attempt to abolish marriage, or the relation of paternity."[1]

This was a perfectly logical argument, robbed of its meaning by the fact that what Vallandigham considered impossible was actually being done. Slavery *was* being abolished by the sword and by proclamation, by fire and by sudden uprising of the spirit; perhaps because there was no other earthly way to do it. The greatest single change in American life arrived without the benefit of any advance planning.

To begin with, the proclamation was taken with deadly seriousness by the people most concerned, the Negroes themselves. To others it might be no more than a piece of paper that would mean much or nothing depending on how the war went; to the Negroes it was the parting of the Red Sea. It meant freedom now and everywhere, as fast as the word could travel, and the Negroes acted on this belief. Even though it had always been buttressed by unlimited force, slavery in America really existed by the consent of the governed. This consent, to be sure, came largely because the governed were utterly helpless, but it was a basic element in the

This is a particularly interesting and significant page of Catton typescript. He begins with a specific thought – actually, a sentence of ten words. Then he drops the thought, hits the spacer a couple of times, starts afresh with "The chaplain of an Ohio regiment . . ." Following this incomplete paragraph, the author makes several random efforts at revising, then returns to the Ohio chaplain and sticks with him to the bottom of the page.

All of it was unlooked for and everyone was unprepared

The chaplain of an Ohio regiment in Grant's army said that the flood of
fugitive Negroes "was like the oncoming of cities", unplanned and ~~xxx~~ uncontrolled;
some of the slaves had abandoned their plantations, others had been themselves abandoned by owners who fled ~~Xxxtkxxxkxx~~ when the Federal soldiers approached, and these
people

There was no way to keep it from happening. The chaplain

Any

There was no way to keep it from happening ~~xxyxmxxxxxtkxx~~ because

The chaplain of an Ohio regiment in Grant's army said that the flood of
fugitive Negroes "was like the oncoming of cities." The army could not keep it
from happening because ~~ixxxxx~~ the movement was beyond possibility of co
                                        uncontrollable; as the chaplain

said

                    the slaves were moved by a force greater than themselves,
greater than any

The chaplain of an Ohio regiment in Grant's army said that the flood of
fugitive Negroes "was like the oncoming of cities". The slaves were responding to
an impulse no one could control: "a blind terror stung them and an equally blind
hope allured them, and to us they came"; and the soldiers took care of them -- after
an exremely sketchy fashion -- simply because the army would be swamped if they did
not. Some of the slaves had fled from their plantations and others had been aban-

On this second page of revising on the typewriter, Catton goes
back to the mid-section of page 1 and picks up the thought, "There
was no way . . ." But now he writes a short sentence and puts a
period at the end. He goes along for five lines, then halts and commences once more. Now the paragraph begins to take firmer shape;
the author seems to be hitting his stride; the copy moves ahead
with pace and clarity.

There was no way out of it. The chaplain of an Ohio regiment in Grant's

army wrote that the flood of fugitive Negroes "was like the oncoming of cities."

were adrift because the
Some of the slaves had fled from their masters and some had been abandoned by their
masters themselves had fled when the armies drew near.
masters, who left the neighborhood as soon as the Federal soldiers arrived, and none

of

There was no way out of it. The chaplain of an Ohio regiment in Grant's

army wrote that the flood of fugitive Negroes "was like the oncoming of cities"x.

xxxxturxlxfxnexxhxyxndxxnyxnxkxxxxnxxlx Some of the slaves had fled from their

masters and some were adrift because the masters themselves had fled when the Fed-

all of them were
eral soldiers drew near, and xhxyxxmmxxxxxxhxxFxdxrxlxxxmpxxblindlyxx helplessxyxx

inxblindxterrxr xpxxplxxlxxtxinxxxwxxkxmxxxxxxixxixnd

rootless and homeless waifs cast xdxiftxby loose in a baff-

ling world where the only certainties they had ever had were gone forever. They

came to the army camps because they were totally helpless, xixxxxx self-reliance and

initiative being traits which had never developed under slavery; Thxx they came to

the army camps because they could think of no other place to go and knew only that

they had to be on their way somewhere, and as the chaplain said "a blind terror

stung them andan equally blind hope allured them, and to us they came.

For the fifth time, Catton starts anew with the words, "There was." But note that in this version he adds a fresh second sentence: "The soldiers in the field had to do the job . . ." Also note the other variations between the third page of script and the two which preceded it. Always the author is striving for a still better, a still more forceful way of presenting the march of history to his reader.

There was no way out of it. The soldiers in the field had to do the job, simply because they themselves stood in the path of destiny. The chaplain of an Ohio regiment in Grant's army wrote that the in-gathering of fugitive Negroes xxx "was like the oncoming of cities." Some of the slaves had fled from their masters and some were ᵻ adrift because the masters themselves had fled when the Federal soldiers drew near, and all of them were rootless, homeless waifs cast loose in a baffling world where the only certainties they had ever known were gone forever. They came to the army camps because they were totally helpless, self-reliance and initiative being traits which had gone undeveloped under slavery; they came because

they could think of no other place to go and knew only that they had to be on their way somewhere, and as the chaplain said "a blind terror stung them and an equally blind hope allured them, and to us they came."

Another printed page from *Never Call Retreat*. As with the previous example, this one shows (above the shaded portion) the final, final revisions which Catton made before the galley proofs went back to the printer. The revisions are striking indeed, as witness the first change in sentence two: "they themselves stood where the Red Sea waves had parted." What better proof that the professional writer is never satisfied until he has done what, in his own mind, seems to be the very best!

CHAPTER TWO: *Parting of the Red Sea Waves*

There was no way out of it. The soldiers in the field had to do the job simply because they themselves stood where the Red Sea waves had parted. The chaplain of an Ohio regiment in Grant's army wrote that the in-gathering of fugitive Negroes was "like the oncoming of cities." Some of the slaves had fled from their masters and some were adrift because the masters themselves had fled, and all of them were waifs in a baffling world where the only certainties they had ever known were gone forever. They came to the army camps because for the moment they were totally helpless, self-reliance and initiative being traits which had gone undeveloped under slavery. They came because they could think of no other place to go and knew only that they had to be on their way somewhere; as the chaplain said, "a blind terror stung them and an equally blind hope allured them, and to us they came."[5] The army had to take some sort of care of them because otherwise the army itself would be swamped.

So the army set up concentration camps, whenever and wherever they seemed to be needed; near enough to be under army protection, remote enough to be out of the army's way. For shelter there were condemned army tents, or makeshift cabins improvised out of stray bits of lumber. Army rations were issued, supplemented by foodstuffs gathered in the neighborhood and later by produce from little vegetable plots cultivated by the Negroes themselves. Sometimes army blankets and clothing could be had; more often, as the business got organized, such things were sent to the camps by charitably minded folk in the North. There were armed guards, to keep order, and at least in theory medical care was available. This was nearly always inadequate, sanitary arrangements barely existed, and a representative of the Western Sanitary Commission, after inspecting a chain of these camps in the Mississippi Valley, wrote that many of the inmates were a good deal worse off than they had been under slavery.

The death rate, naturally, was appalling. By the middle of the summer a camp near Natchez, Mississippi, was having from fifty to seventy-five deaths every day—rather more than half the number recorded at notorious Andersonville Prison in its worst days, al-

Gordon Carroll

Some further examples of how an editorial pencil can help bring an author's work into focus

Exercises in editing

When an editor gets around to spreading a manuscript on his desk and reaching for his pencil, he's arrived at the point where he must either prove his capabilities or betray the author. His first task, however, is not to fret about grammar, spelling, punctuation, and the like: this can wait upon the copy editor, whose job it is to take care of such items. Although the manuscript is ostensibly the work of a professional writer, it has been bought and paid for, thus endowing the editor with certain privileges. His task now is to shape these pages into the format which his readers, out of habit or preference, expect to find within the covers of a publication or a book.

As you might expect, the better the editor, the better the format. But there can be, quite plainly, no mathematical rules for him to follow, no magic template to place over the manuscript so that the eye tells the hand what to do. No two manuscripts can ever be identical; and even the similarities which often exist must be treated on the basis of *this* manuscript, not the manuscript that went before or the one inevitably coming after. Each sentence, paragraph, and page is part of a whole manuscript, and during the time the editor works with this piece it is the whole he must concentrate on, so that the finished product is not marred by the whims of a careless or capricious pencil.

Whether the manuscript is fiction or non-fiction, the editor has various techniques for getting the job done. But he is aware that his activities are more limited in the short story or novel than in the magazine article or non-fiction book. The reason is as simple as it is sound.

The fictioneer writes out of creative imagination; what he puts on paper is distinctly his own in style, theme, pace, and scope; the manuscript is so individualized, so deeply personal, that the editor is precluded from indulging in mayhem. Although he may use his pencil to good advantage, his task in fiction is chiefly to make changes which he feels, from an objective view-point, enhance the story's readability.

Non-fiction is something else again. Mostly it is writing predicated in advance; it comes out of practical planning and negotiation between editor and author; it lends itself to sharp editing, not only on the score of length and pace but also on that of readership. It might even be said that non-fiction is a "commercial" product, and as such can be shaped to fit a competitive market where content dictates readability – or, if you prefer, salability.

So far I have been talking about a kind of editing in which the editor bears down on the components of a manuscript in order to improve the whole before it goes to the printer. But there's another kind of editing that has grown in importance during the past few decades – the craft of condensing already published articles, stories, books, and novels into the page space allocated to the editor or dictated by such practical factors as mechanical format and production costs. Pioneered chiefly by the *Reader's Digest,* this business of compressing wordage has spread widely in the editorial world, resulting in a welter of pocket-size magazines, magazine supplements, and multi-volume books.

Criticism has been leveled at condensation on the grounds that it dilutes the flavor of the original work, or wreaks injustice upon the author's style, or encourages "capsule culture," or does any of many other injuries to contemporary literature. I find it hard to agree with these strictures. While occasionally some damage may be inflicted upon belles lettres, it is more than balanced by the vast public benefits derived from increased reading at every level of American society. The craft of condensation has helped to bring about this increased reading among a people who, rightly or wrongly, for too long excused their ignorance of many subjects with the excuse that they were "too busy to read."

Brevity – another word for condensation – has so undermined this excuse that millions of people are now exposed to thoughts and ideas once regarded as the vested interest of the scholar and the intellectual. In short, condensation has made a contribution to the democratic procedure – a curious yet demonstrable fact for which we should all be thankful.

In this chapter, I shall present facsimiles of work as it comes from the editor's desk. The variety of examples is wide. Some are quite elemental; some are fairly complicated; still others carry the editor's pencil over an alarming series of bumps and digressions. But behind most editing lies a simple purpose: to refine and bolster an author's work in light of the audience for which it was written.

The editor knows his reading audience better than the writer can know it, and it is here that he can make a major contribution to a mutual effort. Upon his mind and his pencil may well hang the difference between a publishable piece of work and an abortive effort that, despite the author's best intentions, inexorably finds the wastebasket.

A newspaper story

News copy is usually susceptible to editing. This is not to detract from the reporter's or the rewrite man's ability; it is merely to say that the editor knows what he wants for the next edition and knows best how to secure this with his pencil.

The second ~~but by no means the last~~ snowfall of the winter ~~season,~~

~~which doesn't officially begin for a week,~~ struck the Bridgetown area last

night ~~and left a white fluffy layer, six inches thick, which~~ *Leaving a six-inch layer, it* turned high-

ways and local roads into ~~clogged,~~ bumper-to-bumper traffic jams and hos-

pitalized ~~twenty-two~~ *22* pe,sons, though none *of whom,* ~~was~~ seriously hurt. Snow ~~clear-~~ *Clear*

~~ing~~ *weather* is expected ~~to follow~~ *after* an additional inch or two of snow this morning,

to be followed by subfreezing temperatures and high winds ~~out of~~ *from* the north

and northeast.

State police at Northport ~~said that~~ *reported* several accidents ~~occurring~~ on

the Salem Parkway and the State Turnpike, ~~one at Morgantown Avenue, Bridge-~~

~~town were the result of the snow blanket but that no one was badly injured.~~

The most serious ~~of a number of~~ pedestrian accidents ~~reported by~~ *in* North-

port ~~police~~ occurred on Howard Street near Willowbrook Cemetery, when ~~a~~ *an*

~~driver applied brakes on the icy pavement and the~~ automobile hit a hydrant

~~and a fence.~~ The driver was taken to Mercy Hospital with a broken nose

Much of the copy produced in newspaper offices shows a careless hand,
chiefly because the writer is working under the pressure of deadlines.
But there is another reason: behind each writer is the support of the
copy desk, where skilled editors do the kind of revising shown here.

and a possibly fractured left wrist. His car was thoroughly wrecked.

Public Works Department workers sanded all hills by nightfall, but *while*

the depth of the snow required all the city's snow removal equipment un-

til after midnight. Some 85 men from the department cleared and removed

650 loads of snow which was dumped into Long Island Sound at various

points. *& Although,*

The Weather Bureau pointed out that winter doesn't bow officially

until 3:40 A.M. next Sunday. There hasn't been a day since December 5th

in which the temperature has risen above freezing. Average temperatures

since that time have been 8 to 10 degrees below normal for so early in

the season. One year ago the Bridgetown area had a prolonged warm spell

during

in which two days

more to come

Right up to the end of this fragmented page, a pencil is needed to remove extraneous thoughts, excess wordage and repetitive phrases that
add nothing to the reader's enjoyment of a purely local story.

A publicity release

When my company decided to expand its art and writing schools in Westport by adding a course in photography, ten eminent men were chosen for the Guiding Faculty of the Famous Photographers School. For publicity and other purposes, biographies of the ten were needed. When the manuscripts came to my desk, some surgery was indicated.

Out of the ten biographies, I have selected several pages from the story of Richard Avedon to illustrate what a pencil can do in achieving clarity, smoothness, and accuracy *after* a piece of "finished" copy has been submitted. At three points in the margin, I have filed queries for the author, all in the interests of accuracy.

RICHARD AVEDON

[handwritten: in Manhattan]

[handwritten: the often]
At age ~~10~~, Richard Avedon photographed his first ~~picture of a cele-~~
brity, Sergei Rachmaninoff, a neighbor of the Family. *[handwritten: -- who happened to be]* "I used to hide

among the ~~garbage~~ *[handwritten: trash]* cans on his back stairs," he recalls, "and stayed there

hour after hour listening to him practice." Finally, he got up the nerve *[handwritten: enough]*

to ring his door bell and ask permission to take a picture. He used a *[handwritten: "Young Richard" simple]*

box camera his father had ~~recently~~ given him. A decade later, he was a

professional photographer on the staff of Harper's Bazaar and going places

at a phenomenal rate. *[handwritten: Today,]*

~~Still fond of using a small camera, the Rolleiflex,~~ he is now "the

wonder boy" of fashion photography, widely acclaimed for ~~his~~ introducing

~~of~~ a revolutionary concept in his field -- namely, that models need not be

mummies and manikins, but can be photographed as human beings, albeit high-

ly romanticized.

Born ~~May 15,~~ *[handwritten: in]* 1923 in Manhattan of well-to-do parents, young Avedon

The editing on this page is self-explanatory. Mostly it is done for the
sake of "smoothness"—a hard-to-define word which covers a great
multitude of writing sins.

attended Public School No. 6 and De Witt Clinton High School. Later,

he took extension courses in literature at Columbia.

In his boyhood and early youth, Avedon aspired successively to be

a politician, a dancer and a poet. The first, at age 9, was nipped in

the bud when, armed with a letter from Mayor LaGuardia, he was about to

leave for Washington and a visit to the Senate when he was suddenly

stricken with hives (caused by stage fright, he says) from which and

politics he soon recovered simultaneously.

He tried emulating Fred Astaire for a while, but with little suc-

cess. He then turned to poetry, becoming poet laureate of the New York

City high schools in 1941 after winning an inter-high school competition

between 31 schools. Some of his poems actually got into print, in the

Journal-American and in H. I. Philipps' column in the New York Sun. The

25 cents a line received for his literary efforts supplemented a regular

weekly income he was getting on his job, as errand boy for a small photo-

graphic concern.

Most of this page can be removed: it's full of words, but the words
are unimportant. Avedon's youthful interest in politics, dancing and
poetry is of no consequence to anybody.

no ¶

a photographic
The first stirrings of ~~the future Avedon~~ career ~~as a photographer~~

Dick leafed through
came while ~~the youth idly perused the~~ fashion magazines -- Harper's

Bazaar, ~~which he particularly liked,~~ Vogue, ~~and~~ Vanity Fair -- in his

what did he do?
(father's office.) He ~~came to~~ admire*d* the work of such fashion and theatri-

ers
cal photograph~~y favorites~~ as Cecil Beaton, Edward Steichen, Martin Munkacsi

went to
and Anton Bruehl, ~~B~~ut that was as far as his ambitions ~~ran in that direc-~~

~~tion at the time.~~ ¶ When World War II came along,

since
~~In 1942,~~ Avedon joined the Merchant Marines. ~~H~~is father had given   *Why did he join?*

him a Rolleiflex as a going-away present, ~~thus, perhaps unwittingly, de-~~

~~ciding his son's fate, for it was the possession of a camera that suggested~~

ied   *what was this?*
he appl~~y~~ for a job in the photographic branch.

The service gave him a technical training in photography and ~~assigned~~

~~him to a group in Sheepshead Bay, where he covered shipwrecks and did identi-~~

snapshots
~~fication snapshots of Marine personnel.~~ In his spare time he took ~~pictures~~

of his fellow merchant mariners ⊙
~~to please himself.~~ One of these was a portrait of two brothers, once focused

Three queries are filed in the margins of this page. These will have to
be answered — and for informational reasons — when the copy is returned
to the original author, who should have been specific in the first place.

sharply in the foreground, the other ~~in the background,~~ out of focus.
[handwritten: out of focus]

Although ~~he did not~~ suspect it at the time, this picture presaged his
[handwritten: Avedon didn't]

coming fame ____ as the man who made the blur acceptable as a photo-

graphic technique.

By the time he was discharged from the Merchant Marines in 1944,

Avedon had ~~definitely~~ made up his mind to become a photographer, speci-

fically a fashion photographer. ~~Having picked his goal in photography, he~~
[handwritten: But first, he needed]

~~wanted to begin right away, if only to accumulate quickly~~ a sample port-

folio. With characteristic ~~enthusiasm and~~ self-confidence, the sailor-

turned-civilian, still in uniform, ~~ran excitedly~~ to Bonwit Teller's on
[handwritten: went]

Fifth Avenue. ~~He~~ asked ~~to~~ photograph some ~~of their~~ dresses, ~~offering to~~
[handwritten: and, if he could]

~~do the job~~ free of charge.

~~Overwhelmed~~ by his eagerness, ~~and push,~~ the store ~~lent him some~~
[handwritten: Impressed] [handwritten: agreed & Dick]

~~dresses, he~~ hired an expensive model, and soon returned with pictures that

the management thought ~~were~~ good enough to hang in their store elevators.

~~About~~ a year later, armed with these ~~and other~~ pictures and ~~including~~ the
[handwritten: a portfolio that included]

The working editor is constantly amazed at the number of words,
phrases and sentences that can be revised or removed from a manuscript without wreaking the slightest injury on the first (or second or
third) draft.

A brochure chapter

Editors are often cozened by friends into giving a helping hand on copy. The sample here was brought to me by a young writer who had been asked to prepare an industrial brochure – and had agreed eagerly, since he needed the money. The writer asked me to "smooth out" the copy, and this is what I did on the first two pages.

¶1 National Aniline Division's brand-new plant in South Carolina is designed

to produce fine denier nylon in an integrated operation starting with li-

quid monomer supplied in tank-truck quantities from another Allied Chemical

plant. It makrs NAD's first venture into the fine denier field.

¶2 The physical plant structure is designed around chemical and mechani-

cal process equipment supplied by SNIA VISCOSA, an Italian firm headquar-

tered in Milan. Much of the key equipment, therefore, was manufactured

in Europe, and bears unfamiliar names. But all the rest of the plant build-

ings and equipment is unmistakably American in design, appearance, form,

and shape. And so skillfully hidden for functional and aesthetic reasons

are the intricate complexes of pressure vessels and pipe runs that a passer-

by would hardly suspect that the handsome exterior houses such a comprehen-

sive array of chemical equipment. This plant is indeed a far cry from

typical "chemical plants" generally found sprawling near the rear of in-

dustrialized neighborhoods; this one, could proudly take its place at the

par some-where else

to p.2

pleasantly situated on rolling slopes in front of river-edge woods,

As indicated above, the lead for this industrial piece is contained in the top 2 and bottom 3 lines of the page. Lines 3 and 4 belong somewhere else—and were put there before the editing was finished.

→ back to ¶ 2, p. 1

~~front of~~ any modern industrial development.

¶ 3   ¶ Key to the modernistic exterior ~~appearance~~ is a tasteful combination
of geometric shapes and natural colors. ~~pleasantly situated on gently-
rolling slopes in front of river-edge woods~~. South Carolina's famous red-
dish-brown jumbo brick forms the ~~perimeter~~ walls of the single-story plant,
broken by bold vertical stripes of shadow-wall concrete block, painted gleam-
ing white. Roof-line monotony is broken by two ~~prominent~~ penthouses whose
sides of enameled ~~corrugated~~ aluminum match the warmth of the jumbo brick.
And wide ~~welcoming~~ windows of an ell-shaped low-silhouette office wing,
centrally spotted, add further variety to the fifth-of-a-mile-long plant.

¶ The Imagination and ingenuity displayed on the outside are ~~carried out equally well on~~ matched cleverly on
the inside. Production areas, ~~house~~ containing brightly-painted process equipment and
filament machinery; ~~these areas~~ are bounded by ~~perimeter and fire~~ walls of
either jumbo brick or glazed tile, done with a random pattern of contrasting
color. A view of the 100-foot-square ~~A hundred-foot-square~~ courtyard between office wing and plant ~~can be~~ is

The descriptive passages in lines 3 and 4 were placed at the bottom of
page 1, where they belonged. Then we go back to line 5 of page 1,
which stands as paragraph 2.

An academic essay

When a pedagogue sets out to write, the results are often fearsome to behold. He very likely knows his topic, and knows it well, but when he gets to his typewriter his style can become so turgid, so professorial, that even a freshman is repulsed. The pedagogue's defense is that he is writing solely for his colleagues, who understand his lingo. Perhaps so — but why not let an editor put it into more straightforward English so that even laymen might profit from the professor's findings! The excerpt here is taken from a piece on teacher evaluation.

lead is on next page

lead from p. 2

A further difficulty arises out of the fact that ~~the~~ concept of ef-

ficiency is nowhere well defined. Here, as with the definition of teach-

ing ~~there are many different concepts of efficiency.~~ The opinions are

so varied among teacher educators, administrators, and teachers that each

~~person can be said to have~~ a more or less private system of evaluation all

~~of~~ his own. This is not a mere ~~statement of opinion~~ but a matter that has

~~been~~ amply substantiated by research. The amount of divergence ~~that one~~

~~would expect to find~~ in a ~~particular~~ situation ~~would~~ depend, of course,

upon the composition of the group making the evaluation, the extent to

which ~~an attempt has been made to standardize criteria and provide train-~~

~~ing in their use~~ and the particular teacher or aspect of teaching being

evaluated. In uncontrolled situations the judgments of a group of super-

visors, administrators, and teacher educators, all observing the same

teacher at the same time, under identical conditions, may rate a particu-

lar teacher as among the ~~very~~ best ~~that they have observed~~ and others as

This passage is lifted direct from a manuscript of 24 pages, containing
several sections. The lead for this section is on page 2, and if you will
look to the next page, you will see how the proper lead starts in line 1
and then jumps back a whole page.

among the ~~very~~ worst teachers ~~that they have observed.~~ Much that is im-

portant ~~in providing~~ good schools depends upon the accuracy with which

teachers are evaluated. *Unfortunately, however,* → *back to p.1*

[handwritten: lead is here]

¶2 One of the facts brought home ~~time and time again~~ by these investi-

gations, is that researchers ~~in this area employ a very~~ extensive vocabu-

lary in describing teacher effectiveness. Not only is the list ~~of des~~-

criptive terms used to describe teacher effectiveness and its prerequisites

very long, but there is a tendency to use words in a ~~non-technical layman's~~

~~sense~~ rather than in a ~~manner characteristic of~~ scientific ~~study.~~ Even

~~where the~~ investigators define terms, they are likely to define them in a

manner ~~personally~~ prefereable to ~~the investigator rather than in more uni~~-

versally useful ways. This problem is one that has long plagued the

behavioral sciences. There are very few operational definitions.

Even were the vocabulary more adequately defined there is an over-

whelmingly large number of terms employed in discussing the assessment

[handwritten annotations in margins and interlinear: "to maintaining", "use too", "a)", "too", "also", "lay", "sense", "when", "themselves", "The result is a lack of", "¶2", "back to p.1", "lead is here"]

Paragraph 2 of the piece starts here, at line 4. The last 5 lines on the page offer a superb example of words wasted on trivial (and super-fluous) topics.

and prediction of teacher effectiveness. ~~There are too many terms em-~~
ployed to ~~make~~ meaningful communication ~~possible for the many~~ individuals _between_
who ~~need to communicate~~ about ~~teacher effectiveness and make predictions~~ _pass upon_
~~as in~~ the selection, education, and placement of teachers in pre-service
programs ~~of teacher education~~ and in the supervision, administration, and
improvement of ~~the~~ staff in-service. To ~~secure~~ more ~~manageable lists~~ of _insure_ _accuracy in_
descriptive ~~terms, both~~ individual and group ~~attempts~~ have been ~~made~~ to _ions,_ _tried_
combine, condense, and telescope these many terms into shorter lists ~~of~~
~~one sort or another; on the objective side, factory analysis has been~~
~~employed.~~

\####

How easy it is to do away with words – if the editor pits his sense of
objectivity against the writer's sense of subjectivity. It is this latter
sense that, more than anything else, clouds an author's vision when he
looks at his own work.

A magazine article

Chapter 7 of this book consists of an article written for the *Famous Writers Magazine* by Morton Freedgood, who at the time was a member of the school's instructional staff. Later, when he turned his talents to writing copy for our public relations department, I asked him whether we might use the article as an item of supplementary teaching material – use it, that is, in an abbreviated and edited version.

He agreed to the request but, being a modest man, said he was the editorial pencil in his stead? I had no choice in the matter – not objective enough to work over his own copy. Would I wield and the visual result appears on the pages immediately following. The author was happy, our students have learned much from his expository prose, and our teaching program has been improved by still another assist from the non-fiction category.

The wide world of non-fiction

For reasons having little to do with ~~anything so disagreeable as~~
reality, the fiction writer currently enjoys more "status" in the eyes
of the public than the non-fiction writer does. ~~Like most questions
involving status, this one is as bright and iridescent as a soap bubble,
and just about as substantial. As writers themselves know, the sole
valid standard for measuring status in the world of writing is quality.
Whether a man writes fiction or non-fiction, only one thing matters --
how well he writes.~~

Bedazzled by the occasional "~~runaway~~ best seller" and ~~the occasional~~
Broadway smash hit, the public tends to regard the novelist and the
playwright as literary Glamor Boys. But this view is a mirage. The best
seller and the smash hit constitute a tiny minority of all the novels that
are published and all the plays ~~that are~~ produced. And even in the case
of these rare birds, glamor is no more than skin deep. Just beneath the
surface are the blood, sweat and tears of hard work and dearly acquired
craftsmanship. So far as writing goes -- any kind of writing -- the glamor
is mostly in the eye of the beholder.

It would be foolish, in defending the status of non-fiction, to do so
at the expense of fiction. Each genre has its place in the scheme of things,
each reinforces the other, both together are vital forms of communication in
a world which may depend for its survival on the ability to communicate.
Whether because of ~~the~~ this myth of glamor or not, fiction is chosen by a
good many beginning writers whose talent might be better suited to non-fiction.

Starting with line 3, I begin to take out sentences which, although they
indicate a casual if lively style, are not necessary to the piece, especially
if the piece must be abbreviated for special use.

Actually, a good argument could be advanced -- if such arguments were
anything but fruitless -- for persuading students and beginners that
opportunities in the non-fiction field were, if anything, greater than
fiction. Certainly this is true in terms of the marketplace. Glamor
or no glamor, many a non-fiction writer, to quote a popular entertainer,
cries all the way to the bank.

At a conservative estimate, the non-fiction writer produces roughly
95 percent of all the words that are printed and read. Does this figure seem outlandish? Let's examine it. We can quickly list the writing the fictionist does: novels, plays, short stories, movies, television shows. Everything else in the expanding universe of writing
falls to the province of the writer of non-fiction. This includes
books and articles on every possible subject in the human spectrum,
ranging from A for Autobiography to Z for Zoology. It also includes
the ingredients of a cough syrup and the instructions for operating an
electric can-opener. It includes the reading matter on a dollar bill
and everything that is printed in a newspaper. It includes the contents of legal documents and circulars and fliers and birth certificates and passports and the Articles of War and the charter of the
Elks. It includes advertisements, publicity, captions, accompanying
photographs, traffic information on road maps and letters from collection agencies. It includes the manual for operating your convertible
top, your air-conditioner, your hair drier and your lawn mower. It
includes mail-order catalogues and theater programs; greeting cards
and subway cards; rubber stamps and postage stamps; speeches, orations

The removal of the top 3 lines merely continues what was started at
the bottom of page 1. Now, at the bottom of this page, more detail
can go out, since it was placed there originally to emphasize a point
that can be covered in considerably fewer words.

~~and eulogies; announcements and pronouncements and political platforms;~~
~~and the copy on a gum wrapper.~~

It includes the news and the weather and the commercials on radio and television; radio and TV documentaries and station breaks and
charity appeals; dictionaries and encyclopedias and how-to books of
every conceivable -- and occasionally inconceivable -- description;
the major portion of all ~~the~~ books written for the burgeoning juvenile
market, which in recent years has favored non-fiction over fiction in
ever-increasing proportion; reminiscences and memoirs and personal histories; chronicles from the Bible to Winston Churchill.

The catalogue could be continued indefinitely. But perhaps it
can be most neatly summed up with this revealing little paradox: barring the fictional examples ~~that~~ are quoted, every word contained in
the two volumes of the Fiction Course of the Famous Writers School is
non-fiction!

A relevant point about each of the varied forms of non-fiction
~~writing~~ cited above is that somebody got paid for writing it. But, important as this is, it's not the only point. The same ~~operative~~ satisfactions that exist for the writer in the "glamor" field of fiction
exist in the not-so-mundane-as-you'd-think field of non-fiction.

Granted, few souls would conclude that they had fulfilled the
American Dream by writing the instructions for assembling a beach
chair, or composing the directions for applying a home permanent but
such huge satisfactions are few in any area of writing. Instead, the

The paragraph of 5 lines, beginning "The catalogue could be continued,"
is not necessary, even though it is an intriguing thought. When condensing a piece, the editor's job is "to get there firstest with the fewest
words."

~~satisfaction is the simple and rewarding one of having written to good~~
~~purpose -- to have communicated and been paid for it. But there are~~
~~additional gratifications.~~ On its upper levels, non-fiction is unqualifiedly creative, and shares with the very best of fiction the permanency of what we call "literature." There are a hundred, or a hundred
hundred, examples that might be adduced of non-fiction books which have
made a seminal contribution to the sum of man's knowledge of himself
and the world he lives in -- great works of science, economics, history,
religion, philosophy.

The argument can be proved -- if it needs proving -- without leav-
ing home. Let's consider the ~~case of one of our own Guiding Faculty,~~ *distinguished historian,*
Bruce Catton. Significantly, Catton started out with the intention of
becoming a novelist. But he was, by his own admission, a poor novelist, and so he turned his creative energies to ~~the writing of~~ non-fiction; specifically, to the Civil War. Working in a field ~~which had~~ already ~~been~~ tilled to near-exhaustion, ~~in which every conceivable facet~~
~~had been turned and re-turned, every fact picked over a thousand times,~~
Catton ~~has~~ produced a series of books ~~which have been~~ hailed all over
the world for having cast new light on their subject.

How did he do it? ~~The answer -- if not the doing -- is simple.~~
He brought to the task the fully dedicated powers of his imagination
and intelligence and perception. In other words, he functioned at the
same white heat of creativity as the good writer of fiction. As the
novelist takes imaginary characters and events, intensifies them, and
brings them to life in a plausible environment, so Catton takes real
people and events out of the past, intensifies them, and makes them

By now, some of my readers may be ready to argue over some of my
editing. However, words *have* to be removed in order to condense a
piece. The question is: which words? My choice is obvious.

live vividly in the present. The point hardly needs making that bringing the dead to life in print, as Catton does, is a fully equivalent
achievement to bringing the nonexistent to life, as the novelist does.

The opportunities to pull off this kind of trick on a grand scale
in magazine non-fiction are limited. ~~But~~, nevertheless, the magazine
writer, too, can experience the high adventure of writing creatively
~~and imaginatively~~. Let's ~~take a~~ look at still another ~~member of the~~ noted writer
~~Guiding Faculty,~~ of non-fiction, J. D. Ratcliff. Ratcliff, who couldn't write fiction if the penalty for failure to do so was burning at the stake,
brings to his non-fiction curiosity, a keen mind, sound editorial
judgment and respect for, but not enslavement to, facts. There's no
question but that he works with as much absorption and devotion on ~~a~~ an
~~brief~~ article for Reader's Digest as a fiction writer does on a short
story. Every one of his articles is massively researched, carefully
thought through, intelligently and creatively attacked. ~~Each is,~~
~~finally, a distillation of fact and balanced opinion that contributes~~
~~its scruple to the weight of man's knowledge.~~

While it's true, as a crude generality, that most writers have
an aptitude
~~a vocation~~ for either fiction or non-fiction (and it's only good sense
to play one's strongest hand), it's equally true that many others work
both sides of the street. Although this jack-of-all trades versatility
is more prevalent in Europe (where the man of letters often does novels,
plays, short stories, literary criticism, political pieces and even

More of what has been going on before. As with Bruce Catton, the
identification of J. D. Ratcliff as a member of the School's Guiding
Faculty was not, to my mind, essential to the article's usefulness or
importance.

journalism), it has begun to flourish in this country as well. Hemingway, whom most people think of exclusively as a novelist and short story writer, is the author of three non-fiction books -- Death in the Afternoon, The Green Hills of Africa and A Moveable Feast; John Steinbeck's most recent best seller, Travels with Charley, was strictly non-fiction; Scott Fitzgerald's famous autobiographical series, "Crack Up," was as widely read as his novels; Saul Bellow, author of the best-selling novel Herzog, frequently writes reviews and criticism; James Michener has published a number of non-fiction books dealing with Oriental art; Mary McCarthy, author of The Group, has published several volumes of non-fiction ranging from literary and theatrical criticism to social commentary. There's no lack of evidence to prove the point -- from Washington Irving and Mark Twain to John Hersey, Herman Wouk and Norman Mailer.

Again, let's refer to the Guiding Faculty of Famous Writers School to illuminate our thesis. For three decades, Faith Baldwin was strictly a fiction writer, and, as such, one of the most widely read of all popular novelists. Then, a half dozen years or so ago, on invitation, she agreed to write accepted the writing of a monthly non-fiction column for Woman's Day. Called "Open Door," the column quickly estab-. lished itself as a prime favorite with the magazine's large audience -- and with Miss Baldwin, herself. She had discovered the wide, wide world of non-fiction and become a convert to its fascinations. Not that she gave up fiction. Instead, she now "mixes 'em up" the way a good baseball pitcher varies the speed of his delivery, writing her

This is a massive cut, yet not truly a debatable one, since the lengthy fill-in on the non-fiction efforts of novelists merely underlines an aspect of the subject that has already been covered in various ways.

non-fiction pieces and continuing to produce stories and novels at the same time.

Miss Baldwin recommends this change of pace highly, but only to those who are suited to it. She's more concerned with those people -- and there's a significant number of them -- who are trying to fit the square peg of a talent for non-fiction into the round hole of fiction.

"Everyone wants to write fiction," she acknowledges, "yet they may be barking up the wrong literary tree. Non-fiction is a tremendous field, and materially, as far as books and magazines are concerned, more rewarding than fiction.... For example, humor is a wide-open field, and both book and magazine publishers are panting for it. Incidentally, everybody now recognizes that humor is not exclusively a man's field. We have a number of women humorists who write books, articles and light verse. The names of Jean Kerr, Phyllis McGinley and Cornelia Otis Skinner spring quickly to mind. And look at other fields, once considered strictly masculine, in which women succeeded -- medicine, physics, engineering, law, the ministry. Why should they not go forward in non-fiction and with enormous success?"

Miss Baldwin continues: "I have found in my particular field of non-fiction more reward, emotionally and spiritually, than I ever knew before. So I hope that other women will bring to this branch of writing their patience, sympathy and comprehension. They make people and places and things come alive for us, make actual struggles real

It's better to quote Faith Baldwin directly than to mix her quotes with explanatory copy. Her words at the bottom of the page are germane — although not vital — to the message of this piece.

~~by understanding both the successes and failures of those about whom~~
~~they write. There is no reason why they shouldn't; they are equipped~~
~~for this kind of writing. More power to them!~~"

¶ Without trying to make invidious comparisons, there's little
question that non-fiction, by its ~~very~~ nature, is a more "outgoing"
form of writing than fiction. From conception to completed work,
the non-fiction article or book contains much of the excitement of
a chase, or a good detective story. The writer tracks down facts
~~wherever they may exist~~ -- in the library, in the museum, in "the
field." In many instances one fact leads to another in a ~~kind of~~
fascinating paper-chase at the end of which is the prize -- perhaps,
if you're lucky, a little gem of information which nobody else has
yet uncovered.

But it isn't all paper work. Much of it involves travel --
not necessarily to far places, but certainly to interesting, off-
the-beaten-track places. And much of it is dealing with people --
interviewing experts, people with unusual personal stories or backgrounds, people with odd occupations, public officials. Then there's
correspondence, not only to gather facts, but with editors and, from
time to time, there will be face-to-face conferences with editors to
discuss one aspect or another of a piece. As a vehicle for getting
to meet people, to learn new things, to enlarge your own preparatory
work -- the research -- for a non-fiction article or book. It comes

At the bottom of the page, the removal of 6 lines brings the reader
quickly and directly to one of the more rewarding thoughts about
writing non-fiction: "It comes as close to being fun," etc.

as close to being ~~sheer~~ fun as anything connected with the serious
business of writing can be.

Writers who inhabit the wide, wide world of non-fiction know all
this, of course, and most of them wouldn't change places with the fiction writer for all the money in the world...well, perhaps for all the
money in the world, but not for a penny less. The non-fiction writer
doesn't pine for the glamor of the fiction writer because he knows it
doesn't exist in any real sense. He knows that all writing, fiction
or non-fiction, is difficult, exasperating, exhausting, terrifying,
discouraging, anguishing, and, ultimately, infinitely rewarding.

So -- if you want to write fiction, fine, go to it. If you feel
you can combine fiction and non-fiction, that's fine, too. But if
your natural inclination is definitely toward non-fiction, don't ~~let
yourself~~ feel for a minute that you're a stepchild. There are no stepchildren in the family of writers, only, as in any family, brothers
and sisters who are slightly and engagingly different from each other.

This last page has been cut more than 50 percent, yet without in-
flicting grave damage on the author's conclusion. The points in paragraph 1 have been clearly made in all the words that have gone before.

A short story

No one needs more help than the aspiring short-story writer. Over the years, hundreds of manuscripts have reached my desk from aspirants of all persuasions, and it is difficult to select any one example as representative of all. The four pages presented here might be called "typical," provided my reader understands that this is the loosest and hence the trickiest of definitions. And also, provided he understands that my pencil was used solely to improve the pace of the story as well as to give it more brevity.

Enough Time Wasted

~~A FAREWELL TO TIGER BABY~~

It was scarcely dawn when I woke. Maybe it had been nightmare or some prairie sound ~~already ended~~ that shut sleep out, but I think mostly it was the sick dread ~~that~~ walking up from my stomach~~, the moment I opened my eyes~~.

Another day, I thought, and after tomorrow there will only be one more and it will all be over. I could feel ~~the cold~~ perspiration ~~coming out~~ on my forehead even though the room was cool. ~~But~~ I can't leave, I told the silence~~, looking around with love.~~ They can't make me go!

~~I threw back the covers and sat up.~~ The clock by my bed said ~~five forty-five, its luminous paint still glowing in the dim room.~~ *A week from now I'll be there~~, I thought~~. I'll wake up in a strange room and ~~I'll~~ be with someone I've hardly met.* In the shadows against the ~~opposite~~ wall I could see the outline of my trunk~~, like a shadow over my life~~.

It was half full now; Mom and I had worked hard ~~on it~~ last night. All the new clothes would finally fill it -- formals, sweaters and skirts, dresses, the three pairs of Bermuda shorts that Mom ~~had~~ insisted were what they wore instead of levis, the bright, costume-like pajamas for "dorm" life. It was a new language, a new world, and I knew I'd never be able to face ~~or understand~~ it.

The first change here is the title, making it more suitable to the story that I had already read through to the end. Then, starting with the second sentence, words and phrases begin to go out, making the manuscript tighter and more coherent. Also, the girl's thoughts in paragraph 2 are italicized, in keeping with accepted editorial style.

Why couldn't my folks understand that I didn't want to go? ~~I asked myself.~~ My home was here on the ~~northern~~ Montana prairies where I ~~had~~ always lived, not in a ~~big~~ city full of strangers. ~~I began dressing, pulling on my worn levis fondly.~~ The new life, the ~~and~~ fun and excitement were fine for other girls, but I was a part of the rolling grass lands that ~~started~~ began under my window and spread ~~out clear~~ to the mountains fifty miles away. Here, with the fat, white-faced Herefords and the half-wild cowponies, ~~was where~~ I felt at home. What could I ever do ~~or say~~ that would ~~make~~ me fit into a ~~big city~~ college for girls?

Tears burned ~~in~~ my eyes as I washed my face and ran a comb through my hair, then put on a shirt and levis. I'm different, I told my ~~re~~ image in the mirror. ~~flection.~~ It'll be just like high school, I won't fit in Morgan Junior College any better than I did Culver High.

~~Keeping my eyes carefully averted from the trunk that symbolized my exile, I went back into my room for my boots and a sweater.~~ The house slept on as I stopped in the kitchen for a ~~quick~~ raid on the ~~cookie jar~~ doughnuts ~~and the package of doughnuts I found on the shelf. My breakfast safely in a heavy plastic sack~~ Then I let myself out into the sweet-smelling ~~gray~~ dawn, where

~~The~~ The air was ~~already~~ cool with the ~~early~~ feel of fall~~, that haunts the north.~~ Winter comes early to these plains, and even the first few days of September can carry hints ~~traces~~ of ~~the soon-coming~~ frost. ~~I sniffed the air, tasting it with a relish I had never felt before.~~

Not all of her thoughts need to be italicized: the editor can use typographical discretion. The sentence beginning, "Keeping my eyes carefully," is typical of needless wordage. This kind of window-dressing can always be removed from fiction copy without injuring the story—and without injuring the author's style or status.

Shivering, I ran across the small lawn that Mom fought so valiantly
to keep alive ~~in spite of the ever-encroaching buffalo grass,~~ and
slipped into the rustling warmth of the big barn.

Pawnee sensed ~~my presence~~ immediately, putting her head over the
stall door and wickering softly. ~~I paused for a moment's greeting,~~
then went to the feed room ~~to get her~~ a ~~short~~ measure of oats.
Buckskin Cat, my father's registered quarter horse stallion, stuck
his head out as I passed, waiting for his morning pat ~~and molasses
cake, which I delivered after pouring Pawnee's oats into~~ her feed
~~box.~~

Was I so wrong? ~~I asked myself.~~ My friends and companions had
always been the horses and the men who worked with them. The only
boys I ~~had~~ dated had come from ~~the~~ other ranches around us and they
were the only ones I wanted to date. Why couldn't they be enough?
What did Mom -- and even Daddy -- want from me?

I rubbed the velvet nose of the Cat, ~~as we called the stallion,~~
and thought of Rob Hodges. His folks had sent him ~~away~~ to college last fall.
I remembered ~~very clearly~~ our last few days together ~~last fall, that~~ the
special last ride. With a pang of loneliness, I knew where I must
~~go today.~~ ride Giving the Cat a final pat ~~and another cake,~~ I left him and
took another measure of oats to Pawnee; it would be a long ride. While

---

The changes on this page are minor—some may seem even trivial—
yet they are made for purposes of crispness and clarity. (This is *not*
"editing for the sake of editing": no editor in his right mind likes to
push a pencil just for fun.) Note how silly little details can be excised
without damage to the manuscript. Usually, such details are redundant.

she was eating, I went back to the house, ~~for more supplies for myself~~
~~and~~ to leave a note.

Mom would be furious, but ~~I thought~~ perhaps Daddy would understand.
He might explain it to her ~~as he had~~ done for me so many ~~other~~ times.
just as he'd
I was like him, except that I lacked the words to make ~~anyone else~~ know
others
how I felt. Was that why she insisted ~~that~~ I go away to school? ~~I asked~~
~~myself, making two quick sandwiches from the remains of last night's~~
~~roast and stuffing three apples into the now-bulging sack.~~ Did she
think it would change me -- make me more like her?

The note I left was brief:

    "I've gone to Banner Springs for the

      day. Be home for supper.

                    Bev."

When I went ~~back~~ outside, I realized I'd have to hurry. The
eastern sky was changing ~~from gray~~ to pink, ~~and I knew that~~ Daddy would
be out to feed the stock soon. I wanted to be gone before I had to
explain ~~to anyone~~ what I was doing ~~or why.~~

Pawnee ~~had finished the oats and~~ was waiting ~~for me.~~ I got her
bridle, but ~~left my~~ saddle ~~on its rack.~~ Today I wanted to be close
not the
to my horse, to feel her muscles against my legs, to be a part of her
~~the way I always felt I was when~~ I rode bareback.

When I led her out, I closed the stall door quickly, ~~leaving~~ the
colt ~~inside. He~~ squealed with fury and frustration, pounding his

The removal of lines 7 and 8 constitutes an "editorial service." More
often than not, the student writer lards his copy with trivial asides, not
realizing that the reader doesn't have to be spoon-fed all the time. By
removing the "sandwich-and-apple" wordage, I have quickened the
story's pace and placed the girl's related thoughts in closer order.

Condensing a classic

Book condensing, as I have suggested earlier, is a special craft that supplies editorial jobs for an ever-increasing number of practitioners. While again it should be clear that no two editors ever achieve the same result, I am presenting here the opening pages of *Les Misérables,* cut deep and hard so that a busy reader of today may get to the body of the story as quickly as possible.

In condensing books, especially novels, the editor takes from here and gives to there. That is, he may remove a great deal from one portion of the book because he knows he will insert it later and elsewhere; he may decide to excise certain characters and events, certain scenes and settings because they are not truly essential to the condensed version.

If such surgery on the written word seems harsh or callous, it is done always for a purpose. Indeed, a book – a classic like *Les Misérables* – cannot be condensed otherwise. The editor's job is to reduce a large and verbose and unwieldy mass of wordage into something more contemporary in nature, and the only way to do this is to use the pencil in every sense as a deep-cutting scalpel.

1804

at the age of 63, was

an unknown parish curé ①

In ~~1815~~, M. Charles Francois-Bienvenu Myriel was Bishop of D——. ~~He~~

But in that year he had gone to Paris

~~was a man of seventy-five, and had occupied the bishopric of D—— since~~

1806. Although it in no manner concerns, even in the remotest degree, what

we have to relate, it may not be useless, were it only for the sake of ex-

actness in all things, to notice here the reports and gossip which had

arisen on his account from the time of his arrival in the diocese.

Be it true or false, what is said about men often has as much influence

upon their lives, and especially upon their destinies, as what they do.

M. Myriel was the son of a counsellor of the Parlement of Aix; of the

rank given to the legal profession. His father, intending him to inherit

his place, had contracted a marriage for him at the early age of eighteen

or twenty, according to a widespread custom among parliamentary families.

Charles Myriel, notwithstanding this marriage, had, it was said, been an

object of much attention. His person was admirably moulded; although of

slight figure, he was elegant and graceful; all the earlier part of his

life had been devoted to the world and to its pleasures. The revolution

At the beginning of a book such as this, the editor may have to do
some telescoping of dates and ages. In order to place M. Myriel in the
proper perspective, I take him back to 1804 (see bottom of page 2)
and identify him as an "unknown parish curé." Then, taking the liberty
enjoyed by the condenser, I insert the sentence: "But in that year . . ."

came, events crowded upon each other; the parliamentary families, decimated,

hunted, and pursued, were soon dispersed. M. Charles Myriel, on the first

outbreak of the revolution, emigrated to Italy. His wife died there of a

lung complaint with which she had been long threatened. They had no chil-

dren. What followed in the fate of M. Myriel? The decay of the old French

society, the fall of his own family, the tragic sights of '93, still more

fearful, perhaps, to the exiles who beheld them from afar, magnified by

fright -- did these arouse in him ideas of renunciation and of solitude?

Was he, in the midst of one of the reveries or emotions which then consumed

his life, suddenly attacked by one of those mysterious and terrible blows

which sometimes overwhelm, by smiting to the heart, the man whom public

disasters could not shake, by aiming at life or fortune? No one could have

answered; all that was known was that when he returned from Italy he was

a priest.

In 1804, M. Myriel was curé of B------- (Brignolles). He was then an

old man, and lived in the deepest seclusion.

The whole of this page, as is true with most of page 1, can be crossed
out, since the complicated background of our hero is, to put it plainly,
quite boring. If this huge book is to be compressed, let's get moving —
and go on to page 3, where some action takes place.

Near the time of the coronation, a trifling matter of business be-

longing to his curacy -- what it was, is not now known precisely took him

to Paris.

Among other personages of authority he went to ~~See~~ Cardinal Fesch on be-

half of his parishioners. ~~He~~ was waiting in the Cardinal's anteroom
when the Emperor chanced to enter @,
~~One day, when the emperor had come to visit his uncle, the worthy cure,~~

~~who was waiting in the ante-room happened to be on the way of his Majesty.~~

Napoleon, noticing that the old man looked at him with a certain curious-

ness, ~~turned around and~~ said brusquely:

"Who is this goodman who looks at me?"

"Sire," said M. Myriel, "you behold a good man, and I a great man.

Each of us may profit by it."

That evening the emperor asked the cardinal the name of the curé, and

some time afterwards M. Myriel was overwhelmed with surprise on learning

that he has been appointed Bishop of D-------.

Beyond this, no one knew how much truth there was in the stories which

---

Now I've placed M. Myriel where he belongs, in the Cardinal's anteroom, where suddenly, Napoleon makes an appearance. Then, at
the bottom of the page, we shall start to jump forward again, to give
the reader a feeling that things are happening, unimpeded by clutters
of wordage.

~~passed current concerning the first portion of M. Myriel's life.~~ But few

families had known the Myriels before the revolution.

M. Myriel had to submit to the fate of every new-comer in a small

town, where there are many tongues to talk, and but few heads to think.

He had to submit, although he was bishop, and because he was bishop. But

after all, the gossip with which his name was connected, was only gossip:

noise, talk, words, less than words -- palabres, as they say in the fore-

cible language of the South.

Be that as it may, after nine years of episcopacy, and of residence

in D-------, all these stories, topics of talk, which engross at first

petty towns and petty people, were entirely forgotten. ~~Nobody would have

dered to speak of, or even to remember them.~~

¶ When ~~M. Myriel~~ he came to D------- he was accompanied by ~~an old lady,~~ his sister

Mademoiselle Baptistine, ~~who was his sister,~~ ten years younger than himself, and

their housekeeper,
~~Their only domestic was a woman of about the same age as Mademoiselle~~

At this stage, we meet the sister, who can be presented in a minimum of
words, just as was the case with M. Myriel. All of the background so
stodgily put together by Hugo can go by the board: the reader of a
condensed classic will not miss it. Indeed, that's why he is reading a
condensation.

~~Baptistine, who was called~~ Madame Magloire ~~and who, after having been the~~

servant of M. le cure, now took the double title of femme de chambre of

Mademoiselle and housekeeper of Monseigneur.

Mademoiselle Baptistine was a tall, pale, thin, sweet person. She

fully realized the idea which is expressed by the word "respectable;"

for it seems as if it were necessary that a woman should be a mother to

be venerable. She had never been pretty; her whole life, which had been

but a succession of pious works, had produced upon her a kind of transpar-

ent whiteness, and in growing old she had acquired what may be called the

beauty of goodness. What had been thinness in her youth had become in

maturity transparency, and this etherialness permitted gleams of the angel

within. She was more a spirit than a virgin mortal. Her form was shadow-

like, hardly enough body to convey the thought of sex -- a little earth

containing a spark -- large eyes, always cast down; a pretext for a soul

to remain on earth.

Madame Magloire was a little, white, fat, jolly, bustling old woman,

In condensing a book, classic or otherwise, the editor has the inner
knowledge that he can cut out something here and, later on, put it
there. Such is the case with this page, where any of the excised material
may be used at other points in the novel, provided the editor so desires.

always out of breath, caused first by her activity, and then by the asthma.

no ¶ → They were

M. Myriel, upon his arrival, was installed in the episcopal palace

with all the honours ordained by the imperial decrees, which class ed the bishop

next in rank to the field-marshal. The mayor and the president made him

the first visit, and he, on his part, paid like honour to the general and

the prefect.

The installation being completed, the town was curious to see its

bishop at work.

M. Myriel Becomes Monseigneur Bienvenu

The bishop's palace at D------- was contiguous to the hospital. the palace

was a spacious and beautiful edifice, truly built of stone near the beginning of

the last century by Monseigneur Henri Pujet, a doctor of theology of the

Faculty of Paris, abbé of Simore, who was bishop of D------- in 1712. The

palace was in truth a lordly dwelling: there was an air of grandeur about

everything, the apartments of the bishop, the saloons, the chambers, the

The cuts and revisions on this page are more of the same. They are designed to eliminate a host of petty details which were acceptable – even important – to the nineteenth-century reader but which hardly entrance the reader of today. Nevertheless, important details must be retained – for valid and obvious reasons.

court of honour, which was very large, with arched walks after the antique

Florentine style; and garden planted with magnificent trees.

In the dining hall was a long, superb gallery, which was level with

the ground, opening upon the garden; Monseigneur Henri Pujet had given a

grand banquet on the 29th of July, 1714, to Monseigneur Charles Brûlart

de Genlis, archbishop, Prince d'Embrun, Antoine de Mesgrigny, capuchin,

bishop of Grasse, Philippe de Vendôme, grand-prior de France, the Abbé de

Saint Honoré de Lerins, François de Berton de Grillon, lord bishop of Vence,

Cesar de Sabran de Forcalquier, lord bishop of Glandève, and Jean Soanen,

priest of the oratory, preacher in ordinary to the king, lord bishop of

Senez; the portraits of these seven reverend personages decorated the hall,

and this memorable date, July 29th, 1714, appeared in letters of gold on

a white marble tablet. *kept to it was,*

The hospital ~~was~~ a low, narrow, one-story building with a small garden.

~~Three days~~ after the bishop's ~~advent he~~ *had* visited the hospital~~,~~ ~~when,~~ *he*

~~the visit was ended, he~~ invited the director to ~~oblige him by coming to~~ the

More and more of the background details can disappear, without harm
to the basic ingredients of *Les Misérables*. What we are interested in
is getting our characters to the hospital, where an important scene is
about to unfold.

palace.

"Monsieur," he said ~~to the director of the hospital,~~ "how many

patients have you?"

"Twenty-six, monseigneur."

"~~That is as I counted them,~~" said the bishop.

"The beds," continued the director, "are very ~~much~~ crowded."

"I noticed it."

"The wards are but small chambers, ~~and are not easily ventilated.~~"

"~~It seems so to me.~~"

"And then, ~~when the sun does shine,~~ the garden is very small for the

convalescents."

"That was what I was thinking."

"~~Of epidemics we have had typhus fever this year; two years ago we~~

~~had military fever, sometimes one hundred patients, and we did not know~~

~~what to do.~~"

"~~That occurred to me.~~"

At last, we come to dialogue which not only informs the reader but also
moves the novel along with a minimum of stage-managing. The dele-
tions here have a purpose: to keep the talk going so that we get a
quick but complete picture of the hospital and its problems.

"What can we do, monseigneur?" said the director, "we must be resigned."

~~This conversation took place in the dining gallery on the ground floor.~~

The bishop was silent a few moments: then he turned suddenly, ~~towards the director~~.

"Monsieur," he said, "how many beds do you think this hall alone would contain?"

"The dining hall of monseigneur!" exclaimed the director, ~~stupefied~~ *horrified*.

The bishop ran his eyes over the hall, ~~seemingly~~ taking measure and making calculations.

~~"It will hold twenty beds," said he to himself then raising his voice, he said:~~

"~~Listen,~~ Monsieur Director, *"he said,* ~~to what I have to say.~~ There is evidently a mistake here. There are twenty-six of you in five or six small rooms: there are only three of us, and space for sixty. ~~There is a mistake, I tell you.~~ You have my house and I have yours. Restore mine to me; you are at home."

The dialogue continues in somewhat compressed form. The process of condensation has brought the conversation closer to today's style, a style in which an economy of words often strengthens the author's prose. Surely there is nothing wrong with this objective, despite carpings about "capsule culture."

Next day the twenty-six poor invalids were installed in the bishop's palace, ~~and~~ the bishop was in what had been the hospital.

M. Myriel had no property, his family having been impoverished by the revolution, but he ~~His sister had a life estate of five hundred francs, which in the vicarage sufficed for her personal needs. M. Myriel~~ received from the government as bishop a salary of ~~fifteen thousand~~ 15,000 francs. The day on which he took up ~~his~~ residence in the hospital ~~building,~~ he resolved to appropriate this sum ~~once for all~~ to the following uses. ~~We copy the schedule then written by him.~~

~~Schedule for the Regulation of my Household Expenses~~

~~"For the little seminary, fifteen hundred livres.~~

~~Mission congregation, one hundred livres.~~

~~For the Lazaristes of Montdidier, one hundred livres.~~

And now we come to the end of this fragment of a great novel. The completed condensation will be quite different from Hugo's original — and well it should be. The purpose of such condensations, as I have remarked elsewhere, is to spread the influence of literature into areas where it might normally not be found.

The instincts of an editor

There seems to be no professional training for a good editor. The really great ones seem never to have been anything else. It seems to be an instinctual thing. It is not just knowing what the public likes, as you can get from some sort of selling experience. It is knowing what they *will* like, slightly ahead of them. Not so far ahead as the critic or teacher is likely to be, but just so far ahead as the editor always is. Ears up, listening, asking what's new, not minding if his own version of the new thing will seem slightly shopworn and shoddy to the intellectuals who've been talking about it for years, but feeling that he's somehow interested in it himself, so his readers will be too. Thus, of course, the better the man, the better the magazine. – L. Rust Hills

A matter of mutual feeling

After the acceptance of a manuscript for publication, the first duty of the editor is to establish the friendliest and most cooperative relation possible with the author. The more mutual trust there is, the happier their whole publishing life together will be. Often this relation has been established long before acceptance. Together, they will not be sure that the manuscript is as perfect in all ways as it can humanly be before it is presented to the copy editor. A whole book could be written about this mutuality of the editor and author. The relation has been compared to marriage and to that of the psychoanalyst and his patient. At any rate it is delicate and difficult – but it can be most rewarding. – John Farrar in *Editors on Editing*.

Discovering talent and quality

Most editors are actually writers to a certain degree: they know the high joy of creation, they know the agony of the rejection slip in the envelope, they know the triumph of acceptance. The know they are dealing with a man's heart and guts and soul. And they are careful to handle these gently and with respect.

Beyond this built-in sympathy for the writer, the editor's chief pleasure is the discovery of talent and quality. Editors stay up late at night wading through piles of manuscripts; they read on trains, in automobiles and in the bathroom, and when they are talking to people at cocktail parties, they are reading, still, in the back of their heads, which gives them a well-merited reputation for being absent-minded companions.

This search for the golden piece of writing goes on perpetually, and each new writer represents a new hope, a wild surmise that maybe this is the time, that here is The One at last. So the writer has a friend in the editor – even if he is only an executioner on his good behavior. – Frederic A. Birmingham in *The Writer's Craft*.

FW

Section VI Publishing

Bennett Cerf and Robert Loomis

An informal, close-up view of the publishing
industry, as seen by two experts who know
the author's problems

The birth of a book

Not long ago, a Staff Seminar was conducted at the Famous Writers School by Bennett Cerf, Chairman of the Board of Random House, and one of his senior editors, Robert Loomis. Messrs. Cerf and Loomis talked for some hours on the techniques and tribulations of the publishing business.

As head of Random House, Mr. Cerf is well aware of what takes place between the time a manuscript arrives at his office and the time it appears as a published book, while Mr. Loomis is a distinguished editor who has brought many an author from obscurity to fame.

The question-and-answer seminar was recorded on tape. For space reasons, the manuscript has been edited and condensed, but essentially it covers all the points discussed between Messrs. Cerf and Loomis, and between these panelists and members of the school's instructional staff. "The Birth of a Book" should prove enlightening and helpful to all writers who wonder what happens to a manuscript – perhaps their manuscript – *after* it arrives at a publishing house.

CERF: All kinds of manuscripts and publishing projects come into the doors of a publishing house, varying from ones sent by unknown people to ideas originated in the house and farmed out to professionals. There's a great difference, of course, between non-fiction and fiction, and a great difference between books from recognized authors or recognized agents and books sent in out of the blue by people who have never been heard of before.

Any good publishing house gets an average of 100 manuscripts a week. When times are good, we might even get 200, in every shape and form. The first thing we demand is that a script be legible, double-spaced. Scripts in longhand are usually sent back unread, since we have no time to decipher handwriting. The second thing the writer should learn is to put his manuscript into a typewriter paper box and send it without trimmings. Manuscripts that arrive in fancy packages, in ribbons, or bound in leather are almost invariably unreadable.

The devices some people use to get their work read are sometimes childish. They will send in a manuscript with three pages upside down – let's say, pages 168, 244, 331 – and when they get them back, still upside down, they assume nobody's read the manuscript. Other people have had the idea of putting a five-dollar bill between pages 101 and 102, and if it's still there, they assume nobody has seen it.

Most people send a letter with the manuscript or separately. It's best to send it *with* the manuscript. The letter should merely say: "I am submitting herewith my novel or book. . . . My address is so and so, and here is return postage." (Some people write eight-page letters telling us what their novels are about. We don't bother reading them.)

Now, let's start with the receipt of an unsolicited manuscript – one properly typed and worth looking at. The first step is to record the entry. We have a girl at Random House whose sole job is to enter the receipt of manuscripts – what day they arrive, what time, where they came from who they are sent to, etc. This gives us an enduring record of every script that comes into the house.

As a first step, manuscripts go to an initial reading group. We have several girls in our office, recent graduates of Wellesley, Vassar, Radcliffe, or some accredited college – girls who have majored in English and who think they're going to meet John O'Hara or Truman Capote. They'd love to be publishers, so they come and stay with us until they learn the business, then get married and disappear. But they are the initial readers who read the unknown books.

Nineteen out of twenty manuscripts are so bad that you only have to read a few pages to know they are hopeless. It seems to me that books are being written by everybody in the United States today, whether he can write or not. But let's take the one manuscript out of twenty that's worth reading.

Now, if the initial reader thinks it's good enough to be considered by an editor, the book is sent up to the editorial department and given to one of our experienced editors to read. If it has great promise, it's sent up with enthusiasm. In that case a senior editor will take it immediately and put it with his preferred manuscripts.

From this point on, publishing procedures differ. At Random House, all senior editors have the right to contract for books they are enthusiastic about, without anybody saying okay. However, we have a loosely run, informal business, so there's no reason why Bob Loomis, for instance, won't be enthusiastic about a book and talk to Donald Klopfer or me about it before he signs it. Of course, if it involves a big advance, we all have to discuss it. But that rarely happens with an unknown author, because the big money doesn't come to writers until you've made them successful . . . and then some other publisher tries to steal them.

How often do these books make the grade? Perhaps we accept one out of every three or four hundred unsolicited manuscripts. That would be a high average.

LOOMIS: I'd say it is tops.

CERF: Now, to give an example of how success does strike once in a while, I'll tell you about a former best seller, *The Snake Pit* by Mary Jane Ward. This is a prize example of an unsolicited manuscript that burst through to glory. It came to us by accident when a girl in Chicago wrote a novel about incest. She was quite a good writer, but the subject was too tough for her to handle . . . and anyway, in those years, incest wasn't being studied by schoolchildren as it is today.

We wrote to her at some length, saying that she had talent but should start with a simpler and safer subject. She wrote back saying she never thought a New York publisher would take time to write a four-page critique of a rejected book. In gratitude, she added: "I think I can do you a favor. A girl who lives down the street from me in Evanston has written a remarkable book. But her agent can't sell it. May I send it to you?"

In came *The Snake Pit* by Mary Jane Ward, a girl none of us had ever heard of. The book was so good that it required virtually no editing. It was a young woman's authentic story of a nervous breakdown and of her incarceration in a badly run state institution.

When Miss Ward came to New York to sign the book contract, I spent a whole afternoon trying to persuade her to change the title, because, I said,

"Women buy most of the novels – and they hate snakes!" Thank God, she told me to go to hell. Now, of course, *snake pit* is part of our language. The book was selected by the Book of the Month Club, became an Academy Award motion picture, and even gave rise to a Hit Parade song. The excitement in our office at the discovery of this book was something I'll never forget.

Now let me add an amusing sidelight on *The Snake Pit*. As a result of the novel, every nut in America came to Random House with a manuscript. Our vestibule looked like the Bellevue Hospital Receiving Room, and I used to sneak in the back way. One day, I was thinking of something else and walked in the main entrance. A little gray-haired lady grabbed me, stuck a manuscript into my arms, and said: "You must read this while I'm here, because I don't dare leave it with you. I'm surrounded by enemies who want to steal it."

I knew I was in trouble, but I couldn't shake her off as she marched me into my office, put the manuscript on the desk, and took a position right behind me, breathing down my neck. I opened the box and started turning pages of manuscript. They were all blank: there wasn't a word on the sheets. I turned around and said: "This is one of the most amazing manuscripts that's ever come to my office. But as you know, we did *The Snake Pit,* and don't you think it would be a mistake for us to do another book on the same subject?"

She agreed, so I put the pages back and sent her over to Doubleday. About an hour later, Ken McCormick phoned and in that literary way of his said, "You S.O.B., we'll get you for this!"

But I've strayed away from the subject of this seminar. I've taken you to the point where a book has been read, sent to an editor and been accepted for publication. Any questions?

Question: At the physical stage of sending a manuscript up to an editor, what happens? Does the reader append a letter or a report of some sort?

CERF: Yes. It has a report attached and the girl downstairs is told to whom the manuscript has been sent. Now, I must admit that sometimes, in our incredibly efficient way, manuscripts get lost and stay lost for quite a while. But this is bound to happen when scripts keep pouring in. If you come to Random House, I'll show you the room where the envelopes appear. Sometimes they're piled to the ceiling and the girl can't enter them fast enough. While she's entering them, a new pile arrives. Nevertheless, we're supposed to know where a manuscript is at any time. Which reminds me of a story. . . .

Some of you may have heard of Harrison Smith the publisher. Jonathan Cape was his first partner, then he went in with Robert Haas. It was Haas & Smith when we took the firm over, back in 1936. Part of the deal was that Harrison Smith would come along for at least a year. We all loved Hal, but he was rather absentminded: Once he put a fountain pen in his mouth and lit it with a match. Another time he had three lunch dates at the same time, all of whom arrived together.

When he finally left us at the end of a year, we moved his desk out and found three "lost" manuscripts under it!

Question: Do you feel the handling of unsolicited manuscripts is worth the effort you put into it?

LOOMIS: Some publishers have tried to discourage unsolicited manuscripts because the percentage of acceptance is so low. The book business is so organized now, because of communications, that any author usually knows another author who has been published and either he sends a manuscript through that author to the editor he knows or the author has an agent and it goes through him. Nevertheless, there are still many unknown authors, and you have to serve them if you're a responsible publisher.

No one at Random House rejects people for the fun of it. Furthermore, a lot of writers seem to think we're doing them a favor when we read their books. The fact is, that's our job. We're always looking for writers. And although we may turn them down, it doesn't mean we're not interested in them. The very fact that so many manuscripts are bad ensures that the fairly good ones will get a chance.

Although the first reader may be handicapped by being just out of college and having read only the "best" literature (one reader's report about a novel of a man in prison said that Arthur Koestler had done a book on this theme and we didn't need another one), it does happen that a reader can become excited by a manuscript because it's above "trash" average. In other words, a reader will usually spot any manuscript that is *readable*. We may still turn it down, but the book will at least be sent to a senior editor.

CERF: Books that have been turned down by many publishers have become best sellers. Remember Vina Delmar's *Bad Girl?* It was first rejected by about eleven publishers. *The Good Earth* by Pearl Buck was not only turned down at the start by practically every publisher but one publisher turned it down twice!

LOOMIS: I think *Lust for Life* was turned down thirty times. *No Time for Sergeants* was rejected by four houses before we got it.

CERF: And we ourselves turned down *Matador* by Barnaby Conrad. This fine novel was rejected by one of our editors because *The Brave Bulls* had been published a year before. He said, "Who wants another book on bull-fighting?" It sounded sensible to us. But the manuscript was taken by another publisher and then by the *Reader's Digest*. The novel never sold particularly well in the trade, but when a book is taken by the *Digest,* it's like hitting the jackpot at Las Vegas.

Question: What about manuscripts that come to you through literary agents?

LOOMIS: A lot of novels that we get from agents are, technically speaking, unsolicited. Nevertheless, we cultivate agents. I take them to lunch; Bennett takes them to lunch; all the editors keep in touch with agents. The agent does two things before he submits a manuscript. One, he screens material as to whether it's publishable; and second, he has a pretty good idea of the kinds of books that a publisher likes.

CERF: A lot of the most famous agents are in the same position as the authors of best sellers. They're being courted. Also, they're making money out of the astronomical literary payments you read about in the newspapers. Just think what an agent can make out of a new book by a Truman Capote or by an Irving Wallace or by a James Jones. Let's say an author's take comes to 700,000 dollars (which has happened on several occasions). The agent, at 10 percent, makes 70,000 dollars. After an experience like this, the agent isn't too keen about going around to publishers, pleading with them over an unknown author for a 1,000-dollar advance, out of which the agent might make 100 dollars. He's just made 70,000 dollars from a best seller. Having tasted caviar, he's not going to Nedick's for a hot dog. A younger agent on the way up is hungrier – and often better – for an undiscovered author.

Question: Do you give an agent priority on your reading schedule?

LOOMIS: Usually an agent sends a manuscript directly to an editor, and this can mean something. Some agents submit helter-skelter and admit not having read the material themselves. Others read books carefully – their reputations go along with the submissions. However, the influence exerted by an agent isn't necessarily strong. In a publishing house, the sense of wanting to discover a new author is more important.

I approach every book with a chip on my shoulder. If I didn't, I'd be trapped; I'd take on too much. So I try to keep objective. Yet I've taken on a dozen books at Random House that I wish I hadn't. I don't know why I did, but there's no way I can stop myself.

CERF: An editor's job is always on the line, because every publisher keeps a record. At the end of the year, you look around and see six books that got nowhere. And you begin to ask what kind of editor is this.

Question: If a writer is backed up by an agent, are you subject to pressure?

CERF: The best pitch an agent can give is not to say the manuscript is very good but to say that Harcourt or Doubleday has been on the phone four times, asking about the book. If you find out this is just an act, you disregard it. But sometimes it's true. Agents may have a book they feel is just right for certain lists and they will therefore call and say that although other people have asked about it, they think it's right for you. If we trust the agent, then this book will get priority reading.

LOOMIS: Pick up any published book and, if someone has praised it, you may like it more than if you didn't know anything about it. But when you finish, you have your own opinion. It's the same way with a manuscript. Nobody is really going to sway you into thinking it's a lot better than it is.

For sending work to a publisher, an agent is not really necessary. In areas outside of book publishing, an agent is very helpful to a writer. Selling to magazines, selling to television, to radio, or the motion picture business requires a skill that few authors possess. So if anybody asks me, I usually say: "You don't need an agent for us, a book publisher, but for anything else, you're much better off."

Question: How long does it take before the author gets some reaction to an unsolicited manuscript?

LOOMIS: Two weeks to a month.

Question: Would this be a report if the book has passed a first reading?

CERF: Ironically, the more we like a manuscript, the longer the reaction may take. If it's turned down by the first reader, it's finished. If we like it, we send word that the book is being considered. This is not an acceptance, but merely to say it's going the rounds.

LOOMIS: Another thing causes misunderstandings. A publisher is not in the business of criticism. People like myself do work with authors once a manuscript is taken on, and our job is to try and get the best possible book. But to turn down a manuscript with detailed reasons has proven (even though authors might not agree) to be dangerous. Why? Because when you're reading so many books, you make snap judgments, and you can say something injudicious to an author. He, of course, will feel that he's gotten the word from Mt. Olympus and may well act on your offhand comment.

Several years ago a book called *Little Mule* was published by John Burress. It concerned a boy and his grandfather on a farm. I was told that at least ten publishers saw it, and the author rewrote the book three times. The first editor said: "We like this but we feel that the boy should tell the story." So the author rewrote the manuscript in the first person. Then the next editor said he liked the novel very much, but the grandfather should be built up. And so it went, from publisher to publisher. Finally, as you can imagine, the book was published in the form in which it went originally to the first publisher.

I have submitted manuscripts that I was fond of to editor friends at other houses, and the reactions I got made me wonder if we'd read the same book. Literally, I was shocked to think what authors must be hearing. So I make it a practice of writing kindly and in general terms, but authors usually don't like it. They are eager to get some answer, some reason, some criticism. Yet, when you're dictating ten letters in a morning, most of them turning down manuscripts, it isn't fair to say something in haste, particularly when you're not going to act on it. Only when we plan to go ahead with a manuscript should we comment in detail, because we're offering the author money to revise and we're going to publish his work if his revisions are successful.

Question: What happens when you do accept a book?

CERF: Before we go into that, I must tell you about one rejected author who was so angry he picketed us. He walked back and forth with a sign: "Random House Is Unfair to New Authors." Finally, we sent him out a sandwich. He ate it – but he wouldn't go. . . .

Now we've gotten to the point where a book is accepted. What happens then? Well, let's pick a date, and say it was a Monday that the manuscript reached Bob Loomis. Speaking in terms of average time, what would you do with it, Bob? Would you read it at your desk or would you take it home?

LOOMIS: I'd read it at home, and promptly, since the enthusiasm of the first reader's report would naturally make me want to get at it. If I liked it, then I'd go to Bennett or to Donald Klopfer and get them to read it, too. In most publishing houses, when you like a manuscript you give it to another editor and he gives it to another, and next the editor-in-chief will read it and you'll end up with three or four reports. Then, at an editorial meeting, you all sit down and discuss the book, whether you like it or not. You may even show it to the sales manager. So, if the book is taken, everybody in the house knows about it.

At Random House, the problem often is that when we accept a manuscript, only one senior editor has read it. You've got to get others to read it, *after* the fact. So I like to have someone read it beforehand, because I know that in the publishing business we need cooperation. Once we have backing for a book, we write the author. If there are reservations, we present them generally so they won't come as a surprise to him. We like to find out whether he is agreeable to revisions or not. And we also offer a contract, with terms outlined in the letter.

If he is sympathetic to revisions (if necessary) and agrees to the terms, we draw up a contract and send it to him. Our contract is a fair one – the same whether the author has an agent or not. If he doesn't have an agent, we'll take over the agent's duties for the usual commission. We will submit the manuscript to magazines, if it has a possibility for a serial. We will sell it in England, France, Germany, and so on. Eventually we may try to get him an agent, because we often can operate more efficiently with an agent involved.

From then on, it's simply a matter of intuition and experience as to how well you get along with the author, how well you can persuade him to do what you feel is best for the book. If he agrees, the relationship can cement him to the house for as long as he writes. Or he may leave with his next book. You see, publishing is a wide-open field. There just isn't any pattern to it.

CERF: Once in a while an author will come to me and say: "I want to stay with Random House but I can't stand my editor. How about another?" So . . . we change. We've done that with a couple of our biggest authors who, after a close friendship, will fight with an editor over God knows what.

LOOMIS: Friendship with an author can become so close that you get calls from him day or night. If he thinks the advertising appropriation isn't big enough, it's your job to explain it to him. If the binding's wrong, if the jacket's wrong, if the copy's wrong, you are the culprit. If the relationship endures, the editor is fortunate, because authors are extremely interesting and rewarding people.

CERF: And don't forget—you can be *too* good! You probably have heard the story of Thomas Wolfe and Maxwell Perkins, the Scribner's editor. Perkins became so important to Wolfe that Tom said: "Everybody thinks these are your books, not mine. Everybody thinks you're such a good editor, I'd be helpless without you. I'm going to prove to the world I don't need you."

So Wolfe left Scribner's and went to Harper's just because Perkins had virtually given his life to helping Wolfe.

Question: Commercially speaking, do publishers take into consideration the success of previous books in the same category?

CERF: May I take a first crack at the answer? I don't believe a really good book can be written to order. When an author sits down and says, this is the market and this is the book I'm going to write, the book usually betrays itself. However, if a book was *in* you, if you felt you *had* to write it, this shows in the book itself. Ninety-nine times out of 100, you can spot a book written to order. It's obviously an inferior copy of something that has gone before.

Question: What about all the books written about Christianity?

CERF: Well, let's look at James Michener. Jim wrote *The Source,* which became the No. 1 best seller in three weeks. Of course, Michener is a built-in best seller, but when he decided to write this book about the cradle of the three great religions he didn't say, "I'm going to write a best seller." He went to Israel and lived there for a year and a half, so that when he started to write, he had six notebooks full of things he'd learned on the spot. When he wrote the book, he was not copying anybody else, he was writing purely on his own.

Question: Don't you think that some very big best-selling authors, like Robbins or Wallace, write "to order"?

CERF: When authors get into this class, they *can* do it. Having Wallace as an author is like having Richard Burton and Julie Andrews together in a motion picture. Anybody who goes to one of these pictures likes the formula and keeps going, even though the formula may begin to fade.

For example, I think the historical novel *per se* has passed its peak. At the time of *The Robe* and others, you opened the New York *Times Book Review* and half the books mentioned were historical novels. Open it today and you find very few. They're not popular now. We aren't interested in most of the historical novels that come to Random House. Also, I said to Bob the other day: "If you bring me another novel about the Deep South and its problems, I *promise* you I won't read it."

Question: Isn't religion still a predominant subject among readers? Look at *Markings* by Dag Hammarskjöld.

C E R F : This is the kind of book that violates every publishing rule. *Markings* first came to Knopf, now part of Random House. We printed 10,000 copies, which we thought was about right. Now it's selling 2,000 to 3,000 copies a week, and total sales are up to a quarter of a million. About once every six months, a book breaks through to the top. Nobody knows why, but once it does, then everybody, including Bob Hope, talks about it. That happened with *Forever Amber, Anthony Adverse, Gone with the Wind,* and *Hawaii.* It happened with a Russian princess who wrote her confessions some years ago. *Markings* has become this kind of best seller and will continue to be one for years.

Question: How important is advertising in making a book successful?

C E R F : This is a subject that publishers and authors have been fighting about for fifty years – and will never solve. We're convinced that advertising is good for a book that has begun *by itself*. In other words, as Maxwell Perkins once put it: If a car is stuck in the mud, one, two, or three big bruisers can't push it. But if the car is moving slowly by itself, a ninety-pound gal can get it really moving. In the same way, if a book begins to show signs of life, the public starts buying.

This happened some years ago with *The Story of San Michele.* An American publisher imported 500 sets of sheets and somebody in San Antonio, Texas, took a liking to the book. The publisher began getting orders from San Antonio – 25, then 50, soon 500 copies disappeared. It was as if somebody had thrown a stone in a pond. The ripples spread. The publishers finally printed the book in the U.S. and sold 200,000 copies. After the book started moving, it was worth advertising. But if the publisher had taken full-page ads, before it came out, I don't think they would have sold 100 extra copies.

Last spring we published a novel that we thought would be a big best seller. It was by a girl who'd had one great success in the past. We had an enormous reprint sale, the movies bought it, everything looked right for this book. But – it hasn't sold. Since we had made money from subsidiary rights, we appropriated an additional 5,000 dollars for advertising – ads in the

Times Book Review and the Chicago *Tribune*. The ads appeared, but the 5,000 dollars didn't sell many copies. The public will not warm to the book — and that's all there is to it.

Question: Does the enthusiasm of the trade have a lot to do with whether a book succeeds?

C E R F : The bookseller is not as important today as he used to be. The personal bookshop has disappeared. When I started in the publishing business, there were at least thirty booksellers who could put over a title with their own enthusiasm. In New York, Ted Holliday could send out 300 copies of a book on his own authority; his customers believed in him so much that not 10 copies would come back. That kind of bookseller doesn't exist today. Now you have the big retail and discount outlets. The books are there in piles. If they sell, they sell. If they don't, they go back to the publisher.

The heartbreak of modern publishing is the failure to put over a fine book by an unknown writer — unless the book gets an unusual break. The bookstores don't even like to stock a first novel. They say to the publishers: "You create the demand and we'll buy the book. But otherwise, don't bother us."

We published a book of short stories, *Roar, Lion, Roar* by Irvin Faust. Superb stories, beautiful reviews. We spent 2 dollars a copy promoting the book, yet the total sale to date is less than 3,000 copies.

Question: Often I pick up the *Times Book Review* and get excited about a book, but when I go to the bookstore, they haven't got it. Why?

C E R F : Usually they blame the publisher. I don't want to start wailing, but you have no idea how often authors complain: "My sister was in Westport yesterday and there were no copies of my book in the bookstore. The bookseller said, 'I ordered the book but the publisher never sent it to me.'" That's the bookseller's usual alibi. It's practically never the truth.

L O O M I S : Books are sold two ways: directly from the publisher's warehouse and indirectly through jobbers around the country. Most books are sold through a jobber; only the largest bookstore will order directly from us because booksellers have to pay postage. The jobber makes money by ordering 100 copies from us at 45 percent off and selling them to the local bookstore at a discount of 40 or thereabouts. But if the jobber goes out of stock and the local bookstore asks for two more copies, the jobber's not going to order just two copies from us. So he waits until he can build up another order. Meanwhile, bookstores tell an author's friend that the book is out of stock. This situation doesn't hurt a big book, but it can kill a small one.

CERF: There's no profit in selling one or two books. To sell one book, you've got to go through the same billing procedure as for 1,000. An order for one or two books represents a sizable loss to the publisher.

Question: What about the sale of books through discount houses?

CERF: We won't sell to a discount house. On the other hand, a couple of jobbers do nothing but supply the big ones. We do sell to them. When they order 500 copies, we fill the order; without unwrapping the books, they send them to the discounter. All we're doing is giving a bigger discount to a jobber – but we're obliged by law to supply him. I consider it vitally important that we protect all the retail outlets we have. But often our hands are tied.

LOOMIS: If the bookstores should go out of business because of the discount houses, we might lose more than we gained. There are only a couple of hundred good bookstores left in the U.S.

CERF: And getting fewer all the time. However, I'm not pessimistic. More and better books are being read all the time. There'll always be a growing market for books, but it's largely going to come not from retail bookstores but from schools, libraries, and institutions, some operating with government funds. Of the billions being poured into education by the government, a good portion is going to drift to the publishers, so the future is bright.

Question: What about paperback books?

CERF: The market is growing all the time. More and more publishers of hardback books either have an interest in a paperback house or own one of their own. Many current books are being published in hardback and paper at the same time – and selling well in both formats. *The Source,* priced at $7.95, sold 200,000 copies in two months, plus many more through the Book of the Month Club. So the market is still there. Even though everybody knows a book will come out in paperback before long, plenty of people want to read it while it's new. So the whole market and all our calculations have changed. When you contract for a book now, you may lose money on the hard-cover edition but you'll make it back in paper.

Question: How is your Modern Library doing?

CERF: It's getting bigger and bigger, because the price of paperbacks has changed so completely. Four years ago, paperbacks were a quarter; try to find one for 25 cents today. First they went to 35 cents; then to 50; then to 95 cents; now they're all the way up to $3.45, so that the difference between paper and hardback has frequently become infinitesimal. A Modern Library hardback today is a bargain, compared to the paperback. It costs a little more, but you get something for your permanent library.

Question: Getting back to handling manuscripts, what about an author who sends you an outline? Is this a good idea?

CERF: We have bought novels that way, but three times out of four, they didn't work out. Even though the outline sounded fine, the finished book was hopeless. In non-fiction, however, you usually know exactly where you're going. Most non-fiction books today are sold on the idea rather than the book itself.

Question: Do you prefer to see a non-fiction book from an unknown author or a novel.

CERF: For a newcomer, it's harder to write a good non-fiction book than fiction, because with non-fiction you've got to have an enormous fund of information, and only the experienced writer knows where to get it.

LOOMIS: I think that most editors would get more excited by finding a new novelist. Few non-fiction books by unknowns come over our transom; I don't ever remember buying unsolicited non-fiction. The non-fiction field has changed a lot since World War II. In the hands of Rachel Carson and similar authors, it became a new "art" form. In the old days, it was *An American Doctor's Odyssey* or *Seven League Boots*. Today, the non-fiction writers are specialists, and good ones: they work like the devil and put a great deal into their books. And once you find a man like that, it's wonderful, because he will turn out book after book.

Question: What is usually the difference between a first and second novel by the same author?

CERF: Most novelists are not novelists at all. They have one story to tell, their own, and they make a success with this book because it's their life. Then they consider themselves novelists, but they have nothing more to say.

The next book is "written to order," and usually falls flat on its face. Nevertheless, the novelist has one advantage. His book, if it succeeds, will live longer than the non-fiction book, which is usually so topical that a year after it's been a best seller, it's a has-been. History is moving so fast today that by the time you've published a book that seemed hot when you bought it, it's ancient history.

Question: How do you explain *The Letters of Fred Allen,* which was high on the best-seller list for two weeks and then vanished?

LOOMIS: A certain number of book buyers love Fred Allen and they bought the book immediately when it came out. The best-seller list is not an indication of total sales but of rate of sales. A book can sell 100,000 copies and never get on the list, because it took too long. You can have a book that sells 10,000 and if it reaches this figure within a couple of weeks, it'll jump on the list.

CERF: You can fake a best seller if you do it carefully enough. A few years ago, a motion picture producer I know bought the film rights to a book, and wanted to keep it on the best-seller list as long as possible. So he found out from the *Herald Tribune* which bookstores were used for compiling its list and sent agents to buy 100 copies a week at each of these stores. In that way, at a cost of some 50,000 dollars, he kept his book on the best-seller list for ten extra weeks. When he was chided for this, he said: "A double-page ad in *Life* magazine would cost me even more!"

And that's just one of the things that goes on in the publishing business every day. No wonder we all stay in it! . . .

A shaft from Mencken

Mark Twain once observed that given a choice between burning in Dante's *Inferno* and reading one of the younger Henry James's later novels, *he* would not hesitate before jumping into the flames. And H. L. Mencken, one of the greatest practitioners of casual literary mayhem, labeled James posthumously as "an idiot, and a Boston idiot, to boot, than which there is nothing lower in the world . . ." Furthermore, according to Mencken, James had known nothing "about women or men or animals or writing" and "could no more write a good book than Bishop Manning can dance a jig . . ." – Myrick Land in *The Fine Art of Literary Mayhem.*

Contributors

Appell, George	a member of the Famous Writers School instructional staff, has sold sixteen novels and more than 250 short stories.
Callanan, Joseph	has contributed articles and short stories to a wide variety of publications.
Carroll, Gordon	has been a newspaperman, a magazine editor and publisher, editor of half a dozen books on a variety of subjects, and is now the Director of the Famous Writers School.
Carter, John Mack	a former editor of *American Home* and *McCall's* magazine, is now editor of the *Ladies' Home Journal*.
Cerf, Bennett	a member of the Guiding Faculty of the Famous Writers School, is the well-known humorist, book publisher and editor.
Eberhart, Mignon G.	a member of the Guiding Faculty of the Famous Writers School, is among the top writers in the suspense story field.
Evans, Bergen	a member of the Guiding Faculty of the Famous Writers School, is a recognized authority on word usage.
Flesch, Rudolf	the author of several best sellers on the craft of writing, is a member of the Guiding Faculty of the Famous Writers School.

Freedgood, Morton — a member of the Famous Writers School editorial research staff, has published many short stories, articles and several novels.

Green, John — a former magazine editor and non-fiction writer, is a member of the Famous Writers School instructional staff.

Hartley, William — a former editor, now collaborates with his wife, Ellen, on free-lance books and articles.

Hood, Robert E. — is the editor of *Boys' Life* magazine, the official publication of the Boy Scouts of America.

Jarman, Rufus — an instructor at the Famous Writers School, is a regular contributor to many national magazines and has also appeared on radio and television programs.

Kostka, Dorothy — a well-known writer of confession stories, is also a columnist for the Denver *Post*.

Lansing, Elizabeth — has written nearly forty books for children and is a member of the instructional staff of the Famous Writers School.

Loomis, Robert — is a senior editor at Random House, one of the country's leading publishing houses.

Lowther, George — a staff supervisor at the Famous Writers School, is a veteran writer of radio and television programs.

Ratcliff, J. D.

a member of the Guiding Faculty of the Famous Writers School, is an eminently successful magazine writer who has interviewed people all over the world.

Rinehart, George

a staff supervisor at the Famous Writers School, is a former book editor and technical writer.

Shulman, Max

a member of the Guiding Faculty of the Famous Writers School, is one of America's most popular humorists.

Smith, Red

a member of the Guiding Faculty of the Famous Writers School, is the distinguished columnist and sports writer.

Van Duyn, Janet

a member of the instructional staff of Famous Writers School, is a novelist who has also written radio programs.

Wachs, Theodore, Jr.

specializes in business and public relations writing, in addition to writing articles for national publications.

Index

This book is set in Times New Roman type.

Adapting the style of the Famous Writers Textbooks,
the format and binding were designed by
Joseph P. Ascherl.